POVERTY, U. S. A.

THE HISTORICAL RECORD

ADVISORY EDITOR: David J. Rothman

Professor of History, Columbia University

THE CHARITABLE IMPULSE

IN EIGHTEENTH CENTURY

AMERICA

Collected Papers

Arno Press & The New York Times

NEW YORK   1971

Reprint Edition 1971 by Arno Press Inc.

LC# 71—137199
ISBN 0—405—03098—3

POVERTY, U.S.A.: THE HISTORICAL RECORD
ISBN for complete set: 0-405-03090-8

Manufactured in the United States of America

Publisher's Note: The selections in this compilation
were reprinted from the best available copies.

CONTENTS

(in alphabetical order)

Gordon, William.

The Plan of a Society for Making Provisions for Widows, by Annuities for the Remainder of Life; and for granting Annuities to Persons after certain Ages with the Proper Tables for calculating what must be paid by the several Members, in order to secure the said advantages.

Hollinshead, William.

An Oration Delivered at the Orphan-House of Charleston, South Carolina, October 18, 1797, Being the Eighth Anniversary of the Institution.

Mather, Cotton.

Orphanotrophium, or, Orphans Well-Provided For.

Society of St. George.

Rules of the Society of St. George: Established at New-York, for the Purpose of Relieving their Brethren in Distress.

Smith, William.

Some Account of the Charitable Corporation, Lately Erected for the Relief of the Widows and Children of Clergymen, in the Communion of the Church of England in America; With a Copy of their Charters, and fundamental Rules. And also a Sermon, Preached in Christ-Church, Philadelphia, October 10, 1769, before the said Corporation, on the Occasion of their first meeting.

AN ACT

To incorporate the *GERMAN SOCIETY*, contributing for the Relief of distressed Germans, in the STATE of PENSYLVANIA.

An ACT

To incorporate the GERMAN SOCIETY, con-
tributing for the Relief of distressed Germans, in the
STATE *of* PENSYLVANIA.

SECTION I. WHEREAS the Arrival of Preamble.
Germans from Europe, and
the numerous Settlements made by them in
Pennsylvania, have greatly contributed to the
present Wealth and Strength of this State; and
the Means of encouraging these Foreigners to
come and settle among us, by removing or lessening their Distresses in a new Country, have, on
sundry Occasions, deservedly engaged the Attention of the former Government of this Country.

SECT. 2. AND WHEREAS a Number
of German Inhabitants of the City of Philadelphia, and its Neighbourhood, by their humble
Petition to the General Assembly of this State,
have represented and shewn, that some Time in
the Year of our Lord one thousand seven hundred and sixty-four, some of the Petitioners and
divers other Persons, all Germans by Birth, or
descending from Germans who had settled in this

A 2 State,

State, moved by the Sufferings of their Country-
men then newly arrived, formed themselves into
a charitable Society, under the Name of "The
German Society of Philadelphia, in the Province
of Pennsylvania," and by voluntary Subscriptions and stated Contributions from Time to
Time, supplied the Poor, the Sick, and otherwise distressed Germans, brought to the City of
Philadelphia, and have aided and assisted such
Passengers as for Want of Acquaintance with the
Language and Laws of the Country, were in
Danger of being oppressed. Also, that some of
the Petioners aforesaid, have purchased two contiguous Lots in the said City of Philadelphia, in
order to build thereon, for the Reception and
Accommodation of their Countrymen, when
Need shall be. Also, that they have it in View
to enlarge upon, and further to extend the Benefit of their first Institution, by applying Part
of the Fund of Money in their Hands, and which
hereafter they may raise for and towards other
charitable Purposes; such as to teach and improve poor Children, both in the English and
German Languages, reading and writing thereof,
and to procure for them such Learning and Education, as will best suit their Genius and Capa-
cities, and enable the proper Objects to receive
the finishing of their Studies in the University,
established in the said City of Philadelphia:
Likewise to erect a Library, and to do any other
Matter or Thing which without any Prejudice
to other Inhabitants of this State, in Charity
they might do for the Relief and Benefit of their
own Countrymen; wherefore they have humbly
prayed, that they might be incorporated by a
Law for this Purpose.

SECT.

[5]

SECT. 3. *Be it therefore enacted, and it is hereby enacted, by the Representatives of the Freemen of the Commonwealth of Pennsylvania, in General Assembly met, and by the Authority of the same,* That Henry Keppele, Prefident, Lewis Weifs, Vice-Prefident, Lewis Farmer and Henry Leighthoufer, Secretaries, Chriftopher Ludwick, Peter Ozeas, Andrew Burckhart, John Fritz, Peter Kraft and Melchior Steiner, Overfeers, Michael Shubart, Treafurer, Henry Kammerer, Solicitor, and William Lehman, Deacon; the prefent Officers of the faid German Society, elected and chofen at the laft Meeting of the Members of that Society, on the twenty-fixth Day of December laft paft, and their Succeffors in the refpective Offices, and all Perfons who have fubfcribed and hereafter fhall fubfcribe the Rules and Regulations of the faid Society, and have continued and fhall from Time to Time continue to contribute towards the aforefaid charitable Purpofes of the faid Society, be, and they are hereby made and conftituted, a Corporation and Body politic in Law and in Fact, to have Continuance forever by the Name, Stile and Title of the *German Society* contributing for the Relief of diftreffed Germans in the State of Pennfylvania.

Society is corporated.

Name.

SECT. 4. *And be it further enacted by the Authority aforefaid,* That the faid Corporation and their Succeffors, by the Name, Stile and Title aforefaid, fhall forever hereafter be Perfons able and capable in Law, as well to take, receive and hold all and all Manner of Lands, Tenements, Rents, Annuities, Liberties, Franchifes and other Hereditaments, which at any Time or Times heretofore have been granted, bargained, fold, enfeoffed,

To hold Eftates heretofore granted to the Society.

feoffed, releafed, devifed or otherwife conveyed
to the faid German Society, or to any Perfon or
Perfons for their Ufe or in Truft for them; and
the fame Lands, Tenements, Rents, Annuities,
Liberties, Franchifes and other Hereditaments,
are hereby vefted and eftablifhed in the faid Corporation and their Succeffors forever.   And the
faid Corporation and their Succeffors, are hereby
declared to be feized and poffeffed of fuch Eftate
or Eftates therein, as in and by the refpective
Grants, Bargains, Sales, Enfeoffments, Releafes,
Devifes or other Conveyences thereof, is or are
declared, limited and expreffed; as alfo that the

And may acquire additional Property, &c. faid Corporation and their Succeffors, at all
Times hereafter, fhall be capable and able to
purchafe, have, receive, take, hold and enjoy in
Fee-fimple, or of any other leffer Eftate or
Eftates, any Lands, Tenement, Rents, Annuities,
Liberties, Franchifes or other Hereditaments, by
the Gift, Grant, Bargain, Sale, Alienation, En-
feoffment, Releafe, Confirmation or Devife, of
any Perfon or Perfons, Bodies politic and corporate, capable and able to make the fame; and
further, that the faid Corporation and their Succeffors, may take and receive any Sum or Sums
of Money, and any Manner and Portion of Goods
and Chattels that fhall be given and bequeathed
to them by any Perfon or Perfons, Bodies corporate and politic, capable to make a Gift or
Bequeft thereof, fuch Money, Goods and Chattels to be laid out by them in a Purchafe or Purchafes of Lands, Tenements, Meffuages, Houfes,
Rents, Annuities or other Hereditaments, to them
and their Succeffors forever, or the Monies lent
on Intereft, or otherwife difpofed of according
to the Articles, and by Laws of the faid Society,
and the Intention of the Donors.

SECT.

SECT. 5. *And be it further enacted by the Autho-* *rity aforesaid,* That at every the four Quarterly Meetings of the said Society, that is to say, on the twenty-sixth Day of December, on the twenty-fifth Day of March, on the twenty-fourth Day of June, and on the twenty-ninth Day of September, in every Year, or when either of those Days shall happen to be on Sunday, then on the Day following, each and every of the Members of the said Society, may propose any Person or Persons to be ballotted for as a Member of the said Society or Corporation, and such Person or Persons, so proposed and ballotted for, upon being elected by Two-thirds in Number of the Members present, by Ballot as aforesaid, and signing the Articles of said Society, and paying the Entrance-Money, shall from thenceforth become a Member of the said Corporation, and whilst he shall from Time to Time contribute towards the Purposes aforesaid, shall remain a Member of the said Corporation, and not otherwise, making nevertheless proper and reasonable Allowance of Delay for his Residence in the Frontiers of this State, or his being engaged in the Land or Sea Service of this State, or any of the United States, or a Prisoner of War, or beyond Sea on a fair Trade.

Quarterly Meetings of said Society.

New Members may be elected, who are to sign the Art. &c.

SECT. 6. *Provided always, and be it enacted by* *the Authority aforesaid,* That the Members of the said Society shall not, at any Time hereafter, be less than seventy-five in Number, nor more than three hundred.

Proviso for limiting the Number.

SECT. 7. *And be it further enacted by the Autho-* *rity aforesaid,* That the said Corporation and their Successors, or the Majority of such as shall be con-

Corporation to make Rules, &c.

convened at any of the four Quarterly Meetings
of the said Society, shall be authorised and empowered, and they are hereby authorised and
empowered, to make Rules, Bye-laws and Ordinances, and to do every Thing needful for the
good Government and Support of the Affairs of
Provided the said Corporation. *Provided always*, That the
they be not said Bye-laws, Rules and Ordinances, or any of
repugnant them, be not repugnant to the Laws of this Com-
to the monwealth, and that all their Proceedings be fair-
Laws of the
State, and ly and regularly entered in a Book to be kept for
are entered that Purpose; which Book, and all Papers and
in a Book other Documents of the said Society, shall, at
liable to all Times, be liable to the Inspection of the
the Inspec- President and Vice-President of the Supreme Ex-
tion of ecutive Council, the Speaker of the General As-
the Presi-
dent, &c. sembly, and Chief Justice of the State, for the
Time being; and that at the General Meeting
of the Members of the said Society or Corpora-
Members tion, on the Days aforesaid, they, the said Mem-
to elect Of- bers, or a Majority of such as shall be present,
ficers an- be authorised and empowered to elect and chuse
nually, &c. by Ballot, one President, one Vice-President, six
Overseers, a Treasurer, two Secretaries, one Solicitor, and one Deacon; the said Officers to be
Inhabitants of the said City of Philadelphia, and
to remain in Office until the next Meeting of
the said Corporation, on the twenty-sixth Day
of December then next following; and in Case
of Death, Removal or Refusal to serve of any
one or more of the Officers so chosen, his or
their Place so dying, removing, or being removed, or refusing, shall be supplied by an Election in like Manner, at the next Quarterly
Meeting; and the Person or Persons so chosen,
shall remain in his said Office, by Virtue of the
said Election, until the next December Meeting
aforesaid.

SECT.

SECT. 8. *And be it further enacted by the Autho-* **How the** *rity aforesaid,.* That the Rents, Interest and Pro- **Profits of** fits arising from the said real and personal Estate **the Estates** of the said Corporation, shall, by the Officers of **are to be** the said Corporation, and their Successors, cho- **applied.** sen and appointed in such Manner and Form as herein before is directed and required, from Time to Time, be applied for the Relief and Support of poor distressed Germans arriving in this State from Parts beyond Sea, for the erecting or sup- porting Schools and Seminaries of Learning, and one or more Library or Libraries within this State, for the better educating and instructing the Children and Youth of the Germans, and Descendants of Germans, and in building, re- pairing and maintaining School-Houses, and other Houses necessary for the Purposes afore- said, for Salaries to Schoolmasters and Teachers, and for such other charitable Uses as are con- formable to the true Design and Intent of the same Society.

SECT. 9. *Provided always, and be it further enacted* **Proviso,** *by the Authority aforesaid,.* That in the Disposal and **regulating** Application of the public Monies of the said Cor- **the Dispo-** poration, the aforesaid President, Vice-President, **sal of Mo-** Overseers, Secretaries, Treasurer, Solicitor and **ney, &c.** Deacon, and their Successors in Office, or any seven of them, the said Officers, may make Or- ders and Directions for the Relief of poor and distressed Persons, and supporting Scholars, Schoolmasters and others, coming under their Notice, and that upon emergent Occasions, when immediate Relief is wanted, an Order signed by one of the Presidents, and two of the Over- seers, directed to the Treasurer, shall be a suf- ficient Authority for the said Treasurer to dis-

B   charge

charge and pay fuch Order. *Provided alfo,* That neither of the faid Officers, fhall at any Time during the Execution of his Office, or afterwards, be entitled to demand, fue for, or recover any Pay, Reward or Commiffion for his Service, in any of the faid Offices refpectively.

Corporation may have a Seal, and alter it at Pleafure, &c.

SECT. 10. *And be it further enaƈted by the Authority aforefaid,* That the faid Corporation and their Succeffors, fhall have full Power and Authority to make, have and ufe one common Seal, with fuch Device and Infcription as they fhall think proper, and the fame to break, alter and renew at their Pleafure.

May fue and be fued, &c.

SECT. 11. *And be it further enaƈted by the Authority aforefaid,* That the faid Corporation and their Succeffors, by the Name, Stile and Title aforefaid, fhall be able and capable in Law to fue and to be fued, plead and be impleaded, in any Court or Courts, before any Judge or Judges, Juftice or Juftices, in all and all Manner of Suits, Complaints, Pleas, Caufes, Matters and Demands of whatever Kind, Nature and Form they may be, and all and every Matter or Thing therein to do, in as full and effectual a Manner, as any other Perfon or Perfons, Bodies politic and corporate within this Commonwealth may or can do.

Provifo, for limiting the yearly Value of real Eſtates and Intereſt of Money, exclufive of ſta-

SECT. 12. *Provided always, and be it further enaƈted by the Authority aforefaid,* That the clear yearly Value or Income of the Meffuages, Houfes, Lands, Tenements, Rents, Annuities, or other Hereditaments and real Eftate of the faid Corporation and Intereft of Money lent, fhall not exceed the Sum of two thoufand and five hundred Pounds, lawful Money of Pennfylvania, to be

taken

taken and efteemed exclufive of the Monies arifing ted Sub-
from annual or other ftated Subfcriptions or Pay- fcriptions,
ments, which faid Monies fhall be received by &c.
the Treafurer of the faid Corporation, and difpofed of by him, upon the Order of the other
Officers, or a Majority of them, in the Manner
herein before defcribed, purfuant to a Vote or
Votes of the Members of the faid Society, ap-
propriating the fame at one of their Quarterly
Meetings.

Signed, by Order of the Houfe,

Frederick A. Muhlenberg, Speaker.

*Enacted into a Law, at Philadelphia,
on Thurfday, the twentieth Day of
September, in the Year of our Lord
one thoufand feven hundred and
eighty-one.*

SAMUEL STERETT, *Clerk of the General Affembly.*

THE
Great DUTY
OF
CHARITY,
confidered and applied
IN A
SERMON,

Preached at the Church in
Brattle-Street, Bofton, on the
Lord's-Day, *November* 28.
1 7 4 2.

By *Jonathan Afhley*, A. M.
Paftor of the Church of CHRIST, in *Deerfield.*

B O S T O N:
Printed by J. DRAPER, for S. ELIOT, in *Cornhill*,
1 7 4 2.

PREFACE.

COURTEOUS READER,

*WHOEVER thou art, into whose Hands these
following Pages may fall; I ask the Kindness,
that thou wouldst read without Prejudice : I can
assure you I had an honest Intention in delivering of it ;
and hope you will have the same in reading ——If what
I have said in the Introduction to my Text may open your
Eyes, when you see the same Disorders in our Churches,
as were in the Church of Corinth, and reclaim you from
them : Or, if it be a Means of removing the Prejudice
of your Mind against Things of a serious Nature,
when you find there were the same Irregularities
in the Church of Corinth (at the same Time that the
Fruits of the Spirit were evidently amongst them) as
are amongst us at this Day of the Grace of GOD, in the
hopeful Conversion of many in our Churches: Or if it
excite in you earnest Prayers and longing Desires after
that Charity which is greater than Faith and Hope,
which is the Life and Soul of Religion here, and the
Happiness of Heaven above ; let GOD have all the
Praise ; my End is answered.*

I am your Servant in the Gospel,

J. Aſhley.

THE great DUTY OF *CHARITY* consider'd and applied.

1 COR. xiii. 1. 2. 3.

THO' I speak with the Tongues of Men and Angels, and have not Charity, I am become as sounding Brass, or a tinkling Cymbal.
And tho' I have the Gift of Prophesy, and understand all Mysteries, and all Knowledge; and though I have all Faith, so that I could remove Mountains, and have no Charity, I am nothing.
And though I bestow all my Goods to feed the Poor, and tho' I give my Body to be burned, and have not Charity, it profiteth me nothing.

WHOEVER carefully reads this *Epistle* of the *Apostle* to the Church of *Corinth*, and examines their State by what the Apostle says to them, and of them, and then brings his Tho'ts down to our own Times, and the State of Religion amongst us, cannot, I think, well avoid running a Parrallel between *Us* and *Them*,

Them : And the Circumstances of Religion in *This Land* will in nothing appear very different, and in *many Things* will exactly resemble *Theirs.*

The Apostle Owns, and blesses GOD for it ; That there was a very plentiful Effusion of the Divine *Spirit* on the Church of *Corinth* in his *extraordinary* Gifts, such as *Tongues, working Miracles, Prophesying,* &c. And in his *common,* and *saving Graces* on the Hearts of Believers ; enlightning and comforting their Souls ; *Chapt, 1. 4,*——8th *Verse,*

And it is fully evident to every unprejudiced Mind, that GOD has remarkably shower'd down his *Spirit* on the Churches in our Land (not indeed in his *extraordinary* Gifts of *Tongues* and *working Miracles* ; for these are not necessary for us, nor to be expected ; but) in his *common* and *saving Operations* on the Minds of Men, in convincing, converting, edifying and comforting his People.

But yet, It is observable, That in the Church of *Corinth* there was much Contention and Division in religious Matters : They fell into diverse Sects and Parties, who were too much void of Charity towards each other : One said he was of *Paul,* another of *Apollos,* a third of *Cephas,* or *Peter,* a fourth of *Christ* ; and each Party was concern'd to exalt it self, and pull down the other ; therefore the Apostle expostulates with them as he does in the 11th, 12th and 13th *Verses* of the 1st *Chapter.* And herein we are not unlike them : Almost endless are the Sects and Parties amongst us ; Some Followers and Admirers of one, and some of another ; nor is there a small Degree of Contention among us : Our religious Debates are the common Topick of Conversation with all.

And then, What was naturally consequent upon the Church of *Corinth's* falling into divers Sects and Parties, they were guilty of a very sinful exalting those Men who were at the Head of their Sects, above the Place of *Instruments* ; and setting them up in the Room

of

of GOD, as tho' they could impart Faith and Salvation to their Followers : Hence the Apoſtle addreſſeth them in the 3d *Chapter* 5th, 6th and 7th *Verſes.* Nor can we excuſe our ſelves in this Point ; for the Perſons of ſome have been evidently had in Admiration ; and they have been ſet above the Place of Means and Inſtruments.

Nor was the Church of *Corinth* free from uncharitable Judging and Cenſuring one another ; and even the Apoſtle himſelf was not ſpared, but fell under their Cenſures ; and therefore he lets them know, it was a ſmall Matter to be judged of them or any other, *Chapt.* 4. *Verſ.* 3, 4, 5. And I need not ſpend Time to ſhow you how far this Evil of Judging and Condemning our Brother is ſpread amongſt us.

And in the Church of *Corinth* there was a Diſpoſition in many to deſpiſe and reject thoſe Miniſters, who had been labouring amongſt them ; and by whoſe Miniſtry they had believed ; and to heap to themſelves Teachers of more Eloquence, greater Zeal and Gifts as they imagined : And hence the Apoſtle reproves them, as he does in the 13th, 14th, 15th, 16th *Verſes* of the 4th *Chapter.* And who can be ignorant that it has been too much the Temper amongſt Us, to lay aſide ſtated Miniſters of the Goſpel, and to ſet up *Novices* without end to be our Teachers ?

Again, Diſcipline in the Church of *Corinth* was almoſt wholly neglected ; they were grown ſo conceited of their Attainments, that they would not ſubmit to Order : Offenders could not be called to an Account : And even a notorious *Fornicator* was let alone : See the 5th *Chapter.* And how greatly is Church-Diſcipline deſtroyed in many Places with us : Some are grown ſo zealous and conceited of their own Graces, that they cannot be brought to ſubmit to the Order of Churches ; and even deſpiſe Reproof.

So alſo in the Church of *Corinth* there was a Diſpoſition to abuſe the Liberty of the Goſpel ; and thereby
diſſolve

diſſolve the civil Relations of Life : The Wiſe to depart from the Husband, and the Servant to rebel a-
gainſt the Maſter, under a Pretence of chriſtian Liberty:
And this moved the Apoſtle to write as he did in the
7th *Chapter* from the 13th to 22d *Verſe.* And it is
well known there has been ſomething of this Spirit in
our Land : Some have been upon the Point of breaking the Bands of theſe Relative Duties becauſe of Uncon-
verſion ; the Wiſe to forſake the Husband, and the
Servant diſobey his Maſter.

Again, We may obſerve in the Church of *Corinth*
an unbecoming Stiffneſs and Unyieldableneſs towards
one another ; not avoiding the Occaſions of Offence to
one anothers Conſcience, as they ought to have done ;
ſome would eat Part of thoſe Beaſts which were ſlain
to be ſacrificed to Idols, and perhaps in the Idol's Temple with their Worſhippers, ſaying an Idol was nothing ;
however offenſive it was to ſome others ; therefore it is
the Apoſtle gives them ſuch Directions in the 8th *Chapter* 10th *Verſe* to the end. And can we excuſe our
ſelves in this Point ? Have we avoided giving Offence
to one another ; and carefully abſtained from Things
indifferent becauſe offenſive to others ?

It is alſo eaſily obſerved from the Apoſtle, that there
was too great Sparingneſs towards the Miniſters of the
Goſpel, who imparted ſpiritual Things to them : Yea,
it ſeems it became a Queſtion with ſome, whether they
were oblig'd to contribute for the Support of Miniſters, ſince the Spirit was ſo plentifully poured out : And
hence the Apoſtle anſwers them, who put the Queſtion
to him, in the 9th *Chapter* from *Verſe* 3, to 14 And it
is too true of us in this Land (in ſome Parts of it at
leſt) notwithſtanding all the Revival of Religion.
There is a greater Backwardneſs to the Support of Miniſters than ever ; as tho' an extraordinary Degree of
Zeal excus'd People from ſupporting their Miniſters.

Again, In the Church of *Corinth* there was the Diſorder of leaving the proper Buſineſs, and Calling GOD
had put them in, and invading the Province and Buſineſs
of

of another. They were guilty of a proud, afpiring Humour, which enclin'd them to fet up for Teachers in the Church: And hence the Apoftle exhorts them in the 7th *Chapter, Ver.* 20, 21. And expoftulates with them with warmth in the 12th *Chapter, Ver.* 28, 29, 30 And who is ignorant that this has been, and is ftill our Cafe? What Numbers of illiterate Teachers have thruft themfelves into the Churches?

Nor was the Church *of Corinth* free of all Pride and Vain-glorying in their Religious Matters: They indulge Spiritual Pride, and this it was that ftirred up fo much Contention. The Apoftle tells u they were puffed up one againft another, 5th *Chapter* 2d *Ver.* They gloried in their Gifts and Attainments, and were forward to difcover them; fo that many prophefyed together: And would to GOD we had been more free from fpiritual Pride and vain Oftentation in Religion! Who is ignorant? There has been no fmall Appearance of it in the Worfhip of GOD's Houfe?

So alfo the Church of *Corinth* fell into great Irregularities and Diforders in their religious Affemblies; feveral taught and exhorted at the fame Time. The Women laid afide their female Modefty, and fet up to be Teachers in the Church: Therefore the Apoftle directs them as he does in the 14th *Chapter* from the 30th to the 35th *Ver.* And who is fo blind that he cannot fee our Diforders defcribed as in a Glafs by the Apoftle in this *Chapter*.

And once more, by way of Comparifon, The Church of *Corinth* was under the Judgments of GOD for thefe Things; fee the 11th *Chapter, Ver.* 30, 31, 32. And have we not reafon to fear GOD is angry with us at this Day, for the many Things which have been amifs: And let us confider wherefore it is his Judgments are ftill continued in many Refpects.

Having thus confidered what the Apoftle fays of the Church of *Corinth*; I afk Liberty of my Hearers to make one Remark, *viz.* " That the Apoftle *Paul*

B " in

" in the Judgment of some modern Teachers, was the
" greateſt Oppoſer that Religion ever had; for he in
" the firſt Place acknowledges the Operations of the
" divine Spirit in the Church of *Corinth,* and then
" proceeds to enumerate, and bear a full Teſtimony
" againſt all the Extravagancies they were guilty of;
" nor did he think he diſſerved Religion by it. "

What I have hitherto ſaid, may ſerve both to let
you ſee the the Reaſon of the Apoſtle his recommending Charity, and giving of it ſo high an Encomium;
and alſo juſtify me in offering the Words read to
your ſerious Conſideration.

The Apoſtle allowed the *Corinthians* to *covet ear-*
neſtly the beſt Gifts; but yet, ſays he, *I ſhew you a more*
excellent Way, 12th *Chapter* laſt *Verſe;* a more excellent
Way for Peace, for Order, for Edification, and to recover
them from their Diſorders and Confuſions; and this he
lets us know is CHARITY: And he told them, and
now tells us, that without Charity we are nothing:
Notwithſtanding all our Gifts, if we have not Charity
we are no real Chriſtians; nothing but empty Noiſe
and Sound. The *Doctrine* I ſhall ſpeak to from the
Words before us is,

> DOCT. *THAT whatever Attainments we may ar-*
> *rive to in Religion, if we are void of* Charity, *we*
> *are no real Chriſtians; nor will they profit us any*
> *Thing.*

Under this Doctrine I propoſe theſe Things,

1ſt, *To open the* Nature *of this Charity, which is ſo*
neceſſary in our Religion.
2dly, *To ſhow that Men may go great Lengths in Re-*
ligion, and yet have nothing of this Charity.
3dly, *That all our Attainments without Charity,*
will neither make us real Chriſtians; nor profit us
any Thing.
Laſtly, *Apply the Truth to ourſelves*

I. I am

I. I am in the firſt Place to open the *Nature* of this *Charity*, the *Apoſtle* ſo recommends ; and without which every Man, as well as he himſelf, will be nothing.

I am ſenſible that Uſe and Cuſtom in theſe latter Days has confined the Term *Charity* to *Alms-Deeds*, or giving our Wealth to the Poor and diſtreſſed ; and ſo it is only a Fruit or Effect of Charity : But that the Apoſtle does not intend *Alms-Deeds* by Charity, is evident from the Character he gives us of it in the Verſes following our Text ; none of which can agree with Charity in the vulgar Senſe of the Word, and are compatible only with that *Divine Love* which is ſo often recommended in the Goſpel.

" CHARITY then is *Love* in the Goſpel-Latitude,
" comprehending *Love to GOD* and *our Neighbour*, in
" *all the Branches of it.*"

And this Charity or divine Love, the Apoſtle tells us is the *Fruit* of the *Spirit*, Gal. 5. 22. A Man cannot poſſibly plant it in his own Soul : All his Care and Pains ; all his religious Duties and Services ; all his Prayers and Tears, will not of themſelves ſubdue that Enmity that is in the Heart to GOD, *Rom.* 8. 7. and bring the Soul to love GOD with a true Love of Complacency, and reſting in Him as a Being of Holineſs and Goodneſs. Nothing but the Spirit of GOD can turn a Man from being not only an Enemy to GOD, but Enmity it ſelf, to love Him with his whole Soul ; ſo as to make choice of GOD for his Portion and Inheritance forever, and account his Favour better than Life.——— The beſt Education and the beſt Means, the moſt pious Counſels, and the beſt Diſcourſes concerning GOD's Goodneſs and Mercy can never beget this Love in us without the gracious Operations of the Divine Spirit on our Hearts. Nor can we without the Help of the Spirit ever love one another in a Goſpel Senſe.——We naturally live in Hatred, *Tit* 3. 3. We may love as *Publicans* did of old, ſuch as were Friends to them, *Mat.* 5. 46. But to love all Men, even our Enemies as our ſelves, is above the utmoſt ſtretch of human Nature,

and

and only the Spirit of CHRIST can enable us to do so.

And this Charity the Apostle lets us know is a necessary Consequent and Attendant on Faith, for *Faith works by Love*, Gal 5. 6. This Love never preceeds, but always follows Faith: A Man cannot love as the Gospel requires, before he believes in CHRIST; but if he does believe he will have this Charity: They cannot be separated from each other, no more than the Cause can from the Effect: And if we have not *Love*, we may assure our selves we are destitute of *Faith*.

And the Apostle informs us, That it is *a fulfilling of the Law* (*Rom.* 13. 10.) in both the Tables of it. It engages a Man to a diligent Attendance upon all the Duties, which the moral and revealed Law of GOD enjoin upon him towards his Maker: He loves to fear obey, and serve Him: He loves to submit to his Will and attend his Worship, and speak his Praise. Love to GOD makes all the Duties we owe him easy and delightful. And as he knows the same GOD that engages him to fear and serve him, has enjoined it upon him, to do Justice to his Neighbour, to speak the Truth, to be courteous and obliging to all: So he takes pleasure in doing so; because it is the Will of GOD he should. And he is not willing to omit one Duty to GOD, or his Neighbour; for Love teaches him none of the Commands are grievous.

And, the Apostle *Peter* tells us, this Love is *without Dissimulation* and Disguise, 1 *Pet.* 1. 22. It consists not in Words, or some courteous and obliging Carriage; but is seated in the Heart; and the truly charitable Man is really and desirous of your Welfare, as he professes to be: He does not speak smooth Words when Gall and Bitterness is in his Heart: He is honest and upright in his Pretension.

And, this Love is a great Preservative to the Christian against the Allurements, the Flatteries, or Threats of the World; and all the Temptations of Satan.

Hence

Hence the Apostle compares it to a *Breast-plate*, 1 *Thessalon.* 5. 8 which preserves the Heart from all Wounds from the Enemy. And could we always keep this Charity in a lively Exercise, how would it keep us from the Temptations of Earth and Hell?

And, the Apostle assures us, That this Charity is a sure Evidence of our being *born of God*, 1 *John* 4. 7. thereby we may know whether CHRIST is formed within us; whether all old Things are passed away, and all Things become new within us; for none but the Regenerate love GOD above every thing else, and their Neighbour in sincerity as themselves.

As to the Fruits and Effects of this Love: The Apostle sets them before us in the Verses following our Text; and they well deserve a particular consideration.

Charity, saith the Apostle, *Suffereth long*; it defers Anger, and does not suffer it soon to boil up in the Mind, and discover itself in bitter Words, and railing Accusations. The charitable Man sets a Guard upon himself: If he has any Injuries and Abuses offered him, he turns his Resentments into Pity, and Revenge into a rendering Good for Evil.

It is Kind. It moves the Affections towards such as need our Pity and Compassion: It softens our Hearts into Compassion: It unlocks our Hands to distribute our Wealth to such as want our Alms: It does not suffer a Man to live to himself; but puts him upon doing all the Good he can, and making himself as useful as possible to his fellow Creatures.

Charity, Envieth not. In the Greek (*au Zeloi*) is not *Zealous*, (i. e) Does not *burn with Bitterness* towards others. Are they Richer than ourselves; it suffers us not to be uneasy. —— Are they endowed with greater Parts, or have they more Credit and Reputation? Charity will not suffer us to be bitter towards them, as tho' they had injured us: Do they differ
from

from us in some things? Charity don't allow us to call for Fire from Heaven to consume them. It will not suffer us to pursue them with Warmth and Bitterness. Charity teacheth us Mildness and Gentleness towards them.

Charity vaunteth not it self; or it may be render'd, *does not act rashly*. The charitable Man does not despise the Counsel of the Wise and Aged: He is not resolute in his own Purposes, in Opposition to all others: He questions himself, and is ready to prefer the Judgment of others to his own.

Is not puffed up: If he is Rich, he does not value himself for it, and despise the Poor; for his Heart is not set upon this World. Is he honoured and applauded in the World; He does not swell with these empty Titles, for he sees they are Vanity.——Has he greater Gifts or Graces than others, he blesses GOD for them; and does not allow himself to be proud of them; for he knows it is by the Grace of GOD, that he is what he is: And he has not made himself to differ.

Doth not behave it self unseemly, or *indecently* or *unbeautifully*; but is a careful Observer of Order and Decency in all Things: It teaches Men to reverence the Superiour, to be courteous and kind to Equals and Inferiours. — The charitable Man observes the Direction of the Apostle, *Chapter* 14, *Ver.* 40. He does not cry out of Order, as hurtful to Religion, and a Dagon that is to be thrown down and destroyed. He does not bring serious Things into all Companies and Places, to be scoffed at and reproached. He is not willing to expose his holy Religion to the needless Reproach of the Prophane.

Charity seeketh not her own. This Gospel Love does not suffer a Man to look altogether at his own Things; but disposeth him to have regard to the Good of his Neighbour, *Phil.* 2. 4. And in many Things Charity teaches Men to forego their own Profit and Advantage for the Good of others.

4

Is not easily provoked. Charity calms the Mind, so that the Passions are not easily stirred up and carried forth to wrong Objects.— And could we always have our Love to GOD and one another in exercise: How much above these small Injuries and Provocations should we be? It would not be an easy Matter to stir up Anger and Revenge in our Minds: Like CHRIST we should bear long and pray our heavenly Father to forgive such as despitefully use us.

It thinketh no evil: It banishes Jealousies and Suspicions from the Mind. It does not suffer us to suspect a Man as vile and wicked, when he does not appear so. The charitable Man will not entertain low and base Thoughts of his Neighbour, when he can think honourably and well of him; he is careful to think the best he can.

Nor does the truly charitable Man *rejoice* when Sin is prevalent, and the Iniquities of Mankind abound: He is sorry when Vice is practised openly, and Righteousness is treated with Contempt: Nor is he glad at the Calamity of others: It is no pleasure to him to see Men evil entreated, injured and abused: But he rejoiceth when the Righteous prosper, and are accounted honourable amongst Men; when Truth prevails in the Power of it: And He takes Pleasure in the Innocent's being vindicated from all those Aspersions which have been cast on them.

Charity beareth all things; or as it ought to be rendered, *covereth* or *concealeth* all things: It does not allow us to divulge the Errors and Mistakes, the Infirmities and the Failings of our Brother: It teacheth to cast a Mantle over them; that they may be hid from the World; that Men may not hate and reproach him.

And the charitable Man is ready to *believe* all things well concerning his Brother: Is any thing spoke in his Praise and Commendation, he believes it is true. He does not say, he don't think he can speak
or

or do fo well: He believes all things that there may be any Foundation for: If he lives Honeftly, he believes him to be fo: If he lives like a Chriftian, he believes him to be fo indeed.

And when there are fome Things to ftagger his Faith concerning his Brother; yet then he keeps up his *Hope*: Is he fpoke evil of, he hopes he is Innocent: Does he err in fome Things, he hopes it is not wilfull: Does he fail in his Duty, he hopes notwithftanding he is a good Man, until it is too evident that Sin is his Delight and what he allows himfelf in. —And it is a plain Breach of Charity, to think our Neighbour unconverted and a Sinner, when his Life is fuch, that we may hope he is a real Chriftian.

Charity endureth all things. It difpofeth a Man to bear all Manner of ill Treatment, with Patience: If we have this Love of GOD in our Hearts, how eafy will it be to be Poor and Low? Divine Love will yeild us more Satisfaction than all the World: How light a Thing will Reproach and Slander be, if we have Love in our Hearts? How little will it affect us to be fpoken all manner of Evil of? Love will make the moft abufive Treatment eafy. — If we have Charity, we fhan't think hard to be made the Off-fcouring of all Things; we fhall not greatly difturb our felves let Men fay or think what they will about us.

And this Charity, if it be once implanted in our Hearts, it will never wholly fail and die; we may lofe it very much as to the Exercife of it; but it never will wholly ceafe, but will be as a *Well of Water fpringing up to everlafting Life*: When we die, we fhall carry it into the other World with us. *Faith*, as it refpects future Things, will ceafe, and end in *Vifion*. *Hope* will end alfo in *Fruition*. But, *Charity* will not leave us; but will abide with us throughout the endlefs Ages of Eternity; and on this Accoun. it is greater than *Faith* and *Hope*, *v.* 13.

But

But I proceed, *Secondly*, to confider that Men may *go great lengths in Religion and yet be void of Charity.* So the Apoftle fuppofes in the Wo ds under Confide-ration, that he might *fpeak with the Tongue of Men and Angels* ; that he m'ght *have the Gift of Prophecy, underftand all Mifteries, and all Knowledge* ; that he might have the *Faith of Miracles,* fo as *to remove Mountains into the midft of Seas, and yet,* after all, *have nothing of this Love to God,* and his *Neighbour.* I May mention fome things Men may attain to, and yet not have this Love the Apoftle fpeaks of.

A Man may be under very *great Conviction for Sin,* and have a lively Apprehenfion of his Danger, and the Wrath of God, which his Sins have expofed him to: He may be under great *Horror* and *Amaze-ment,* fo as to cry out, *The Pangs of Hell have got hold on me.* He may cry out in the Anguifh and Bitternefs of his Spirit: His Flefh may tremble, and his Heart be ready to melt within Him, and yet be void of Charity. It is granted that Conviction preceeds Con-verfion ; and evangelical Love follows it: And it is certain, Convictions, yea very ftrong ones too, do fome-times prove abortive, and don't iffue in Converfion ; and confequently Love is not the confequent of them. *Cain* had ftrong Convictions; faid, *his Punifh-ment was greater than he could bear. Lamech* was un-der great Diftrefs for his Sin. *Judas* hanged h m felf in the extremity of his Horror; yet neither of them had the leaft Spark of this Divine Love. Conviction then is not a Proof a Man has Charity,

So alfo a Man may *reform his Life,* abandon his former finful Courfes; and become fober, grave, and temperate in his Actions ; and yet have no Charity at all. There are many Things may urge a Man to reform his Life: A Fear of Hell, which he fees his Sin expofes him to; the Uneafinefs of his Confcience, fear of Difgrace, or of the Punifhment of the Magif-trate, may put him upon a more fober Life; and yet he have no Love to GOD; and hence it is too too common fuch return again to their former Courfes,

C

like

like *the Sow that was washed, to her wallowing in the Mire, and the Dog to his vomit*; and the evil Spirit returns into them again, and has more Power over them than ever: But if they had this Love of GOD in their Hearts they could not have so sinned; for *their Seed would have remained in them.*

Again, A Man may be *very Zealous,* and yet be void of this evangelical Love. *Zeal* is nothing but the Ardour of the Affections, or the engagedness of the Powers of the Soul; and a Man may be zealous in a *bad* Cause, as well as a *good* one; and even in Religion itself A Man may be fired with Zeal, who is a Stranger to vital Piety, and the Love of GOD. The Pride of a Man's own Heart may fire his Affections, and blow him up into a burning Zeal. Education may Inspire a Man with a great Degree of it. A Man's own Interest may fill him with it. Thus *Jehu* was all Zeal for the Lord of Hosts, when he was actuated by nothing but his own ambitious Views; and never felt the least Spark of the Fire of divine Love in his Heart. Who more zealous than the Papists? And few or none in our Land have yet equall'd them; but who can think many of them have the least Love to GOD. Zeal is therefore no Evidence of Regeneration, and the Love of GOD in the Soul.

Furthermore, A Man may be *greatly distressed and concerned for others*; and yet have no Love to GOD *Himself.* How common is it, when Persons are under Convictions for Sin, and seeking their own Salvation, to look with Pity on their Friends and Companions, who have no serious Tho'tfulness about their own Souls? And these Persons when they have felt the Workings of their religious Affections, may (some of them at least) mistake them for Grace in the Heart; and hastily conclude their own State safe; and now all their Concern is for others: They may be in great Concern for them, and have not the least Fear about their *own* State; and we have reason to fear this has been sometimes the Case when they

have

have had nothing of the Love of GOD in their Hearts.

And what is confequent upon their hoping their Condition is fafe, is a *Joy* and *Delight* in fuch a Confideration : All which may be when they are deceived, and do not love GOD. Men may take fome Pleafure and Satisfaction in religious Duties who are not Regenerate, and confequently do not love GOD : Thus our Saviour tells us of fome who *heard the Word with Joy for a Seafon*, Matth. 13. 19, 20. And the Apoftle tells us of fome who *have tafted of the good Word of GOD, and the Powers of the World to come*, and yet might *fall away*, Heb. 6. 5, 6. The Prophet *Ezekiel*, was as a *lovely Song* to a People who did not love GOD

And this *Joy* may fometimes arife to fuch a heighth, and be fo fudden as to be called a *Rapture* or *Trance* ; and yet they who feel the fame be wholly ignorant of the Love of GOD : The *Imagination* may be raifed to a great Pitch ; and wonderful Things may be *painted upon the Mind* : The Ideas may be lively, and the Reprefentation pleafing ; and yet there may be no Love of GOD in the Heart : This was the Cafe of *Balaam* ; he was in a Trance, *Numb.* 24 beg. ; but who ever imagined him a true Lover of GOD ?

A Man may alfo attain to a *great Degree of Knowledge in religious Matters* ; and yet have no real Charity : So the Apoftle fuppofes in the Text. A Man may by long Study and clofe Application attain a great Degree of Speculation ; he may difpute learnedly and diftinguifh well in the important Points of Divinity : He may unfold many important Truths ; reconcile many feeming Oppofitions in the Word of GOD ; and yet have no love to GOD, nor his Word.——And fome have by a careful Study of the Scriptures, and attentive hearing the Word preached, when under Convictions, in a few Weeks, made fuch Progrefs, that they would talk wonderfully of Things they knew nothing about before ; and yet after a while manifefted themfelves Strangers to a Love to GOD.

C 2   And

And many have attained to a surprizing Art of *addressing the Passions*: They have been able to command the greatest Attention ; have talked as tho' they had the Tongue of Angels, and yet knew nothing experimentally of the Love of GOD and CHRIST: Some Popish Missionaries will stir up all the Passions, and yet ignorant of GOD and CHRIST.   And some of you may remember here, many Years past, a vagrant Preacher addrest you, with all the Force of Oratory, and drew away your Ears and stirred up all your Passions ; and yet I believe none of you in the End supposed him to have the least Spark of divine Love. *

Others have *counterfeited all Grace*, and yet have been Strangers to this Charity: They have appeared exceeding Meek ; speaking meanly of Themselves, and all their Duties ; they have profess'd to be wholly weaned from the World, and all its Enjoyments ; they have talked much of vital Piety, of the Love of GOD and CHRIST ; they have seemed to excell in Holiness and Heavenly-mindedness ; but in the End have discover'd themselves to be Wolves in Sheep's-Cloathing. They deceived the World, and perhaps Themselves too.

And they may go such a length in Religion, be so constant in Duties ; and stir up their own Passions and Affections, till they are confident of their good Estate ; and have banished all Doubts and Fears out of their Mind, and yet know not what It is to love GOD and CHRIST. Confidence is no Evidence GOD loves us, nor we Him: Who more assured of their good Estate than the Pharisees ? They despised CHRIST's Admonition to escape the Wrath of GOD: They told him they were Children of *Abraham* ; and question'd not the Love of GOD to them ; but after all their Confidence, they were a Generation of Vipers.

Again, A Man may take Pleasure in *distributing his Goods to the Poor*: He may give largely in charitable

---

* One Mip.

Use :

Ufes; he may build and adorn Churches; he may give a vaft Eftate, even *all his Goods*, to feed the Poor; a natural Tendernefs of Heart, E ducation, Cuftom, Pride, and other Things may move him to this, and yet he have no real Love to GOD : He may give much to be feen of Men, that he may have much Applaufe from the World.

And laftly, and to add no more here, A Man may arrive to fuch a *Zeal* in religious Matters, that he may *Glory in Tribulation*; rejoice in Stripes; he may go finging to a Goal, and prefer it to a Palace; he may even long to fuffer Perfecution, and pray that it may come upon him; and yet have nothing of this Charity: How many poor deluded *Roman Catholicks* have gloried in Perfecution, and tho't they merited Heaven by it? How many Self deceived Quakers have run into Perfecution being impatient to fuffer for Religion : And the Apoftle fuppofes a Man may *give his Body to be burned*, and yet have no Charity.

Thus I have confidered many Things a Man *may attain to* and yet have no Charity.

I proceed, *Thirdly*, To fhow you, That *if he has all thefe Attainments and many more; yet if he has no Charity, he is no real Chriftian; and they will profit him nothing.*

Firft, After all, He is no *real Chriftian without Charity. I am nothing*, fays the Apoftle, (i. e.) nothing of a Chriftian. He may be one to Appearance; the World may judge him fuch; he may have a *great Name* to live, yet he is *nothing* in reality : he is but empty Noife and Sound.

For, after all his Attainments, he is an Enemy to GOD in his Heart if he has not Charity *He that loveth not, is not born of God*; and every one who not born of God, *is full of Enmity againft Him*, Rom. 8 7. And is it poffible a Man fhould be a real and thoro' Chriftian, who hates GOD? If he hates the Father will he love the Son, fubmit himfelf to his
Go.

Government, and follow his Example? This cannot be; for GOD the Father and Son are One; and he who cannot subject himself to the Laws of one, cannot to the Laws of the other.

Nor has that Man, who is void of Charity, that *Meekness* which is necessary in order to our being real Christians: A proud, arrogant Christian, who has not learned of CHRIST to be *Meek and Lowly in Heart*, seems to carry a Contradiction ; and it is certain, that a Man is no more than a *nominal Christian*, who has not a meek and quiet Spirit dwelling within him.

A Man who does not Love GOD is not *Heavenly-minded*, as a Christian must be : How can he have his Hopes and Desires, his Expectation and his Conversation in Heaven, where GOD is, whom he don't love, and looks upon as his Enemy? He will not have his Thoughts and Views there, if he don't love GOD.

Nor is it possible He should *aim at the Glory of GOD* in all his Ways and Behaviour as a Christian is required to do, if he has not this Charity. He never will seek the Honour and Glory of an Enemy : *Self* will be the ultimate End of all his Actions : The great Idol of *Self* will swallow up all his Views, and employ all his Actions, and GOD will be neglected so long as he don't love him.

And so long as he is destitute of the love of GOD, he will be void of all *true evangelical Repentance* : He may have a *legal* Repentance, and mourn for Sin as it exposes him to eternal Pain and Torment : But if he does not love GOD, he never will mourn over his Sins, as they are against a holy, merciful and righteous GOD. True evangelical Repentance always follows the Love of GOD ; and the Soul repents *because* it loves GOD, and is grieved that it has offended Him.

Nor

Nor has the Man, void of Charity, any *faving Faith*—.*Faith works by Love* ; and if there is no *Love*, there is no *Faith*, where there is not the *one*, there is not the *other* ; for GOD does not feparate them. When he begets Faith in our Souls by his Spirit, he gives a living operating Faith ; and the neceffary Fruit of that is Love. Thus you fee a Man if he has not Charity, will be *nothing of a real Chriftian*.

Secondly, I am to confider, That *all our Attainments in Religion, if we are void of Charity, will profit us nothing at all*.

They never will fatisfy the Demands of that Law we are under the ftrongeft Obligations to yield a perfect Obedience to : The Law denounces Death upon us if we fulfill it not ; and the Apoftle affures us, *Love is the fulfilling of it*. Without Love therefore to GOD and Man we become Debtors to the Law, and fall under the Condemnation of it.

Nor will any of thefe fuppofed Attainments in Religion, ever atone for our paft Breaches of the Law: We have finned, and are become Guilty before GOD : His Law condemns us: and its vain to think any Thing we can attain to, fo long as we are deftitute of Love to GOD, will atone for our Sin.

Nor will they ever move GOD to pardon us and acquit us from the Sentence of Death we are under : They may move Men to overlook our paft Mifcarriages and forget our Failings ; but GOD fees the Heart, and if there be Enmity to Him, he will look upon us Enemies, and condemn us as fuch.

Nor will thefe fuppofed Attainments in Religion ever entitle us to the Obedience and Sufferings of CHRIST : It is upon the Account of thefe alone we can be juftified before GOD ; thefe are the Righteoufnefs GOD will accept : And if we are not entitled to thefe, we muft perifh ; for after all we can poffibly attain to, fo long as we have not Faith in CHRIST, which *works by Love*, we have no Intereft in the *Righteoufnefs of*
the

the Son of GOD. It is only by that Faith, which works by Love, that his Righteousness is *imputed* to us.

Nor will all these Attainments fit us for Heaven, and entitle us to it, if we have not Charity: After all our Zeal and Fervour ; if we are void of the Love of GOD we are utterly unfit for that World of Light and Love above: GOD never will admit such as hate him, there ; and he will certainly exclude us if we are void of that Love, which is the Business and Happiness of Heaven.

And after all the Pains we have taken and the Attainments we have made, they will serve only for a more pompous Descent into Hell, if we have no love to GOD. The more Knowledge and Zeal we have, the greater our Name and Profession has been, the more fearful and amazing will our Fall into Hell be, if we have not Charity; we shall only be more fit Companions for Devil and damned Spirits. Thus you see all your Attainments if you have not Charity, will neither bring you to Heaven, nor save you from Hell ; you will be nothing but most miserable and wretched Creatures, if you live and die without the Love of GOD. Which leads me to the *Application.*

APPLICATION.

Use I. Of *Information.* And what has been said may convince us how *falsly many Judge about Religion:* It is to be feared the most place it in something it does not consist in. Some think it is enough if they are Sound and Orthodox in their Notions and Conceptions about Things ; if they understand the Principles of *Calvin,* and believe them, it is enough : Others think Religion consists in being of *this* or *that* Denomination of Christians : Some think Religion consists in a *round of Duties,* without any Life or Spirit attending them: Others are well pleased with themselves because they have been *Zealous* in some Circumstances of Religion ; and discovered a Vehemency against such as have differed from them : But few think. Religion consists in what it really does, in that *Charity* which is the Fruit and Consequent of Faith in the Son of GOD,

                                                        What

What has been faid, alfo gives us too much ground to fear, the *Religion of many will after all their Pains profit them nothing*: There feems to be too little figns of Love either to GOD, or their Brother: A certain Bitternefs feems to be too much intermingled with their Religion, they don't feem to love GOD more than the Creature, nor their Neighbour fo fincerely as themfelve.

And we may *try ourfelves by what has been faid, and examine the State of our own Souls*: It is of great Importance for us to know how Matters ftand betwixt GOD and our own Souls: And there is nothing we can try ourfelves by more fafely than the *Love of GOD.* He that *Loveth is born of GOD.* And if we can fatisfy ourfelves in this one Point we can know what the true State of our Soul is. If we love GOD we are born of GOD, and are intitled to eternal Life; but if we love not GOD, we are in a State of Nature, under the Curfe of the Law, and a Sentence of eternal Condemnation.

So alfo we may examine our *religious Duties* and Services, by what we have heard; and fee how far they are acceptable to GOD, and profitable to u; for GOD is no farther well pleafed with them, nor does he accept of them, only as they are done in Faith, and attended with Love; nor will they ever be any farther Advantageous to us, than they proceed from *Faith in Chrift*, and are performed in *Love*: GOD never will own nor will he reward thofe Services which are attended with Hatred to Himelf and Rancour to our Neighbour: for *GOD is Love*.

What you have heard may alfo teach you, to *fit a high Value on Charity*. Some of late have endeavoured to depreciate, and undervalue it, by cafting the moft opprobious Terms upon it: But the Apoftle valued it above *Faith* and *Hope*; and furely we ought to efteem it above *Zeal* and *party Spirit*, or a *great Degree of Knowledge*: You cannot overvaue the *Love of GOD*, and your *Neighbour*. It is what every one
D   fhould

moſt highly eſteem and pray earneſtly for it : It will be better to us than Ten Thouſand Worlds : If we love GOD, he will love us to all Eternity, and we can't be miſerable in his Love : It will make us happy and give us inexpreſſible Satisfaction thro'out Eternity.

Uſe 2d, Of *Humiliation* and *Self-Abaſement.* Let us all be aſhamed and humbled before GOD, that we have *ſo little of this Goſpel-Charity*, in which Religion conſiſts : We profeſs to be the Diſciples of a lovely Jeſus, who has loved us unto the Death : We have his Example ſet before us, and his ſpecial Command to *love one another* : We all profeſs to ſeek the ſame Felicity above, and hope to live for ever together in Heaven, loving GOD and CHRIST; and one another : And is it not a Shame that we love one another ſo little here on Earth? Charity is almoſt baniſhed from us : Bitterneſs, Cenſoriouſneſs and Clamour have almoſt drove Charity out of the Land : But can we be eaſy whilſt we love ſo little and have ſo many Heart-burnings towards one another? Can we think how CHRIST loved us when Enemie, and not be aſhamed that we cannot love our Brethren? Let us all ſee wherein we have been faulty in this great Goſpel-Duty of *Loving one another*, and confeſs our Sin before GOD.

Uſe 3d, Here ſuffer me to enforce a *Caution* upon every one, to ſee to it that he does not deceive himſelf in this important Point. Miſtake not a natural Tenderneſs of Conſtitution for this Charity : You may have a more tender Heart; and your Affections be more eaſily moved than others : You may be leſs cruel and moroſe : You may have a polite Education, and know how to ſpeak the Words of Decency and Comelineſs, and be a Stranger to this Charity. The *young Man* in the Goſpel, addreſs'd our Saviour in a delightful Manner; and CHRIST as Man, lov'd him ; but he had no Love to GOD : His Affections were upon this World.

This Charity is a Fruit of the divine Spirit, moulding you into the Frame and Temper of the Goſpel ; exciting in you all the gracious Diſpoſitions of a virtuous

tuous and holy Life : And if thefe attend not your Charity, it is not fuch as the Apoftle means, and tells you
without it you are nothing.

Ufe 4th, Of *Motive* to us all, to pray earneftly to
GOD to *pour out a Spirit of Charity from on High upon
us* : It is only GOD can fill our Souls with Love to
Himfelf and one another : It is He alone can deftroy
that Enmity there is in our Hearts; and he will be
fought to for this as well as all other Graces : And
when we confider thefe Things, fhall we not all wifh
and defire and pray for this Charity

Firft, It is the *beft* and *only Way*, in order to our *pro-
fiting under the Means and Advantages* we are favoured
with. We are lifted up to Heaven in Privileges; but
how Barren and Unfruitful are we under thefe happy
Advantages? And whence comes it to pafs, but from
hence, that there is fo little Charity amongft us? We
don't love GOD, therefore we don't fear, ferve and
reverence him, as we fhould do. We have Envying,
Strife and Debate amongft our felves, therefore we don't
grow in the Chriftian Life and make Advances towards
Heaven ; but was Charity fervent and lively, how much
fhould we profit.

Secondly, This is the only excellent Way *to retrieve
us from the miferable* Confufions *and* Animofities *we are
run into.*—— Every one may fee they are great and
melancholy; and happy would it be could we recover
our felves out of them. This is the only excellent Way
for Peace and Order amongft us, *to put on Charity* : So
the Apoftle told the *Corinthians*, and his Words are
inftructive to us : And wou'd all Sects and Parties put
on Charity towards one another, we might foon expect that Things would return to their due Order a-
gain ; but it's in vain to expect it, if Love to GOD and
one another does not fill our Hearts.

Thirdly, Charity, or Love to GOD, and one ano-
ther, is attended with *a great deal of Pleafure and
Satisfaction here on Earth* ; if there was nothing of
Duty

Duty in it, it would be well worth our Pains to practice it as much as possible we could : It calms the Passions ; casts out Uneasiness, and Melancholy ; makes the whole Soul chearful : It destroys Anger and Envy, which are *rottenness to the Bones.* Charity saves us from that Jealousy, which is as *cruel as the Grave.* Charity gives a Pleasure to all the Cares and Business of Life ; and it drives away Uneasiness. It is a Sort of Heaven in the Mind : And whilst other Men carry a Hell in their Souls, the charitable Man enjoys the Blessedness of the Spirits above. Who does not long to feel this Love in his Soul ?

Fourthly, By this it is we *become most like to* GOD *and* CHRIST. How noble is it to be like GOD ? and herein we can resemble Him ; we cannot imitate him in *Faith* and *Hope,* these Things cannot agree with the Divine Nature : But *GOD is Love* ; there is pure and perfect Love in GOD ; and the more we love, the more we are conformed to his Image. And how much like our LORD JESUS CHRIST do we become by *Charity ?* How pure, how fervent and constant was his Love ? Shall we not long to be like the great GOD, and our ascended LORD, who is full of Love to his Church and People on Earth.

Fifthly, Without Charity *we never shall be fit for, nor can we possibly arrive to an heavenly World* : That is a World of Love, and inconceivable Delight, where there is no Uneasiness and Hatred ; and it is only Spirits who are filled with Love, who are fitted for that State of Blessedness. What Pleasure could a Man take in Heaven who delights in Envying, Revenge, and Strife ? And GOD never will admit any to Heaven, who have not their Enmity subdued, and their Minds cast into the Mould of the Gospel, and prepared to love GOD, and all the Spirits of Light and Holiness.

Lastly, The more we love on Earth, the more our Affections and Desires are drawn out after GOD, and the more we put on Charity to one another, so much the

the more *Happy* shall we be when we arrive to the *Paradife* above : The more we encreafe and enlarge our Love here ; fo much the larger and extenfive will it be in Heaven ; and confequently the more Happy and Bleffed we muft be. Who can think of this, and not pour out his Soul to GOD that he would give him fuch a Faith in the Son of G O D, as fhall fill his Soul more and more with Love to G O D and Christ and all the Children of GOD on Earth. Let us wreftle with G O D in Prayer for this Charity : And will GOD of his Grace grant to each one of us to *love* the Lord our GOD with all our Heart, and our *Neighbour* as ourfelves.

F I N I S.

Dr. *Chauncy's*

SERMON

Preach'd before the Society

For *encouraging Industry,*

AND

employing the Poor.

August 12. 1752.

The *Idle-Poor* fecluded from the *Bread* of *Charity* by the *Chriſtian Law.*

A

SERMON

Preached in BOSTON, before the Society for

encouraging Induſtry,

A N D

employing the Poor.

Aug. 12. 1752.

By *Charles Chauncy,* D. D.

Drowſineſs ſhall clothe a Man with Rags : But the diligent Hand maketh rich.   SOLOMON.

B O S T O N: Printed by *Thomas Fleet,* 1752

The *Idle-Poor* fecluded from the *Bread of Charity* by the *Chriftian Law.*

2 Theffalon. 3. 10. ——— *This we commanded you; that if any would not work, neither fhould be eat.*

THE Law of Love is, in a fingular and diftinguifh-ing Manner, the Law of Chriftianity. *This is MY Commandment,* fays our Saviour, *that ye love one another.* And again, *A NEW Commandment give I unto you, that ye love one another.* And yet again, *By THIS fhall all Men know that ye are my Difciples, if ye have Love one to another.* And by *this* were the firft Chriftians diftin-guifhed from other Men, and known to be the Difciples of Jefus Chrift. And they difcovered their Benevolence, *not in Word only, neither in Tongue, but in Deed and in Truth ;* never *forgetting to do good and communicate,* as they had Op-portunity. They did not judge, they could ever do too much, in a Way of Charity, for the Relief of the poor and needy.

And no Inconvenience, one would think, could arife from the Liberalities in which they abounded. And yet, it was owing to this, in part at leaft, that among thofe who took upon them the Name of Chriftians, there were fome who indulged to *Idlenefs ;* either not working at all, or not with a becoming Diligence.

Of

Of this Character there feems to have been a confiderable Number among the Chriftians at *Theffalonica*. The extraordinary Charities, common in that Day, might encourage thofe, who were before difpofed to be idle, to neglect the Bufinefs of their proper Callings. The Hope of having their Wants fupplied, by the Bounties of their Chriftian Friends and Neighbours, might infenfibly flacken their Diligence, and betray them into an indolent inactive way of Life.

But, from whatever Caufe it might arife, *Idlenefs* was the Fault too prevalent among the *Theffalonian* Chriftians. The Apoftle *Paul* feems to be concerned about it; and is particular in his Care to do whatever might be proper to correct and amend it. And to this Purpofe it was, that, among other Things, he fpake the Words of my Text, *This we commanded you, that if any would not work, neither fhould he eat.* In difcourfing to which Words I fhall endeavour the following Things.

I. I fhall fay what may be proper to afcertain the true Senfe of the Command, *If any will not work, neither fhall he eat.*

II. I fhall mention a few Things, as the Time will allow, to *juftify the Wifdom and Reafonablenefs of the Command.*

III. And, Finally, I fhall *apply* what may be offered to the *Occafion of our being now together.*

I. I am to explain the Command in my Text, *If any will not work, neither fhall he eat.*

Some perhaps may think, that it ought to be interpreted *univerfally*, as extending to *all,* the Rich, as well as the Poor; infomuch that they ought neither of them *to eat, if they will not work.* But fuch an Interpretation does not fall in with the Defign of the Apoftle in this Place. For he is here fpeaking, not of thofe who are able, without Labour, to maintain themfelves; but of poor People, who, if they won't work, muft have their Expectations of Relief from the Charities of others.

Not

Not but that it is a shameful Thing for any *to eat the Bread of Idleness.* If Persons possess ever so great an Abundance, this gives them no Licence to be lazy. They may indeed reasonably exempt themselves from the lower and more servile Parts of Business: But still they ought not to be idle. Indulged habitual Idleness is a Reproach to any Man, whether he be high or low, rich or poor. We were made for Business. Both our Souls and Bodies are so constituted, as that Exercise is a great and necessary Means to keep them in an healthful and vigorous State; and without it we shall soon contract a strange Hebetude of Mind, as well as Inability of Body to all the Functions of Life. If the great and rich would but thoroughly realize this, it might happily tend to lessen their love of Ease, and put them upon Activity and Diligence in the Employment of their Time and Powers to some or other of the valuable Purposes of Life.

But the *Rich,* as I said, are not the Persons the Apostle has here to do with, but the *Poor* ; whose Circumstances in the World are such as that, *if they won't work,* they have nothing to depend on but the *Charities* of their Friends and Neighbours. And it is with respect to this kind of Persons, in special, that the Apostle has commanded, *if any will not work, neither should he eat.*

And the *Manner* in which he has worded the Command is observable, and clearly ascertains its true Meaning. *If any WILL not work.* Those that *will not work,* not those that *cannot,* are the Persons here pointed out. Such among the Poor as are *willing* to work, but can't get Employment, are not the Persons secluded from the Bread of Charity. Neither are they restrained from eating of this Bread, who would be willing to work, but are incapable of Labour, by Reason of Sickness, or Lameness, or the Decays of an infirm old Age.

As for disabled Persons, it was never the Design of the Apostle to command, that, *if any would not work, neither should they eat :* No; tho' their Incapacity for Labour was brought upon them by their own Follies and Vices. It is very unhappy indeed when this is the Case, as, God knows, it too often is. And such **Persons** have infinite Reason to

look

look back upon their paft mad and finful Conduct with Grief and Shame: But yet, if they are really unable to do any Thing, in a way of Labour, towards their own Support, they are by no means to be neglected. They are, in common, with other difabled Perfons, the proper Objects of Charity, the Poor of this World, concerning whom it is the Will of God, that they fhould be pitied and help'd. And the Rich fhould look upon themfelves obliged to fhew Compaffion towards them. If any fhould *fee a Brother or Sifter*, of this Character, *naked, and deftitute of daily Food*, they fhould not only *fay to them, depart in Peace, be ye warmed and filled, but give them thofe Things which are needful to the Body*; fuiting their Charities to their particular Wants and Circumftances.

But we are under no fuch Obligations with refpect to the other Sort of poor People, thofe who *can* work, but *won't*; who may have Work to do, and have Activity of Body to do it, but no Will to employ themfelves in Labour. Concerning thefe Poor, it is the Command of an infpired Apoftle, *that they fhall not eat*, i. e. fhall not be maintained at the Charge of others; fhall not live upon the Charities of their Chriftian Friends and Brethren.

Some, perhaps, may think this a very unreafonable Command. Doubtlefs, it will be complained of as hard and fevere by the indolent and lazy among the Poor. But it is really one of the moft equitable Commands; a Command founded on fo much Reafon and Juftice, yea, and Goodnefs too, that not a Word can fairly be objected againft it. And this leads me, as was propofed,

II. In the fecond Place, to fay what may be thought fufficient to *juftify* this Command of the Apoftle, and point out its *Reafonablenefs, Equity and Goodnefs*. And the following Things may be briefly offered to this Purpofe.

1. The eftablifhed Laws of Nature are fuch as render it impoffible, that Mankind fhould be fupported, if they are generally lazy. Our Bodies are fo made as conftantly to require Food and Raiment: Nor can thefe Neceffaries be fupplied but by Labour. The Conveniencies and Comforts of Life are more numerous, and require ftill greater

Care

Care and Pains. The Almighty, it is true, if he had ſeen
fit, could have maintained the humane Race, without the
Concurrence of any Endeavours of their own, by making
Nature ſo rich and fruitful, in every reſpect, as to have
rendered Art uſeleſs, and Induſtry ſuperfluous. But he
has ordered Matters otherwiſe ; and, no doubt, for wiſe
and good Reaſons. Our Food does not ſpring out of the
Earth without Culture ; neither does our Raiment naturally grow on us, as it does on the inferiour Creatures. The
Birds of the Air ſow not ; neither do the *Lillies of the Field
toil or ſpin :* But we are obliged to do both. The eſtabliſhed Order of Nature is ſuch, as that, if we don't, we
muſt unavoidably ſuffer, if not periſh, for want of Food
to eat, and Raiment to put on.

Now if Labour is thus neceſſary for the Support of
Life, it is contrary to all Reaſon, that thoſe ſhould eat
the Bread of Charity who won't work, while yet they
have Ability therefor. What Right have the lazy and indolent, who are both healthy and ſtrong, to live on the
Fruits of other Men's Labour ? Wherein lies the Fitneſs
of this ? If without Labour the World can't ſubſiſt, for
any to ſit idle, depending upon a Supply from other Men's
Induſtry, is certainly incongruous to an high Degree. Why
ſhould ſome Men labour and toil to get Bread for thoſe
who are as able to work as they are, but chuſe rather to
ſpend their Time in doing nothing ? The Suppoſition is
abſurd. It is not fair ; it favours neither of Reaſon nor
Juſtice, that the diligent and laborious ſhould, by their
Bounties, relieve the Wants of thoſe, who are poor and
needy, not thro' Incapacity for Bodily Exertions, but becauſe they are ſluggiſh and idle.

2. The *poſitive Will of God* has appointed *Labour* the
Means in order to a Livelihood in the World. To this
Purpoſe are thoſe Words of the Almighty, which, tho'
originally directed to *Adam*, are yet obligatory upon all
his Poſterity, *Gen.* 3. 19. *In the Sweat of thy Face thou
ſhalt eat Bread, 'till thou return to the Ground.* As this Appointment of Heaven was publiſhed after the *Fall* of Man,
and as a Puniſhment for Sin, it ſhould ſeem as tho' humane Labour had but an ignoble Original. And ſo it
    B   had

had, if confidered as to *Kind* and *Degree :* But as to the *Thing it felf,* it was as truly the Requirement of God from Man in his *innocent,* as in his lapfed State.   Even *Adam* in *Paradife* was not fo wholly provided with every Thing by the fole Bounty of Nature, but that it was neceffary he fhould be employed in Labour.   We therefore read, not only that he had Work to do in his innocent State, but what it was, namely, *to drefs and keep the Garden of Eden,* Gen. 2. 15.   If therefore Sin had not entered into the World, Men would not have lived without Labour ; tho' it would have been of a *nobler* Kind, and in a *lefs Degree.*   In thefe refpects, Sin has made a difference.   We muft now fweat and toil.   Nature calls for this Sort of Labour, and will not furnifh us, upon any lower Terms, with fuch of her good Things as we ftand in need of :   And it is the *exprefs Will of God,* that, in this Way, we fhould earn our Bread.   Laborious Diligence is the *Means* by which he has *ordained* we fhould fupply ourfelves with Food, and other Neceffaries of Life.

If any therefore indulge to Idlenefs, who have Ability for Labour, they virtually fet afide *the Method* God has been pleafed to direct to, and enjoin, in order to their being fupported in Life.   And is it reafonable they fhould be maintained in any other ?   Is it fit, if Men won't work, when they can, that a different Way, from what the Wifdom of God has inftituted, fhould be taken for their Supply with Bread ?   And yet, by fupporting the needy in Idlenefs, we conftructively oppofe the *Appointment* of God, and fubftitute a Method for their Maintenance of our own devifing.   And is this reafonable ?   Can it be juftified ?   Ought Perfons to be maintained in plain Contempt of the Conftitution of God ?

I am fenfible, it has fometimes been pleaded, that, however it might be in former Days, the Cares of Religion now, in a great Meafure, fuperfede the Affairs of the World ; infomuch that if Men neglect their temporal Bufinefs, provided they do it that they may have Time to attend on the Spiritual Concerns of their Souls and another World, they ought to be confidered and helped ; and that it is a *Chriftian Duty* to fupport fuch pious Perfons upon the Bread of Charity.   A

A specious Pretence this for Idleness, in contempt of the Government of God; but a very poor one; as being founded on intirely wrong Notions of the *Christian* Religion, which requires its Professors, not only to mind the Things of another World, but the Affairs of this also. And it is particularly observable, Christianity is so far from allowing Men to be slothful in the Business of their proper Callings, that it has reinforced the *Law of Labour* given to *Adam*, and in him to all Mankind, by adopting it into its Scheme of Morals. Says *Paul*, the Apostle of Jesus Christ, addressing himself to the *Thessalonians*, and in them to all Christians, *We command and exhort, by our Lord Jesus Christ, that with Quietness they work, and eat their own Bread;* as we read in the 12th *v.* of my Context. Very observable is the Manner, in which these Words are delivered, *We command, and exhort, by our Lord Jesus Christ.* He does not satisfy himself with *exhorting* only; but he *commands.* And he does it *by our Lord Jesus Christ,* i. e. by his Authority, as commissioned, and empowered by him. So that whosoever, in this Article, *despiseth, despiseth not Man, but God;* for here the Contempt does finally terminate, as our Saviour himself has taught us, in *Luke* 10. 16. *He that despiseth you, despiseth me; and he that despiseth me, despiseth him that sent me.*

Industrious Labour is therefore the Law of *Christianity.* Instead of altering this Method appointed by God, from the Beginning, for the Support of Life, the Gospel has confirmed it. So that Idleness is a Reflection upon the governing Wisdom and Authority of God under the *Christian,* as well as former Dispensations. And to support Man in Sloth, tho' they should disguise their Guilt under the Cover of the most pious Pretences, is a virtual setting up our own Wisdom in opposition to the Wisdom of God, and subverting the Method he has established, both in *the nature of Things,* and by *positive Revelation,* for the supply of Mankind with the Necessaries and Conveniences of Life.

3. The Command, in my Text, is founded on the *publick Good.* For there cannot be a flourishing People, without Labour. It is by Improvement in Arts and Trade, that they must grow in Wealth, and Power, and become

possessed

possessed of the various Emoluments tending to the Benefit and Pleasure of Life; and these Arts take their Rise from, and are carried on by, the Industry of particular Persons. And this is so evident, that while some Nations have increased in Riches, and Grandeur, and Power, by being industrious, tho' great Obstacles, and discouraging Difficulties have stood in the Way; others, thro' Sloth and Indolence, have been kept low, and sunk in Oblivion, tho' under great *natural Advantages* to have got into flourishing Circumstances: Or, it may be, they have become a Prey to other more active and enterprising Nations, who knew how to make a better Use of their Advantages. And the Truth is, the *natural Advantages* a People are favoured with, whether for Husbandry, Navigation, Fishery, Manufactures, or any other Source of Wealth, will be, in a great Measure, lost, and, as it were, thrown away upon them, without Labour and Industry, in making a wise and good Use of them.

The *Athenians* were so sensible of this, that *Idleness*, in that State, subjected the guilty Person, whoever he was, to a Prosecution at Law, as an Injury to the Commonwealth: And they made Inquiry of each Man and Woman, *quâ Arte se Alerent?* By what Trade they supported themselves? And so long ago as the Days of *Pharoah*, it was taken for granted that a Man could not be without *some Occupation*, or other. Hence that Question of his to *Joseph's* Brethren, upon their coming into *Egypt*, Gen. 47. 3. *What is your Occupation?*

The Law, in my Text, is therefore connected with the *publick Good*; as it tends to encourage Industry, by restraining us from Distributions to the lazy and slothful. And it is indeed a great Hurt to a *Community*, when private Persons dispense their Charities to such, among the poor, as keep themselves so by an Indulgence to Idleness, while yet they are able to work. For the *Public* loses the whole Benefit of the Labour of those, who are thus supported in Idleness; and not only so, but is liable to suffer all the Inconveniencies which are to be looked for, in Consequence of their indulging to Sloth, and doing nothing.

And it is observable, the *Apostle* had it particularly in
his

his View to guard againſt theſe *public Inconveniencies,* when he gave the Command in my Text. Hence he adds, in the Words that immediately follow, giving the Reaſon, at leaſt one Reaſon, of the Command, *For we have heard, that there are ſome among you which walk diſorderly, working not at all ; but are Buſy-bodies.*

You obſerve, theſe Perſons who did not work, and were the Occaſion of the Command in the Text, were *diſorderly.* And this, in a Senſe, is always the Caſe. Whenever Perſons are *idle,* they are *diſorderly :* For an idle Life is, in the whole of it, a *Diſorder.* It ſubvert the Order God has eſtabliſh'd for the Support of Mankind, and would introduce another Method of Livelihood than *that,* infinite Wiſdom has contrived and appointed.

Nor is this the only Senſe in which idle Perſons are *diſorderly.* They are too often *Tempters to others to neglect their Buſineſs.* Having none of their own, and being inclined to none, they endeavour to find, or, if they can't do that, to make Perſons as idle as themſelves, to the great Detriment of the Public, and, many Times, the intire Ruin of their Companions in Sloth. And who are ſo much noted for the moral Diſorders of *Lying* and *Stealing,* as thoſe who have ſettled into an Habit of Lazineſs ? Their Lazineſs reduces them to Straits and Difficulties ; and theſe, as the readieſt and eaſieſt Way to ſupply their Wants, put them upon deceiving the kind and charitable by artfully invented Falſhoods, or elſe upon ſecretly robbing them of their Money, or their Goods. And who more given to *Tipling* than the Perſons who have accuſtomed themſelves to Idleneſs ? The Drones in a Place are commonly the People who doze away their Time and Senſes over their Cups, There are indeed no *Diſorders,* but the idle are liable to them ; and their Danger lies in their Idleneſs. Were they diligently employed in Buſineſs of one Kind or another, their Thoughts and Time would be properly taken up ; but having ſettled into a Temper inclining them to ſit idle and do nothing, they lie open to every Temptation, and are in danger of being betrayed into moral Diſorders of every Kind.

And theſe idle Perſons were not only diſorderly, but

Buſy-

Busy-bodies. We hear there are some who work not at all, but are Busy-bodies. This may seem an Inconsistency; but it is most commonly the Truth of the Case. None more ready to *busy* themselves in other Men's Matters, than those who neglect all Business of their own. Not minding their own Affairs, they have Leisure, and generally Inclination, to intrude into other Men's. Hence that Character of some, in the Apostolic Times, *They learn to be idle; wandring about from House to House; and not only idle, but Tatlers also, and Busy-bodies, speaking Things which they ought not.* 1 Tim. 5. 13. And none indeed are, usually, more free with their Tongues than *idle Persons*; none wander more about from House to House; none are more ready to meddle in Things which don't belong to them; acting in the Sphere of others, tho' they won't in their own. And I need not say that this intermeddling in other Men's Concerns, greatly tends to *public* Hurt;—for it kindles Contention, creates Feuds and Animosities; and is indeed a main Scource of that Variance and Strife, which disturb the Peace of Society.

And is it any Wonder, when *Idleness* is connected with such Damage to the *Public*, which might be as much benefitted by *Industry*, that we should be restrained from supporting those who won't work, thro' Slothfulness of Disposition? It is certainly a most reasonable Restraint: And the Command that lays it, is so far from being hard and unjust, that it kindly and equitably consults the *public Good*. And it is an Honour to the Christian Religion, that it can boast of this, and a great many other Commands, which, the more critically they are examined, the more wise and equitable they appear to be.

4. The Command we are considering is admirably adapted to promote *private* as well as public Good. For industrious Labour is the Way for *Individuals*, as well as *Communities*, to thrive and flourish. Men, it is true, may come to the possession of Wealth by Inheritance. But Wealth, even in this Case, was originally the Purchase of Labour; and it is only in this Way, that it can be improved to Advantage. Idleness naturally tends to *Waste*, and will, in Time, reduce the greatest Estate to nothing,

thing. But however it be as to Men of Subſtance, thoſe, who have their Fortunes to make, muſt certainly take Pains. They may as well expect to be learned without Study, as to be rich without Diligence. If a Man's Circumſtances are low, he can riſe. and proſper in no other Way, but that of Induſtry. To this Purpoſe are thoſe Proverbs of *Solomon,* Ch. 10. v. 4. *He becometh poor that dealeth with a ſlack Hand : But the Hand of the diligent maketh rich.* And in the 12th Ch. v. 24. *The Hand of the diligent ſhall bear Rule : But the ſlothful ſhall be under Tribute.* And ſo neceſſary an expedient is Diligence in order to Wealth, that if Men are idle, they will unavoidably be poor. Hence that Obſervation of the wiſe Man, *Prov.* 23. 21. *Drowſineſs ſhall clothe a Man with Rags.* And again, Ch. 24. 30. 31. 34. *I went by the Field of the ſlothful, and by the Vineyard of the Man void of Underſtanding : And lo, it was all grown over with Thorns, and Nettles had covered the Face thereof, and the Stone-wall thereof was broken down. —So ſhall thy Poverty come as one that travelleth, and thy Want as an armed Man.* And it is obſervable, one of the Arguments the Apoſtle *Paul* uſes, to enforce the Duty of Labour, upon the ſlothful among the *Theſſalonians,* is its Tendency to ſupply their Wants, ſo as that they ſhould have no lack of outward good Things. 1. *Theſſ.* 4. 10, 12. *We beſeech you, Brethren, to do your own Buſineſs, and to work with your own Hands—that ye may have lack of nothing.* Induſtrious Labour is, you ſee, in the *Apoſtle's* Opinion, an effectual Expedient to prevent Want. If Perſons are idle, they may expect to be needy : Whereas, if they *do their own Buſineſs,* and *work with their own Hands,* they will have lack of nothing ; nothing for their Supply either with Neceſſaries or Conveniencies.

It is therefore for every Man's *private Intereſt,* that the *Apoſtle* has commanded, *if any will not work, neither ſhall he eat.* And indeed charitable Donations, ſupplying the needy without Labour, inſtead of being a Kindneſs, is a real and great Diſſervice to them ; as it tends to ſettle them in Idleneſs. For if idle People find, that they can be ſupported by the Charities of others, inſtead of employing themſelves in Labour, they will indulge to Sloth, 'till it becomes their habitual permanent Temper; than which there is not a more certain Presage of their Ruin. For Idleness naturally and powerfully tends to keep Men in Poverty, or to reduce them to it. If they are low in the World, it will unavoidably keep them so: and if they possess Estates, it will soon waste them away, or sink them into nothing. Nor is this the only bad Effect of Idleness. It has a strange Influence to enfeeble the Powers both of Mind and Body, and render Men useless to themselves as well as others. Besides all which, it is the great Inlet to all manner of Wickedness, and tends to corrupt Men's Morals, and make them Scourges to themselves, as well as Plagues to Society. It is therefore a real and great Hurt, not only to the *Publick*, but to *private Persons*, individually considered, to support them in Sloth; and the Command, in my Text, restraining us herefrom, is therefore an Instance, not of Severity, but of Love and Kindness to them.

I have now said what may be thought sufficient to justify the *Apostle*'s Command, by shewing that it is so far from being arbitrary and unreasonable, that it is connected, in the Nature of Things, with the Good of Mankind, considered both *individually*, and as coalescing in *Society*, and carries in it all the Marks of Fairness, Equity, and Goodness.

III. It remains now, in the last Place, that I make some suitable *Application* of what has been discoursed.

And, was it upon another Occasion, I should bespeak the poor, those among them especially who are idle, in the Language of the Apostle, in the Verse but one following my Text, *exhorting and commanding them by our Lord Jesus Christ, that with quietness they work, and eat their own Bread*:—But considering the Design of our being together at this Time, with the Character of the Persons here convened, it may be more proper to confine my Discourse to the *rich*; who are as truly concerned in the great *Gospel Command* we have been illustrating, as the poor.

You are hereby, my Brethren, restrained as to the Distribution of your Charity; not being allowed to dispense it

pro-

promiſcuouſly, but obliged to take due Care to find out
ſuitable Objects ; diſtinguiſhing properly between thoſe needy People who are *able*, and thoſe who are *unable*, to employ
themſelves in Labour.

You can ſcarce be too liberal in your Charities to thoſe,
who, in the Providence of God, are reduced to Straits, not
thro' Slothfulneſs, but real Incapacity for Work. The
Chriſtian Law, requiring Charity, was made with a ſpecial View to this Kind of needy People: and you may,
under no Pretence, ſhut up the Bowels of your Compaſſion againſt the Cry of their Wants. Charity is the Way,
the infinitely benevolent God has ordained for the ſupply
of their Neceſſities. And you ſhould be ready, in this
Way, to miniſter to their Relief, according to your Ability, and as you have Opportunity. But it is ſuperfluous
to urge you upon this Head ; for, as touching charitable
Miniſtrations to the *truly neceſſitous*, we may even boaſt of
this Town. The good Lord reward into their Boſom, an
hundred fold, all the Kindneſſes they have ſhewn to the
diſtreſſed, eſpecially in the late Day of general Calamity.

But tho' you can't be too generous in your Charities to
the poor, yet, as I ſaid, you muſt take Care to diſtinguiſh
between them. For as to them who *can*, but *won't*, work ;
who have Ability for Labour, but no Diſpoſition, you are
reſtrained from ſupporting them in *Idleneſs*. The Command in my Text is plainly a *Statute of Heaven*, tying up
your Hands from Charitable Diſtributions to the ſlothful
poor. And, ſo far as appears to me, it would be an evident Breach of the Law of the Goſpel, as well as of Nature, to beſtow upon thoſe the *Bread of Charity*, who might
earn and eat their *own Bread*, if they did not ſhamefully idle
away their Time.

This, if I miſtake not, is both a ſeaſonable and important Truth ; and if it were duly attended to, there would not
be ſo much miſplaced Charity, as that certainly is, which is
given to *meer Drones*. Many ſuch there have been among
us ; and perhaps it may be too much owing to the un-
diſtinguiſh'd Kindneſs and Compaſſion of the Benevolent,
that they have ſo increaſed upon us, to the great Detriment
of the *Public* ; which is intirely deprived of the Labour of

C   great

great Numbers, who, inſtead of living upon the Charity of others, might eat *their own Bread.* It is to be hoped, there will be a better Care taken upon this Head for the Time to come; and the rather, as there is now a Way wherein the charitably inclined may be aſſiſting even to the *ſlothful* among the poor. They may be thus helpful to them by their Donations to ſtrengthen the *Society,* not long ſince formed, *for encouraging Induſtry, and employing the Poor.*

My Text evidently countenances the formation of ſuch a Society; the Deſign whereof is one and the ſame with that of the Apoſtle *Paul,* who delivered the Command contained in it, *viz.* the putting poor People, who are able, upon maintaining themſelves by their own Labour and Induſtry, conformable to the Conſtitution of Nature, and the Appointment of God from the beginning of the World.

And in what more proper Way can we ſhew Kindneſs to the poor of this Sort, than by contributing to ſuch a generous Deſign of ſetting them to Work, that with quietneſs they may Labour, and, as the Fruit thereof, eat their own Bread. We ſhall herein concur with the infinitely good God himſelf, who does not give Men Food and Raiment, and other Neceſſaries immediately from Heaven, but by adding his Bleſſing to their laborious Induſtry.

As this *Society* has not ſubſiſted for any long Time, it cannot reaſonably be ſuppoſed, they ſhould have accompliſhed any great Things: And yet, more a great deal has been effected, than Strangers to the Execution of their Scheme may be ready to imagine. According to the Information I have received, ſome thouſands of Yards of good *Linen Cloth* have been already fitted for Market; a Specimen whereof, you have there before your Eyes. And it is eaſy to determine, that, in order to this, Employ muſt have been given to a very conſiderable Number of Labourers, in raiſing Flax, in preparing it for the Wheel, in ſpinning it into Thread, and then in weaving it into Cloth. Some hundreds of Women and Children have, by this Means, been kept at Work, whereby they have done a great deal towards ſupplying themſelves with Bread, to the eaſing the Town of its Burthen in providing for the poor. And, as one good Effect of the ſetting up this

Linen

Linen Manufacture, it may with Truth be ſaid, there is now to be found, in the Town, many a virtuous married Woman, and young Maiden (ſome Inſtances whereof are there preſented to your View) who may be characterized in the Words of *Solomon*, *She ſeeketh Flax, and worketh willingly with her Hands. She layeth her Hands to the Spindle, and her Hands hold the Diſtaff. She maketh fine Linen, and ſelleth it to the Merchant.*

Perhaps, ſcarce any Deſign of this Nature has afforded a more hopeful Proſpect in its Beginning, notwithſtanding its Interruption, for a conſiderable Time, by the late general Prevalence of the *Small-Pox* ; and, if duly encouraged, and vigorouſly proſecuted, there is good Reaſon to think, it will ſoon become extenſive in its Uſefulneſs ; finding Employ for great Numbers, eſpecially among the Female Poor, both Women and Children, and by this Means enabling them to aſſiſt in the ſupport of the Families to which they belong, to the great Advantage of the Community. It is indeed a Scheme, ſo far as I am able to judge, well calculated to promote Induſtry, and, its Companion, Frugality ; than which nothing will more powerfully tend to deliver us from that Poverty to which we are reduced by our Idleneſs and Extravagance. And every one concerned for the Good of his Country muſt be ſenſible, it is high Time to lend an helping Hand towards the bringing into Effect every wiſe Projection to raiſe us out of the low Condition we are in, and make us a flouriſhing People.

It will, perhaps, be urged by ſome, that the ſetting up the *Linen Manufacture* is *too great* an Undertaking for ſo poor and ſmall a People, and an *unwiſe* one, at this Time, when the Price of Labour runs ſo high. But as poor and ſmall as we are, we need Linen of moſt Sorts, and can't do without it. And if, notwithſtanding the high Price of Labour, we can make it ourſelves ſo as that it ſhall turn out cheaper than if we imported it from abroad, as it is now known by Experience that we can, it is certainly a Point of Wiſdom to do ſo : And the rather, as thoſe may be employed, to good Purpoſe, in this Branch of Buſineſs (Children in particular) who have hitherto

C 2

been suffered in a great Measure, to spend their Time too much in Idleness. And it ought farther to be considered, there is no *Manufacture* our Soil and Climate are better fitted to encourage the setting up, and endeavouring to cultivate and bring to Perfection, than the *Linen*. And, as this is not the *Staple Manufacture* of *Great Britain*, we have Reason to hope they will strengthen us in it. To be sure, it looks as tho' it would be for their Interest to do so, as, in Time, if it should extend it self thro' this Province, and the neighbouring Colonies, and be brought to any considerable Degree of Perfection, it might, in a good Measure, supply them with what they are now obliged to pay their Money for to other Nations.

Others, it may be, may fear, if this *Manufacture* should be encouraged, and succeed, that it might hurt them in their Trade abroad, by lessening the Demand for, or lowering the Price of, the *Linen* they import for Sale. But such are evidently too much under the government of a selfish Spirit to be regarded in this Matter. And indeed, if their Fears are justly grounded, there cannot be a stronger Argument, so far as we consult the public Weal, to set forward the present Scheme with the utmost Vigour; as the professed Intention of it is, the *Good of the Community*, and not the *private Interest* of any individual Person whatsoever.

There may be still others, who may think much of the Expence that must attend the effectual carrying this Design into Execution, and imagine it better it should drop than be supported at any considerable Charge. But what Projection of this Nature was ever formed, but upon the Supposition of Charge in executing it to Purpose, in the Beginning? The only proper Question is, Whether this is a likely Scheme, under proper Cultivation, to counterballance, with Advantage, the Expence necessary in order to its taking Effect? And there does not seem to be much Room for Debate upon the Point, thus stated. The *Linen Manufacture* has proved a noble Scource of Wealth to other People. And why may not we reap the like Benefit from it? Our natural Advantages to carry it on are well adapted to the Purpose. We are in these Respects, exceeded

ceeded by no People on the Earth. And if it be not our own Fault, we may soon find our Account in the Prosecution of this Branch of Business. It will certainly, if not neglected, or discouraged, save a great deal of that, which is now exported, either in Money, or other Things, to purchase the Linen that is necessarily consumed in the Country; besides which, it will employ a great many needy idle People, who instead of being supported by *private Charities*, or *public Taxes* levied for that Purpose, may be fed and clothed with the Fruit of their own Labour; by Means whereof, instead of continuing burthensome, they will become useful and valuable, Members of the Community. And these Advantages alone, if there were no other, are sufficient to justify the present Undertaking, as a very wise and good one.

Upon the whole, it is not easy to conceive, but that every Lover of his Country should wish *God-Speed* to this disinterested Scheme for its Welfare: Nor is it doubted, but that many will assist, by their Donations, towards its being vigorously carried more and more into Effect. It is indeed a difficult Day. We are in a low impoverish'd Condition. But this is a Consideration powerfully suited, not to shut, but to open wide, both the Hearts and Hands of those who have Ability to help forward the present Design; as it was at first projected, and then entered upon, directly with a View to relieve us under our Poverty, by opening a new Scource of Industry, well adapted to better our Circumstances, and that can't well fail of doing so, if properly encouraged, and wisely improved.

It is to be hoped therefore, the Gentlemen, to whom it is principally owing, that we have a *Linen Manufacture* now set up, and so far under Improvement, as to exhibit sensible Proof of its being a *capable Fund* of rich Advantage to the Public, will continue their Supscription, till it has got more Strength, and is better able to support it self. The same Benevolence of Spirit, which at first prompted you to encourage so useful a Design, will powerfully urge you to go on doing so, that it may, at length, get so well establish'd, as to be in no Danger of coming to nothing. *Be not weary of well doing; for ye shall reap if ye faint not.*

The

The Society here prefent gratefully acknowledge the Help they received the laft Year, in this Place, not only from the Subfcribers, but other well difpofed Perfons; who will now alfo have an Opportunity, if they pleafe, to contribute towards the farther carrying on of their good Defign. And this I can heartily, and would earneftly, recommend to every one profeffing a Love to his Country, in proportion to his Circumftances. You cannot, my Brethren, be too liberal in your Donations upon this Occafion. For what you give for the encouragement of Induftry, and the Relief of the poor, as the Effect of their own Labour, you may depend is well-placed Charity. Even God himfelf exercifes his Benevolence towards Men conformably to the *great Law of Induftry.* And can you have a better Pattern? It is indifputably kinder and wifer to beftow your Money to encourage and enable poor People, according to the Law of their Nature, and the Law of God, to feed and clothe themfelves by their own Labour and Induftry, than to fupport them in Idlenefs and Ufelefsnefs. And this is the Method of Charity you are now invited to. And if only a Part of that Charity might be put into the Hands of this Society, which has been formerly loft and thrown away, by being beftowed on *Drones,* who are Burdens, without Profit, to the Community; it would enable them to go upon this Defign with Spirit, and to profecute it with fuch Vigour, as that it would probably foon gain Strength, fo as to convince us all by Experience, that a noble Scource of Riches was thereby laid open, within ourfelves, fufficient to raife us out of our prefent Poverty, and make us a happy and flourifhing People. The good God profper this, and all other Schemes that may be projected for fo defirable an End.

Amen, and Amen.

FINIS.

The Reasons for forming the Society, to whom the preceeding Sermon was preached, as originally published by themselves.

WHEREAS it is found by Experience, that this Province is not adapted for raising Sheep, by reason of our long and tedious Winters; and therefore the Inhabitants have been and must forever continue to be under a Necessity of importing large Quantities of Woollen Goods from our Mother Country, Great Britain, *which with Pewter, Brass, and other Commodities bro't from thence, that we cannot subsist without, nor produce ourselves, will require all we can procure for Exportation to make Returns : And inasmuch as considerable Sums are yearly exported to purchase* Linens, *that are not the Produce or Manufacture of* Great Britain, *but imported there from* Germany, Holland, *&c. and which this Province is very capable to Produce and Manufacture; and, if done, would be much for the Benefit of our Mother Country, as well as our selves, as it would enable us to apply our Exports to pay for Woollen and other Goods their Produce, and employ our own Women and Children, who are now in a great measure idle :* ——For these Reasons, a Number of Gentlemen have formed themselves into a voluntary Society, by the Name and Title of, *The Society for encouraging* Industry *and* employing the Poor.—— And we do hereby invite all well-disposed charitable Persons to join in promoting the good Ends above-mentioned.

THE

THE many Advantages arifing from a well regulated Society of this Sort, as they are exceeding
apparent, fo it is prefum'd the Defign will meet with
a chearful Reception, and extenfive Encouragement.
——In the prefent State of this Province, we are not
perhaps in a Condition greatly to enlarge our Exports, it becomes neceffary therefore, that by all prudent Methods we contrive as much as poffible to
leffen our Import. This will be confiderably effected, by promoting a *Linen Manufacture*; for which
it is computed that £. 50,000 Sterling are annually
fent to *Europe*, when at the fame Time it may be
carried on to fuch Advantage, as that Linen of all
Sorts may be made cheaper among ourfelves, as is
now found by Experience.—Befides, the Hufband-
man will from hence receive Encouragement for
raifing of Flax, to which the Lands in this Province are known to be well adapted, and fo a new
Source of Riches laid open to that ufeful and neceffary Body of Men, extracted in the moft natural
and unenvied Way, as being the Product of our own
Soil: Hereby alfo fundry Tradefmen and Handi-
crafts will receive further Employment; fuch as the
Makers of Looms, Spinning Wheels, Heckles, Reels,
and the like; but the moft immediate Advantage is
that, which will arife from the Employment of the
Poor, at prefent a great Burthen to this Community,
by the heavy Taxes levy'd for their Support. Many Thoufands of thefe may be employ'd in this
fingle Manufacture, and taught not only to fupport
themfelves, but to become ufeful and valuable Members of the Community. By this Means the *Price of
Labour*, fo much and juftly complained of, will
gradually be leffen'd, as more Hands will be in-
duftrioufly

duſtriouſly employ'd ; the Poor will be decently cloath'd, and fed with the Fruits of their own Diligence ; the publick Taxes abated, and in general a Spirit of Frugality, Induſtry and Virtue will probably take place among us.

This Town has remarkably ſignalized its ſelf, for its Charity and Compaſſion to the Poor ; who for ſome Years paſt have been an encreaſing Burthen, and yet the Supplies that are annually furniſh'd, are very far from being an adequate Relief to their Neceſſities ; and what is worſe, there is no Proſpect of diminiſhing this Burthen in the preſent Way of diſtributing our Charity ; on the contrary, it muſt be expected to increaſe by the continual Addition of new Objects, from which nothing but their Death will be likely to releaſe us, while a new Succeſſion of them will daily preſent themſelves in the Room of thoſe, who are at reſt from their Miſeries : Every Man of Senſe muſt ſee, and every Lover of his Country will deplore the Calamities that muſt ariſe from increaſing Poverty, Idleneſs and Vice ; but every Chriſtian will feel the Miſeries of ſuch a State, almoſt as if they were his own, and be uneaſy till ſome Method be entered upon, for providing an effectual Remedy againſt them.——Temporary Methods of Relief are very commendable, till ſomething better can be eſtabliſhed ; but theſe are of the Nature of Palliatives only ; it muſt be a laſting and permanent Scheme, that may be expected to reach the Root of this Malady : The **Linen** Manufacture, when thoroughly underſtood, will appear to be ſuch a Scheme, and under proper Cultivation will, it is apprehended, enlarge it ſelf into a noble Deſign, ſo as not only to yield **preſent** Relief to great

D   Num-

Numbers of poor People, but by gradually extending it felf to all Parts of the Province, feems to promife a perpetual Eftablifhment ; and if it be enter'd upon with a proper Spirit, and vigoroufly fupported in the Beginning, it will foon add a new Branch of Riches to the Province, will cloath the naked, find Bread for the hungry, and Employment for the idle.

IN hopes of accomplifhing the good Ends above-mentioned, and depending upon the Bleffing of Almighty GOD, to give Succefs to the Under-taking, we the Subfcribers do promife to pay unto
hereby appointed Treafurer to us the Subfcribers, within one Month from the Date of thefe Pre-fents, the Sums annexed to our refpective Names, for promoting and carrying on a Linen Manufac-ture, and fuch other Manufactures, as the Society fhall hereafter think proper to encourage. We likewife promife to pay quarterly the Sums fub-fcribed by us, as they fhall become due, until we fhall give Notice to the Society of our Defire to be excufed.

Merchandiſe and Hire

HOLINESS TO THE LORD.

The Merchandise of a People
HOLINESS TO THE LORD.

A
SERMON,
Preached in part at the
Publick Lecture in *Boston*,
July 1. 1725.

In part at a *private* Meeting
for *Charity* to the *Poor*,
March 6. 1726.
And now publiſhed as

A *Thank-Offering* to GOD
for repeated ſurpriſing *Bounties*
from *LONDON*
for *Uſes* of *Piety* and *Charity*.

By *Benjamin Colman*, D. D.
And *Paſtor* of a Church in *Boſton*.

2 Cor. ix. 9. *He hath diſperſed abroad, he hath given
to the Poor, his Righteouſneſs remaineth for ever.*

BOSTON, in *New-England*,
Printed by *J. Draper*, in Newbury-Street,
1 7 3 6.

To the HONOURABLE

Samuel Holden, Esq;

of *LONDON:*

SIR;

THE generous Things You have been doing from Year to Year for *my Country*; for many of the *Churches of Christ* in it, whom You have enrich'd with Means of *sacred Knowledge* and *practical Religion*; and for the *pious Poor* in it, both *Ministers* and *Others*, who have tasted of your Bounties and their Souls have blessed You; have led me into this open Acknowledgment, to the Glory of God, from whose Hands we would receive what You and Others have sent us from Time to Time, *an Odour of a sweet Smell, a Sacrifice acceptable, well pleasing to God.*

Sir,

Sir, I hold my Self highly indebted to the Governing Providence of a gracious *God*, which led me in my Youth from my *Native Land* to see That of our *Fathers Sepulchres*; and in my Way thither was pleas'd to *strip* me of the Little I had, that I might be invited by the excellent *Saint* your dear *Mother*, who *took in the Stranger*, and for a Course of Years together regarded him as a *Son*, while her Soul longed after *You* at *Riga*.

What the *Holy God* was then doing I could little know at the Time, but He has made me to perceive since, " That He led me into Mr. *Parkhurst's* House, and from thence to *Bath*, to bring me into a more immediate & extensive Acquaintance with *Persons of Distinction for Learning and Religion*, for my greater *Usefulness* in the Times that have passed over me, and to be *the Hand* thro' which his purposed Benefactions to our *College*, to many of our *Towns* and *Churches*, and to many poor *Members of Christ* in these Parts, should flow.

By the Help of God, I humbly hope that I have willingly done the Part of a *faithful Almoner*, as well in *advising* when I have been writ to, as in *observing the Directions* of Those who have intrusted me; which is all the *Honour* I may pretend to in *the Administration of this Service, which is abundant by many Thanksgivings to God*; some of *which* You have seen and read, as from the Hand of worthy *Ministers*, so *One* especially from the *Angelick Pen of a* * *Gentlewoman*, who *in the School of Affliction* made a roficiency in *Grace* and sacred *Science*, even beyond all that *the School of the Prophets* among us has been able to boast! and as soon almost as *She* had wrote what I sent You, lay down and *died* in perfect Peace.

Mrs. *Gerrish* of *Cambridge*.

I

DEDICATION. iii

I know Sir You are no Stranger to *the Profusion of Bounties* which for a Course of many Years our *College* received from the most pious and munificent *Thomas Hollis*, Esq; whose worthy *Heir* has soon followed him to the Grave, after he had made a good *Addition* to the Foundations laid by his *Uncle*, and adorn'd us with a rare *Orrery*; and now we have the Tydings of the Death of *John Hollis*, Esq; the worthy *Brother* of our great Benefactor, and a *Heir* with him of the same *Grace*; who was also a *Father* to poor *Orphans* here, as well as at Home.

And if it were permitted me, I would now have nam'd *Another*, a younger *Gentleman*, whom God has *inrich'd with all Bountifulness* us-ward; of whose Liberality our *Churches* and our *Poor* have heretofore largely tasted; and this Year brings me the Joy of an *Order* from him for schooling, cloathing, feeding and lodging of *twenty Indian Children* at *Housatonnoc*, a *Tribe* who have lately received the Gospel with a marvelous Joy, and are now under the *Pastoral Care* of the Reverend and Learned Mr. *John Sargent*.

You will easily think, Sir, how placid the *Surprise* of such a Benefaction is, and tho' I see not how the *Donor* of so public a Charity can be kept *secret*, any more than *a City set on a Hill can be hid*; yet the *Thing* ought to be told to the Glory of God, and in this open Manner I would let the *bidden Donor* know the Sense we have of the *Goodness of GOD* to us thro' Him, and our *Prayers* for Him, that *his Fath.r which seeth in secret will reward him openly.*

I

I own, Sir, that I mean a *Dedication* of the following *Discourse* to this namelefs *Benefactor* alfo, who would account it an Honour to be nam'd after *You*; Whom God has fet in the *Chair* among your Brethren the *Diffenters*, and honoured You before the Greateft Men at *Court* as well as in the *City*, for Wifdom, Modefty and Integrity.

That your *Days* may be multiplied, even crofs to your own *Wifhes* of a fpeedy Entrance on a better Life; for your greater and longer *Ufefulnefs* in your Generation, and your more abundant *Reward* in the Day of Chrift; and that a gracious God may alfo pleafe to *multiply Grace and Peace* unto ou *Other Benefactors*, is the hearty Prayer of,

S I R,

Your moft Obliged *Friend,*

and very Humble *Servant,*

Bofton, May 5. 1736.

Benjamin Colman.

To the *Gentlemen* of the Town of *Boston*, who usually attend the *weekly Lecture*,

And to *Those* in particular who attend the *Quarterly Meetings* for *Collections* for the *Poor* in *Cornbill*.

Gentlemen,

WHEN the following *Discourse* was preach'd to *You*, a part of it at the *public Lecture*, and a part in your more *private Meeting*, You were then address'd in the *Close* of those *Sermons* in the following *Words*, which I think good *now* to bring to your *Remembrance*, and also to lay before Others.

" I speak unto a *Trading Town*, and I thank God
" unto a *People* us'd to *Charities* and *liberal Things*.
" Need I provoke you to *Emulation* by what is
B " written

" written of the Men of *Tyre* ? And God forbid
" that *they* should *rise up in Judgment against Us,
" and condemn us.* Shall not *your* Merchandize and
" *your* Hire be *Holiness to the Lord,* when *theirs* was
" so, when the *Gospel* came among them ! Surely
" *we* have carried *our Profession* as high, and *our Ob-*
" *ligations* are at least as great as Those of *Tyre and*
" *Sidon.*

" One *natural Benefit* of Trade and Commerce
" to any People is, that it *enlarges their Hearts*
" *to do generous Things.* God grant that every
" Thing of that Nature done among us, or *by O-*
" *thers for us,* may be so done as to carry in their
" *Front* the glorious *Inscription* of HOLINESS TO
" GOD. So let it be in your *secret Gifts* and Dis-
" tributions, so in your private and more bounti-
" ful *Subscriptions and Collections,* whether they be
" for God's *Poor* or for his *Worship.* And I wish
" the *Proposals* which were lately printed for the
" yearly Gathering a small *Stock* or *Fund* in parti-
" cular *Congregations* for pious and charitable Uses,
" might find *Acceptance* in our Churches, and
" prove a happy *Means* of fulfilling my *Text* among
" us.

" But there is *one* Thing, the Work and Duty
" of the present *Day,* which I may not *omit,* if I
" would be *just* either to my *Text* or to my *Country*;
" which is — *That your Merchandize and Hire must*
" *be for Them which dwell before the Lord, to eat suffi-*
" *ciently and for durable Clothing.* How shall it be
" called *Holiness to the Lord* without this ? You
" must make Conscience of supporting your *Mini-*
" *sters,* who serve in the *Sanctuary* and at the *Altar*
" of God. Money *falls,* you all *raise* your Mer-
" chandise

" chandise, and you are *unjust to Christ* and *his Mi-*
" sters, (that is to say *unholy*). if you do not *raise*
" their Support. It is impossible that *They* should
" *eat* sufficiently, or have *Clothing* for their Families,
" if their Support rise not while all your Trade
" and Hire *rises* after so prodigious a Manner.
" This is to your poor *Ministers*, like a *hundred lit-*
" tle Streams uniting on *them*, and bearing them
" away as with a *Flood* ; or like *a sweeping Rain*
" that *leaves no Food*. You must up instantly or it
" will *wash away* the Field of God, his *Worship* from
" off the Face of the Land. You must minister
" more of your rising Hire to the *Temple* of God,
" or let drop any Pretence to my *Text*.

" This Matter belongs in the first place to the
" *Government* over us, who have had it under Con-
" sideration in their present *Session* * and piously
" *resolved*, That it is the *Indispensable Duty* of the
" several *Towns, Precincts* and *Parishes* of the Pro-
" *vince*, to make such *Additions to the Salaries or*
" *Maintenance* of their respective *Ministers*, as may
" honourably support and encourage them in their
" Work : The *Court* did therefore most earnestly
" recommend a speedy and chearful Compliance
" with this their *Judgment*, to the several *Congrega-*
" *tions* and *Religious Assemblies* within the Province.

" To *Them* it indeed belongs nextly and more
" immediately, whose Profession in a *Church-State*
" is this *Holiness to the Lord* ; and it is the Duty of
" the respective *Members* in every Congregation to
" see to it that *their Merchandise and Husbandry* be
" so, and that *their Pastors* have *Meat sufficient* and
" *durable Clothing*. —— For with what Face and

" Confcience fhall every One of you rife a *Penny*
" or a *Shilling* in your Hire and Merchandife, Year
" after Year, and not rile alfo in the Support of
" your *Miniſters* ? I leave it to the *Heart* of every
" *Merchant* and every *Labourer* to judge in this
" Thing. †

" I have but one *Word* more to add in this *public*
" *Audience.* and that concerns the *College* ; to mind
" you that the many great and prudent *Benefactions*
" made of late Years to that *Society*, have (I truſt)
" this *Inſcription* of *Holineſs to the Lord* upon them.
" The *Bounties* of the pious Mr. *Hollis* in particular,
" his humble Offerings to *Chriſt* and his Munifi-
" cence to *us*, his *Lectures* and devoted *Students*
" wear *This* on their Forehead. " *The LORD raiſe*
" *up of our Sons for Prophets, and of our Young Men for*
" *Nazarites. That our Sons may be as Plants of Righ-*
" *teouſneſs ; and our Garners full, afficrding all Manner*
" *of Store ! Happy the People that are in ſuch a Caſe, yea*
" *happy is that People whoſe God is the Lord.*

The *Addreſs* to *You*, with which the *Sermon* cloſ'd
in your *private Meeting*, was in the following Words,

" *Finally*, Should our *Merchandiſe and Hire* be
" *Holineſs to the Lord* ? it gives a ſpecial *Countenance*
" to, and puts great *Honour* on, your *preſent Meeting.*
" This *Evening Lecture* is on a *double* Account *holy*

---

† Since *that Day* many or moſt of our *Churches* have made
conſiderable *Additions* to the Support of their *Miniſters*, but
in very few Places I think in a juſt *Proportion* to the Fall
of *Money*, and the Rife of *Goods*. So that every *New Year*
or two ca'ls for a *new Proviſion* ; ſuch is our miſerable
ſinking *Condition* ; alas without Proſpect of any *Remedy* !
May the *Dews of Heaven* come down more abundantly on
the *Places* that conſider of it !

' to

(v)

" to God ; as in Respect of the Religious Exercise
" of *Worship* so also in Respect of our intended *Col-*
" *lection for the Poor.* The *Design & Intention* of our pre-
" sent Meeting is entirely sacred to *Christ* & to his
" *Poor.* We come to cast our *Mites* into the *Lord's Trea-*
" *sury* for the Use of the *Widow* & the *Fatherless.* Let
" us seek the *Divine Grace* that we may so *worship,*
" and so *give,* as becometh *Holiness* ; in holy Man-
" ner, with holy Frames, from holy Principles, for
" holy Ends, to the Increase of holy Fruits in our
" Hearts & Lives, to the Glory & Praise of God.

" Write now, if you please, *Holiness to the Lord* on
" these *Doors* ||, here opened to us for the sake of
" *Charity* and *Devotion* ; which *two* will never *fail,*
" no not when *Faith* and *Hope* shall cease, within
" the *Holy of Holies.* The *Rich* are invited hither,
" not for their *own* so much as for the *Poors* sake.
" *The Bowels of the Poor are refreshed by Thee, Brother,*
" in your *calling the Rich to your House* : It is to *feast*
" *the poor, the maimed, the lame and the blind,* and *Thou*
" *shalt be recompenced at the Resurrection of the Just.*

" This *Meeting* is a Witness that our *Widows* and
" the *Fatherless* are not neglected in the daily Mi-
" nistrations. By *Inclination* you are led, and some
" of *You* more especially are by * *Office* bound, un-
" to this Service. And *God is not unrighteous to for-*
" *get this Labour of Love,* which you are *showing to*
" *his Name, in ministring to his Saints.*

" We have had a *hard and long Winter* †, which
" some may think has impoverished the *Town,* but

|| Deacon *Williams's* in *Cornhill.*   * The *Deacons* of the Churches.
  † March 6. 1726.

                                            " God

" God has carried us thro' it, and provided for the
" *Poor.* Yet *they* must needs be left the more *bare*
" and necessitous, and laden with little *Debts* it may
" be, which you *Brethren* are now met to *pay,* with
" a willing Mind ; that they may begin a *New*
" *Year* with *Thanksgiving* to God on your behalt.——
" I need not *urge* you to what you are so *ready* of
" your selves. You are *met* for *this* very End, *to*
" *pray us to accept the Gift,* and to *continue in this Fel-*
" *lowship* of ministring to the Saints. Like *Titus,*
" I am defired in *my Turn* to minister unto *the finish-*
" *ing in you* the *Grace,* which God has long since
" begun. *And God is able to make all Grace to abound*
" *toward you, that ye always having Alsufficiency in all*
" *Things, may abound to every good Word and Work.——*
" *Now He that ministreth Seed to the Sower, both mini-*
" *ster Bread for your Food, and multiply your Seed sown,*
" *and increase the Fruits of your Righteousness, being en-*
" *riched in every Thing to all Bountifulness, which*
" *causeth thro' us Thanksgiving unto God.*

OUR

Merchandise and Hire

HOLINESS TO THE LORD.

Isaiah xxiii. 18.

And her Merchandise, and her Hire shall be Holiness to the Lord.

*T*YRE is the *City* here spoken of; and a very good and great *Word* it is that is here spoken of her. It is a *Prophecy* of the *Conversion* of the *Tyrians* by the preached *Gospel*; and how they should use their *Wealth* in the Day when God should convert them. And what is here written concerning them is for our learning, being a Direction and Precept to us, that *our* Merchandise and Hire should be *Holiness to the Lord.*

Tyre

Tyre was a *Gentile City* of great *Antiquity*, and Re-
nown for *Trade* and Wealth, ſcituate on the *Me-*
diterranean Sea, near to the Lot of the Tribe of *Aſher*.
It was built by ſome Colony of the *Zidonians*, and
is therefore in our Context called *the Daughter of*
Zidon.

In *David* and *Solomon's* time we find the *Tyrians*
faithful Allies and Friends of *Iſrael*. And as one
well obſerves, " Trading Cities ſeldom prove dan-
" gerous Enemies to their Nei'bours ; for they ac-
" quire and maintain their Grandeur, not by the
" Conqueſt of others, but by Commerce with them.

The Inhabitants of *Tyre* were now grown the
moſt skilful in *Sea Affairs* of any in the World. A-
bout the ninth Year of *Hezekiah*, *Salmanezer* the
Aſſyrian invaded and beſieged them both by Sea and
Land. By Sea they beat the *Aſſyrian and Phænician*
Fleet of ſixty Sail, with *twelve* Ships only· This
gave 'em a Name for *War* as well as Riches, and
made 'em the Terror of the Ocean. The *Aſſyrian*
Army then block'd 'em up by Land ; for *Old Tyre*
was built upon the *Continent*, and the *new City* after-
ward upon an *Iſland* ; which *Siege* they bare for
five Years, and were at laſt delivered by the Death
of *Salmanezer*. Upon this Succeſs they were puff'd
up with new Pride, and grew hau'tier than ever,
which provoked the *Holy God* to utter the
Burden and Prophecy againſt them, in the *Chapter*
before us, wherein is foretold, 1. The miſerable
Overthrow of the *Tyrians* by *Nebuchadnezzar* and the
Chaldean Army ; and 2. Their *Reſtoration*, like their
Nei'bours the *Jews*, after *ſeventy* Years ; when they
ſhould recover their ancient *Liberty*, *Trade* & *Riches*
again. --- This is the Danger and Miſery of Places
of *Commerce*, that as they grow rich and *opulent* they
                                                    alſo

alſo grow *ſenſual, prophane* and *inſolent, unjuſt* and unrighteous ; and ſo *forfeit* the Bleſſings of Providence, and *incur* its dreadful Judgments ; as *Tyre* did.

Nebuchadnezzar found it a hard peice of Work to conquer *Tyre* *. He began its Siege about *two* Years after the Deſtruction of *Jeruſalem* and the Captivity of *Judah.* It held him *thirteen* Years before it was taken, when he took a terrible Revenge and utterly raſ'd it. An Account of this is given us by the Prophet *Ezekiel*, Chap. xxix. *v.* 18. *Son of Man, Nebuchadnezzar King of Babylon cauſed his Army to ſerve a great Service againſt Tyre; every Head was made bald and every Shoulder was peeled; yet had he no Wages nor his Army for Tyre, for the Service that he ſerved againſt it.* The ſhort Account of this Matter is, " That the *Tyrians* finding him too hard for them by *Land*, while yet they were Maſters by *Sea*, they built themſelves *a new City on an Iſland* about half a Mile diſtant from the Shore, into which they removed the moſt and beſt of their Effects; ſo that when *Nebuchadnezzar* enter'd the *old City*, after his long Seige and hard Service of *thirteen* Years, he found *no Riches, no Spoil* in the Place, to repay him for his vaſt Expence or to reward his Soldiers; the Inhabitants having paſſ'd with their Stores into the *new City*, which was afterwards a moſt mighty *Maritime Power* and *Mart* of the Nations, ſtill called TYRE; riſing as a *Phænix* from the Aſhes of her *Dam.* —— It is probable, ſays the noble *Hiſtorian*, that after the King of *Babylon* had deſtroy'd the *Old Town*, thoſe that retir'd into the *new* one came into *Terms* and ſubmitted to him ; and ſo

---

See the learned Dr. *Prideaux*'s Connection of the *Old and New Teſtament.*

C continued

continued in a ftate of Reftraint and *Servitude* to the *Babylonians* and *Perfians* for Seventy Years; altho' they were not captivated and difperfed, were not carried away to *Babylon* and *Chaldea*, as the *Jews* were.

Such was the Accomplifhment of the *Burden of Tyre* utter'd by *Ifaiah*! So it was *laid wafte*, at which all her *Ships* are call'd to *howl*. This was the *End* of the *joyous City*, whofe *Antiquity was of ancient Days*, *her own Feet carry'd her away*! her Pride and *Highnefs* of Spirit, the *Sin* of rich and thriving Places did it! for it prefently runs a Place into Irreligion, Senfuality and Unrighteoufnefs. The fame *Pride*, that caft down the *Angels*; and deftroy'd *Sodom* in her Fulnefs of Bread, leaving the polluted Cities as the *Image* on Earth of *everlafting Burnings*; laid *Tyre*, *the crowning City*, defolate; whofe *Merchants were Princes, and her Traffickers the honourable of the Earth*: The LORD OF HOSTS *did it to ftain the Pride of all Glory*.

Thefe things are written *for our Warning*; for a warning to the *Maritime Powers of Europe*, to *England* and *Holland* in particular, on whom *the Ends of the World are come*. So criminal is the *Pride of Life* in the Eyes of a *Holy God*, and odious! See it in the Judgment of *Tyre*, as the moft eminent Inftance, *Ezekiel* xxviii. init. " *Son of Man, fay to the Prince of Tyre, Thus faith the* LORD GOD, *Becaufe thine Heart is lifted up, and thou haft faid, I am a God,* (a kind of *Neptune*, God of the Seas) *I fit in the Seat of God, in the midft of the Seas: Yet thou art a Man and not a God, tho' thou fet thine Heart as the Heart of God: Behold thou art wifer than Daniel* (who had it feems fuch a Name and Fame for *Wifdom*, thro' the Kingdoms and Provinces of the *Eaft*, that it might pafs

for

for a *Proverb* among them, " *as wiſe as Daniel) and
with thy Wiſdom and Underſtanding thou haſt gotten thee
Riches, Gold and Silver into thy Treaſuries, and thy Heart
is lifted up ;* (art a *golden God* in thy own Eyes, making *thy Gold thy Hope,* and ſaying to it, " *Thou art
my Confidence !* ") *Therefore thus ſaith the Lord God, Behold I will bring Strangers upon thee, the Terrible of the
Nations, and they ſhall draw their Swords againſt the
Beauty of thy Wiſdom, and they ſhall defile thy Brigh-
neſs ; they ſhall bring thee down to the Pit, and thou ſhalt
die the Deaths of the Slain in the midſt of the Seas : thou
ſhalt be a Man and no God in the Hand of him that ſlayeth
thee.*

All this God bro't on proud and hau'ty *Tyre* for
her Sins. But in the *Cloſe* of the *Chapter,* where my
Text is found, we have " a *Time* fix'd for the Continuance of her Judgment, and a *Prophecy* of the Re-
covery of her ancient Glory, " v. 15. *Tyre ſhall be
forgotten ſeventy Years, according to the Days of one King ;
after the End of ſeventy Years ſhall Tyre ſing as an Harlot :*
By the Days of *one King* we muſt underſtand the
Succeſſion of *one Family* of the Monarchs of *Babylon,
Nebuchadnezzar,* his *Son* and *Grandſon ;* and by her
ſinging again as an *Harlot,* we muſt underſtand, " her
" Return to her State of former *Proſperity,* Mer-
" chandiſe and Traffic ; and her uſing all *Arts* and
" *Means* (as ſhe had done before) to draw Trade
" and Cuſtomers to her : Like as an *Harlot* that
" has been ſometime under Reſtraint and Correc-
" rection for her Leudneſs, when ſhe is at Liberty
" again returns with a violent Bent to her old Arts
" of Temptation * ; *Such was Tyre* when at the End
of 70 Years ſhe recovered Freedom, Trade and
Riches. She did all ſhe could to *allure* the Commerce of the Nations to her again ; the *Tyrians*
were as much ſet upon worldly Gains, were as in-

---

* See *Henry* in loc.

ordinate

ordinate in their Defire and Love of Wealth, and in taking all Methods to get it, as they had been before; and *rejoyced* in their Acquifitions as heretofore. This is the *Harlotry* here imputed to her, an *inordinate Luft* after Riches, and Pleafure in it; which in *Scripture* is called fpiritual *Fornication*. And accordingly the *Prophet* goes on to brand and expofe *Tyre* for her Love of Money, v. 16. " *Take an Harp and go about the City, thou Harlot that haft been forgotten! make fweet Melody, fing many Songs that thou mayft be remembred.* Nothing can be more *elegant* than this predicting" the *various Artifices* and even *difhoneft Practices*, whereby the City of *Tyre* regaining her Iiberty, would return into her *wonted* Commerce with *all* the Nations, and *entice* the *Merchants* of the Earth into their ufual Dealings with her. *So fhe turn d to her Hire, and committed Fornication with all the Kingdoms of the World upon the Face of the Earth,* v. 17.

But then in the *laft Verfe* of the Chapter, which is my *Text*, there is *one* Word of *Good* concerning *Tyre*; *one* Word of *Grace* refpecting her; and *that* is --- " That having recovered her rich and opulent State, *a Time* would come wherein She fhould make *a better Ufe of it* than fhe had done formerly; fhe fhould in Procefs of Time come to *ufe it religioufly, to the Honour of God and in his Service*; " Her *Merchandife* and her *Hire* would then be *Holinefs to the Lord*: And this is *explained* in the following Words, *It fhall not be treafured and laid up*; neither as *Mifers* hoard up their Bags, nor as the *proud* and *vain* lay out and lay up their Moneys in Fineries & Jewels; but " *her Merchandife fhall be for them that dwell before the Lord*, for the Support and Maintenance of *Religion* and the *Minifters* of it; for them *to eat fufficiently, and for durable Clothing*.

What

What more could we hope to hear of *Jerusalem* the Holy City, at any time! or of any other *City* of God in Gospel Times! --- What more than *this*, " *Her Merchandise and her Hire shall be* HOLINESS TO THE LORD? The *High Priest* of God, in his *Attire* of Holiness and Glory, on the *great and solemn Day*, wore no more *sacred Inscription* than this was! yet *this* shall be written on the *Merchandise of Tyre*! marvellous *Word*! written for the Generations *to come*, and that *the People to be created should praise the Lord*.

But *when* was this to be? and *wherein* should it be so? --- Why, In the Day when *Tyre*, and other *Nations*, should come, 1. *Not to treasure up* their Gains, from a Spirit of Covetousness, or of Ambition and Pride, or of Confidence in their Riches; but 2. when their Gains by Trade should be devoted to *God's Honour* and employ'd in *his Service*, in Works of *Piety* and *Charity*; for the Establishment and Support of the *House and Worship* of God, and for the Relief of *his Poor*: for sufficient and durable *Food* and *Clothing* for the *Pastors* and the *Poor* of Christ's Flocks.

But, *was there ever* such a Time as this, for *New Tyre*? and *when* was it? --- I answer, There were such Times; and *two Periods* may probably be referr'd to;

First, The Time of *Judah's Return out of Babylon*, when tho' the *seventy* Years of *Tyre* were not quite expired, yet *new Tyre* had attained more than *fifty* Years Growth, and was able to furnish the *Jews* toward and assist them in their *rebuilding of the City* and their *second Temple*. The *Tyrians* actually did this, partly *in Obedience to the Edict of Cyrus*, to whom they were subject, and partly from Interest

and

and Inclination, having been Fellow-Sufferers with and in the Captivity of *Judah*. Accordingly we read in *the Book of Ezra*, of *Meat and Drink, and Oil given to them of Zidon and of Tyre, to bring Cedar-Trees from Lebanon to the Sea of Joppa ; according to the Grant by the Hand of Cyrus King of Persia*. Chap. iii. 7. So early was the Merchandise of *new Tyre* Holiness to the Lord, for the rebuilding of his *Temple*, and for the furnishing of his *Priests and Worshipers*. And it is greatly to be observed to the Honour of the *Tyrians*, That as the *Fathers* in old *Tyre* had a special Hand in Materials for building the *first* Temple, so had their *Posterity* in the *second*.

But *secondly*, The *Prophecy* in my *Text* looks to be sure to some Time *long after* the Return of the *Jews* from *Babylon* ; even *to the Days of the Messiah* and the *Conversion* of some in *Tyre* by the *preached Gospel*. The Prophecy plainly supposes that *Tyre* would for a *long* Term of Years return into her *old* Course and Way of living, and continue *Pagan* ; tho' in a Way of *Trade* it might be *friendly to the Jews* their Neibours. In this there was little or *no* Religion ; their *Idol* Gain and worldly Wealth was served in it. But in the Day of the *Conversion of the Nations* to the Christian Faith, *Tyre* also received the Gospel. And then it was that her Merchandise and Hire became *Holiness to the Lord*, being used by a Number of Gods chosen and called there in the Services of *true Religion and Godliness*, the Support of his Worship, Ministers and Poor.

In *Nehemiah*'s Time we read of the *Men of Tyre dwelling at Jerusalem*, and we may suppose from that Time to the Day of *Christ* many a Gift and Offering from *Tyre* to the Altar of God at *Jerusalem* ; wherein the Words of *David* in the xlv *Psalm* might be fulfilled, as they doubtless were in his own Day ; " *The Daughter of Tyre shall be there with a Gift.*
In

In *Christ's* Time we find many of *Tyre* and *Zidon* better disposed to have received *Him* and his *Gospel* than the Men of *Israel*; for if *his mighty Works had been done among them they would have repented in Dust and Ashes.*

In the Days and *Acts* of the *Apostles* we find *Christians* at *Tyre*, Chap xxi. 3, 5. with whom *Paul tarried seven Days,* and who *thro' the Spirit* warn'd him of his *Danger* and Sufferings if he went up to *Jerusalem*; and when he departed from them *they bro't him on his Way with their Wives and Children,* so reverend and fervent was their *Love* to him for the Gospels sake, *till he was out of the City,* where *they kneeled down on the Shore and prayed, and took Leave one of another.* After this *Christianity* flourished in this *trading City,* and then her *Merchandise* became *devoted,* in part, to the Worship and Glory of *Christ.*

So that we plainly find in my *Text,* 1. A Prophecy of the *Conversion of the Tyrians.* 2. How they should then *use their Wealth*; that it would be *consecrated to God* in pious Uses, and *holy* to his Worship. 3. This *Spirit* and Example of the *Tyrians* is for the Learning and *Imitation* of other Places, Cities and Countrys, among the *Gentiles.* Let the Christians of *Tyre* teach us, that where ever the Gospel is received, in the *Love and Power* of it, it will bring forth *this good Fruit*; the Merchandise and Hire of the People *will be* Holiness to the Lord. " So " *Christians* should use their Estates in the Service " of God, and unto *pious Uses,* and count that best " laid up, which is so laid *out.* Both the Merchan- " dise of the Men in *Trade,* and the Hire of the " Men of *Labour,* should be devoted to God. The " *Tithe* was so under the *Law,* and there is a *Due* (and surely an *equal* one) under the *Gospel.*

New Tyre has the Honour of teaching us *this* under the *New Testament*; and in all Places of the
World

World, thro' all Ages, the *Gospel* is to be thus honoured. As it is written, Zech. xiv. 20. *In that Day there shall be upon the Bells of the Horses Holiness unto the Lord; yea every Pot in Jerusalem and in Judah shall be Holiness to the Lord of Hosts.*

And here let me *pause* and obſerve to you, *The Advantage that trading Places have beyond others by their Merchandise and Commerce;* and the *Obligation* they are under to *improve* their Advantages, *for getting and propagating the ſaving Knowledge and Worſhip of God.* This was *Tyre's* Happineſs and Benefit by her Situation for *Traffic*. She was much the more known to *Iſrael*, and knew ſo much the more of *her God and Worſhip*, than other Places. Her *Merchandise* put her in the Way hereof. Many a Man of *Tyre* went a trading to *Jeruſalem*, and heard of the *true God*, his Law to and his Works for *Iſrael*, and ſaw his *Sanctuary*, the Order and Worſhip of his Houſe.

Many of the *Jews* alſo were led to *Tyre* by their Trade, where they accidentally ſpake of the *Lord God* of their Fathers, his Worſhip, Laws and Works. Other Places it may be took up ſtrange and odd Notions of that *ſeparate People*, as a ſingular ſort of Folk; but the *Tyrians* ſaw they were *a wiſe and underſtanding People*, had *Statutes and Judgments moſt righteous*, and excelled other Places in Sobriety and Juſtice as well as in Devotion. And who knows what Influence this might have on that Degree of *Union*, which there was between *Jeruſalem* and *Tyre* in the Days of *David* and *Solomon* ? 1 Kings v. 6. *My Servants ſhall be with thy Servants.*

But this we know, That *Chriſtianity* has been greatly ſerv'd by Trade and *Merchandise*, by means whereof a great Part of the World has been *goſpeliſed*. For

For the Knowledge of Chriſt has been *propagated* by Trade far and near. The *Earth* and *Sea* have thus help'd the *Church*, and as *Daniel* foretold it would be, *Many have run to and fro'* (croſs the Ocean) *and Knowledge has been increaſed.* God has us'd the *Loadſtone* and the *Mariners Art* in the Service of Chriſt, and *the Ends of the Earth have ſeen his Salvation.*

And to add yet one more Benefit of *Commerce*; it *enlarges* Peoples Hearts to do *generous* Things, for the Support of Divine Worſhip and Relief of the Poor. We always ſee moſt of this in Places of Trade. And ſo it has been from the firſt Days of *Tyre*, of whom we read, " *The Daughter of Tyre ſhall be there with a Gift :* She *firſt* and more *free* of her Gifts than others. This is moſt natural to Places of *Commerce*; Something to give and a Heart to give. May it be always found ſo in *trading* Places! but eſpecially we wiſh them a Heart to make the *beſt* Gift, *Themſelves* with their Eſtates, and this in the beſt *Manner*; as the Churches of *Macedonia* are celebrated for ever for doing, 2 Cor. viii. 1,—5. *The Riches of whoſe Liberality abounded in their deep Poverty,* praying the Apoſtles *with much Entreaty that they would accept the Gift, and take upon them the Fellowſhip of miniſtring to the Saints; firſt giving their own Selves to the Lord, and then to* the Apoſtles *by the Will of God.* " When Converts *joyn themſelves to the Church* then they come *with a Gift,* devoting their *Seed and Subſtance* together with their Perſons, Gifts and Powers, to his Service and Glory.

It is high Time I now come to the *Doctrine* which my *Text* leads me to enlarge on, which is,

" *That the Merchandiſe and Hire of a People, their Trade and worldly Buſineſs, their Gains and Riches, ſhould be Holineſs to the Lord.*

D

The

The *Enquiries* under this *Doctrine* must be 1. Into the *Meaning* of the Phrase, *Holiness to the Lord.* 2. When the *Traffic and Wealth* of a People may be so called? 3. *Why* it must be so?

I The Meaning of this *Phrase, Holiness to the Lord* must be look'd into. And the *first* time that we find it us'd, than *which* there could not have been found any more *eminent*, was the *Divine Order* concerning the *High Priests Vestments*, his *Garments for Glory and Beauty*, wherein *he* was to approach before the *Lord*, and minister unto Him upon the *most solemn Occasions*: Exodus xxviii. 36, 37, 38. *Thou shalt make a Plate of pure Gold, and grave upon it like the Ingravings of a Signet, Holiness to the Lord : And thou shalt put it on a blue Lace, that it may be upon the Mitre, upon the Fore-front thereof ; upon Aaron's Forehead, that he may bear the Iniquity of the Holy Things which the Children of Israel shall hallow in all their Holy Gifts ; And it shall be always upon his Forehead, that they may be accepted before the Lord.*

Now we may observe in this first Appointment of this *Title & Inscription*, that it plainly was meant to signify, 1. The infinite Holiness of the *God of Israel*, and of *Christ* the *great High Priest* of our Profession. 2. The Holiness of the *Priesthood and Ministerial Office*, their special *Consecration* to holy Ministrations, and their special *Obligations* to be *Holy* to the Lord. 3. The *Holiness of God's Worship*, and that all his People must take Care to be very *holy* in all their Approaches to Him, in all the *Institutions* of his Worship. Psalm xcix. *The Lord is great in Zion, and high above all People : Let them praise thy great and terrible Name, for it is Holy ; Exalt the Lord our God, and worship at his holy Hill ; for the Lord our God is Holy.*

So

So that in this *Title Holineſs to the Lord* we have
1. the Holineſs of *God*: 2. a *Conſecration* to Him,
or theSeparation of a Perſon or Thing to *holy Uſes*:
3. *Actual Uſe* and Imployment therein: and 4. in
a ſpecial *Relation* to his *Worſhip.*

1. *Holineſs to the Lord* ſuppoſes, and in the higheſt
manner declares, as *in ſhining Capitals of Gold,* the
infinite, unutterable, incomparable, inconceivable
Holineſs of Jehovah,the only true God; that He is the
Holy One, and *alone* Holy, *glorious* in Holineſs, the
thrice Holy; and there is *none* Holy like Him or be-
ſide Him. This is his *Glory* in both *Teſtaments* [*],
in his *Temple* above and in that below: " *I ſaw the
Lord ſitting upon a Throne, high and lifted up, and his
Train filled the Temple: Above it ſtood the Seraphims,
covering their Faces, andOne cried unto Another and ſaid,
Holy, Holy, Holy is the Lord of Hoſts! the whole Earth
is full of his Glory.* And if the bleſſed *God* were not
Himſelf thus *Holy,* why and how ſhould Perſons
and Things be called *Holineſs* unto *Him.*

2, It ſpeaks a *Conſecration* of Perſons and Things
to God, a *ſeparation* of them to his more immediate
Service and Glory, to be of holy *Uſe* according to
his Will. So *Aaron* and the *Prieſthood* were of old
ſeparated and devoted to God, and therefore had
this Name written on them, *Holineſs to the Lord.* So
the *Sabbath* is conſecrated Time, and in the *Hebrew*
called *Holineſs to the Lord,* Exod. xxxi. 15. In like
manner the very *Fruit of the Trees in the fourth Year
were holy to praiſe the Lord withal:* Levit. xix. 24.
The Hebrew Word is *Holineſs;* being given to the
Prieſts and to the *Poor.* And the ſame is ſaid of the
Veſſels of Silver and Gold, Braſs andIron, in *Jerico.*

---

[*] Iſaiah vi. 1, 2, 3. Revel. iv. 8, 9.
D 2   Joſh.

Joſh. vi. 19. Thus *Iſrael was Holineſs to the Lord*
(Jer. ii. 3.) by the Covenant of *Circumciſion*, their
Dedication to God therein ; and in like Manner
do all *Chriſtian People* by their *Baptiſmal Dedication*
to God wear the ſame Words, as on their *Foreheads*.

But moreover, 3. *Holineſs to God* imports the
actual Uſe and Improvement of Perſons and Things
in the *Service* of God and to his *Glory*. When *Aaron*
put on his *Mitre* it was actually to *officiate* before
the Lord. He was then in a more ſpecial manner
to intend, deſign and act for, the ſanctifying God's
Name in holy Miniſtrations. *De facto* there was
Holineſs to the Lord in his right Diſpoſitions, and
Diſcharge of his Office : Elſe the Prieſthood and
Worſhippers *profaned the Holineſs of the Lord which
be loved.* Mal. ii. 11. Otherwiſe, *in their ſet Office*
(" in the Diſcharge of their Office to which they
were *ſet apart* ") *they ſanctified themſelves in Holineſs.*
2 Chron. xxxi. 18. Then, and *then* only, were they
Holineſs to the Lord, in *Deed* and in *Truth*. And
ſo are we to *Chriſt*, if we are holy in Heart and
Life ; if we *live to Him in all holy Converſation*, as in
our *Baptiſm* we have bound our Selves.

4. And laſtly, This *Motto, Holineſs to the Lord,*
has a more particular Regard to the *Worſhip* of God,
his *Miniſtry* and *Sanctuary*, his *Ordinances* and *Inſti-
tutions.* So *Iſrael* as Worſhippers, and *Aaron* as a
Prieſt, and the *Sabbath* as the Day of weekly Worſhip, and the *Firſt-fruits* as offered in Worſhip, were
dignified with this *Style* of Holy to the Lord. So
when *we* by the Grace of God devote, uſe and imploy *our* Souls and Bodies, our Gifts and Powers,
our Time and Eſtate, in the Services of Religion,
and for promoting his Worſhip, they become *Holineſs to the Lord* We become in our *Perſons* as
                                        Temples

Temples of the living God, and God is *sanctified in us* as in them *that draw nigh to Him* ; and our *Powers* of Mind and Body, with the *Fruit* of our Bodies, our *Time* and *Estate,* our *Interest* in the World and our *Influence* among Men, are as so many *Offerings* to God at his *Altar,* which *consecrates* the Gifts.

Having thus enquired into the *Meaning* of the Phrase *Holiness to the Lord,* I come now to enquire,

II. *When* the *Traffic and Wealth, Merchandise and Business* of a Person or People may be so called ? To which I answer in *three* general Heads,

1. When Men seriously devote, dedicate & consecrate, first *Themselves* and then of their *worldly Substance,* a due Part, to the Glory and Service of God. 2. When what is so consecrated to God out of our Estates is *actually used and imployed* in his Service, according to his Will, *in Acts of Piety and Charity.* 3. Always provided that what we so devote and use is *acquired honestly & righteously* in God's Fear and Way, and is *given* by us with a *spiritual Mind and Heart.*

I. Then, is our *Merchandise and Trade,* Wealth and worldly Business, *Holiness to the Lord,* when we seriously *devote, dedicate and consecrate,* a due Part of our *Substance,* together with *our Selves,* to the *Glory and Service of God.*

First, I must say *our Selves,* for the *Person* must be sacred and dedicated to God before his *Estate* will be so ; the *Person* is first *holy* and then his *Gift.* This is the Order of *Nature* and of *Grace* * ; for which

* 2 Cor. viii. 5. Matth. xxiii. 17.

is

is *greater*, the Gift or the Giver! how much *lefs* is a Mans Eftate before God, than the *Man* himfelf? according to the *Apoftles* juft Eftimation of the *Macedonians* and their *miniftring to the Saints*, ' *Who firft gave their own Selves to the Lord.* God looks to a Mans *Heart* and Soul in all his Offerings to Him, whether of *Praife* or *Alms*. It is the *Perfon* who wears upon his Forehead the Infcription, *Holinefs to the Lord.* If the Perfon be unholy before Him, *his Sacrifice is an Abomination.* He profanes and pollutes his own Gift; as *Cain* did his Offering, bringing it with a wicked Mind. If we have not given our *Selves*, our *Hearts* to God, we may give *all our Goods* to feed the Poor, or give it to the *Church*, (for *Them that dwell before the Lord*) and yet there will be nothing of *Holinefs* in the one or in the other ||.

Yet the *Eftate* muft go with the Perfon, as it is in *Marriage*; and it has pleafed God to *efpoufe* unto Himfelf the Soul that gives it felf to him; * *I am married to you, faith the Lord.*

The *firft Offering* from Man that we read of, acceptable to God, was the *Perfon* with a part of his *Eftate*; I mean *Abel*'s Offering. *Cain* allo bro't of the Fruit of the Ground, but God had *no Refpect* to his Offering becaufe he *had not firft* given *himfelf* to Him. *Abraham* having refigned up Himfelf to the Divine Will and Call, gave his *Tythe of all unto the Prieft of the moft High God*; the famous *Type* of his *Lord and Saviour*, after whofe *Order* Chrift is *a Prieft for ever*; and he was *bleffed* by him. So *Jacob* vowed, firft *that the Lord fhould be his God*, and then a *Tenth* of all that God fhould give him. So *David* having firft render'd his *Heart* to God in Flames of

---

|| 1 Cor. xiii. 4.   Jerem. iii. 14.

Devotion, then gathered *vast Stores* which he confec ated for *a Temple* to the Name of the Lord ; and his *Princes* followed his Royal Example, 1 Chron. xxix. 16. 17. " *O Lord our God, all this Store that we have prepared cometh of thine Hand, and it is all thine own : I know also my God, that Thou triest the Heart and hast Pleasure in Uprightness : As for me in the Uprightness of my Heart have I willingly offer'd all these Things, &c.* Here was the Offering *of the Man after God's own Heart.* And we find in the Gospel when the *young Man* came and offered *Himself* to Christ, our Lord demanded of him also the Use of all his *Estate,* and he *went away sorrowful.* It is added, *for he had great Possessions* * : He might then, one would think, have been the more ready to have given *freely* to the poor out of it : Or, did he think his *Riches* of more Price than *himself ?* poor *Soul !* it seems as if he would not have offer'd himself to Christ, had he tho t himself half so good as his Possessions ! his going away *sorrowful* shew'd that he was not *sincere* in the Offer of Himself. On the contrary *Zaccheus* being a sincere Penitent, gave *half his Goods to the poor,* and Christ accepted of his *Person,* and said to him, " *Salvation is come to thy House* †.

So the *first Christians* || when they had given up *Themselves* to Christ in *Baptism,* gave in all their *Goods* into a common Stock. It was on an extraordinary *Occasion,* and under an extraordinary Effusion of the *Holy Spirit* The Churches Needs call'd for it, and *the Spirit of God* directed to it. *Ananias* and his *Wife* had only given their *Names,* not their Hearts ; and keeping *back* part of the Price *died* for the Sacri-

---

Matth. xix. 22. † Luke xix. 9. || Acts iv. 34, 35.
v. 1, 2.

lege,

lege, and their *Lying to the Holy Ghost*. On the contrary, the *Macedonians*, whose Praise is in all the Churches for Evermore, having given both their *Names and Hearts* to Christ, gave liberally of their *Estates* for the Relief of the *poor Saints*, even *beyond their Ability*. Thus was their *Merchandise* Holiness to the Lord. Neither will the Estate do without the *Person*, all his Heart and all his Soul ; nor the Person do (if that could be) without the *Estate*, for it will go with the Heart and Love. ─ But I prevent my self on the *second* Answer to the Enquiry I am upon:

II. Our Merchandise and Wealth is *Holiness to the Lord*, when what is consecrated and devoted out of our *Estate*, is actually *used* and imployed in the *Service* of God, according to his *Will*. " *When thou vowest a Vow, defer not to pay ; why should God be angry at thy Voice* * *? Vow and pay to the Lord thy God ! let all that be round about Him bring Presents unto Him that ought to be feared.* Present *thy Self*, and then remember that thou hast implicitly and virtually, if not most explicitly and expresly, vowed to him *his Dues out of thy Estate*. Bring these *Presents* to Him as long as thou livest, in their returning Seasons, *Better it is that thou shouldest not vow, than that thou shouldest vow and not pay.*

It is to be feared that many *Christians* do not eno' apprehend and consider, that their *worldly Estate* enters into their *general Vow*, and is always a Part of it, in their *Self-Dedication* to God But God's Part is *holy to Him* whether we consider it or no ; and if we render Him his Part, the *whole* is sanctified unto us. There is not *Holiness to God* written

---

on our Perfons, Faculties and Powers, nor on our
Eftate, till both one and the other are *ufed* to
holy Ends and Purpofes, in actual Miniftrations to
the Glory of God. But if we are actually honouring God with our whole Man, Soul and Body,
the Powers of the one, and the Endowments of the
other, the *Spirit of the Living God* dwells and rules
in us, and has *graven on us,* as in Letters of Gold,
Holinefs to Himfelf. And if we are *honouring the
Lord with our Subftance, and with the Firft-fruits of our
Increafe,* we may *read* with Pleafure the fame *Infcription* on our *Eftates,* & others may *fee* it on us. 2 Cor.
iii. 2. *Ye are our Epiftle written in our Hearts, known
and read of all Men : Ye are manifeftly declared to be the
Epiftle of Chrift, miniftred by us, written not with Ink,
but with the Spirit of the Living God ; not in Tables of
Stone, but in flefhly Tables of the Heart.*

Now if it be ask'd, *Wherein* a Part of our worldly
Eftate is to be *us'd* to the Glory of God ? it is eafily
anfwer'd in the *two* general and known *Inftances,*
Works of *Piety* and *Charity.* The *firft* is the very
Thing in my Text, and the *other is like unto it,* and
never to be feparated ; the *firft* is a more direct Expreffion of Love to *God,* the *other* to our *Nei'bour ;*
on which *two hang all the Law and the Prophets,* and
confequently the whole of *Holinefs to the Lord* is
contained in them.

Firft then, Our *Wealth* and worldly Bufinefs is
Holinefs to the Lord, when with a true and right
Heart it is ufed and imployed in *Works of Piety toward God, for the Support of his Worfhip.* When it is
*for them that dwell before the Lord to eat fufficiently, and
for durable Clothing.* That is to fay, When Men
make Confcience of giving unto God a due Proportion out of their Eftates for the Support of *Re-*
E *ligion*

ligion and the Maintenance of God's *Minifters*, to feed and clothe them, and that fufficiently and *honourably*; eno' to eat of plentifully, and to clothe their Families decently, and leave fomething to them when they die. —— The *Tithes* of old were fuch a Provifion for the *Levites*. And as they that ferved at the *Altar* liv'd of it, fo has the Lord ordained *that they who preach the Gofpel fhould live of the Gofpel*, 1 Cor. ix. 14. The Bread of *Minifters* is the Bread of *God*, and we muft allow Him to be a good *Houfholder*, & to keep a good *Table*. He does not feed his Houfhold by *Miracles*, but by his referved *Dues* out of the Eftates of his People. He will have it done by *their* Hands, that they may do Him Duty and *Homage*, and pay him *Tribute*. There is always a part of your *Moneys*, whereof he fays to you, " *Whofe Image and Superfcription is this ?* and you muft anfwer, *It is Gods.* Then *render to God the Things that are his.* Matth. xxii 21. Do it by miniftring out of your *Eftates* to his Houfe and Worfhip, according to the *Ability* which he gives you.

When People expend prudently and pioufly for the fetting up, and carrying on, the *Worfhip* of God where they live, or in other Places ; or in fending the Gofpel to People deftitute thereof, and perifhing for lack of Knowledge ; and in making Provifion for a more private Inftruction of Children in fuch Places ; their Wealth in this *Ufe* of it becomes *Holinefs to the Lord.* It comes into a *Relation* to divine Worfhip, even as *Aaron* and the *Holy Things* of old belonging to the *Tabernacle.* —— But unto fuch Works of *Piety* for the Support of God's *Worfhip*, we muft add

Secondly, Works of *Charity and Mercy*, which are as much in themfelves, and render us as much, *Holinefs*

liness to the Lord, as the other. Thefe belong to the *fecond Table of the Law,* as thofe to the *firft.* Pity to the poor and needy, in Obedience to God & Conformity to Him, is Piety and *Sanctity* in his Sight. They are the Lord's *Receivers* as well as his Prieſts, and we have them *always with us.* And the *pious poor* are among his *fpiritual Prieſts,* rich in Faith, chofen of God and *called.* He that gives to them, for their comfortable Eating and Clothing, with a right and charitable Frame of Spirit, *lends to the Lord, and honours Him with his Subſtance.* Thefe are fpiritual *Sacrifices* with which God is *well pleafed.* There is Worſhip and *Incenfe,* an *Odour of a fweet Smell* in them, as well as in Offerings at the *Altar* of God. The *Alms* of Believers go up for *a Memorial* before God, with their *Prayers*; as did thofe of *Cornelius.* The *Great High Prieſt,* at the *Golden Altar* within the *Vail,* prefents the one and the other in the *Cloud of Incenfe,* his own Merits & Interceſſion. *He,* the *Holy One* of God, was *Holiness to the Lord* above all the Sons of Men; and his Miracles of *Mercy* were like his Prayers and Devotions beyond number, and alike honorary to God. God will have *his poor* fed, as well as his *Miniſters.* And why not? are they not together *Heirs of his Kingdom* ? and has he not put them together again and again, the *Levite* and the *Poor* *, in his Peoples rejoicing before him on his *folemn Feaſts* ?

But give me leave more *particularly* to prove, by three or four *Arguments,* that Works of *Charity to the poor* are proper *Holiness to the Lord.*

1. They are *Obedience to the Law of God* which is moſt holy. The *Word* of God is the Rule of Holi-

---

* Deut. xvi. 11, 14. xxvi. 11. 13.

nefs,

ness, and one of its grand Rules and Laws to us is *Alms-deeds*, and acts of Charity. These are an eminent Branch of that *Holiness* which the Lord requires, Zech. vii. 9. *Thus saith the Lord, Shew Mercy every one to his Brother.* Only let what we do be done in Obedience to God, for his Glory, and with a pure Respect to his Will, not *to be seen of Men* ; having true *Compassion one of another, loving as Brethren, pitiful, courteous, tender-hearted* ‖ ; otherwise there is no *Holiness* to the Lord, nor *Reward* from our *Father that is in Heaven.*

2. To give to the *poor* out of our Estates is *Holiness to the Lord,* because it is our *Conformity to God, and Christ in their Bounties and Mercies to the indigent and miserable.* Conformity to the Holy God is *Holiness,* but *Compassion* and Mercy to the poor is Conformity to God ; *who maketh his Sun to rise and his Rain to fall on the evil and on the good ; Be ye therefore perfect as your Father in Heaven is perfect.* Mat.v. 45, 48. So *Christ* approved Himself to be the *Holy One* in the Days of his Flesh, by filling up his Life with Acts of *God-like Charity and Mercy.* They *cried after Him,* laid themselves in his Way, *and he healed them all.* This was *Holiness to his Father,* and in the Sight of Men, and we should lay up in our Hearts his memorable Words, Acts xx. 35. *It is more blessed to give than to receive.*

3 A right and charitable Disposition is *the Fruit of the Holy Spirit* in us, & therefore can be no other than *Holiness to the Lord.* " *The Fruit of the Spirit is Love* †. There is much of the *Spirit* of God in Bowels of Pity to one another. " *If there be any*

‖ Matth. vi. 1.   1 Pet. iii. 8.   Ephes. iv. 32.   † Gal. v. 22. Phil. ii. 1.   Col. iii. 12.

Fellowship of the Spirit, if any Bowels and Mercies. The Communion of the *Holy Ghost*, and the Communion of *Saints*, is experienced & exhibited in these *Bowels*, which we are therefore exhorted to put on, as the *Elect of God, holy and beloved*; and because this Charity is *the Bond of Perfectness.* See the Argument and *Demonstration* of the Apostle *James* on this Head, Jam. ii. 15, 16. *If a Brother or Sister be naked, and destitute of daily Food; and one of you say unto them, Depart in Peace, be you warmed & filled: notwithstanding ye give them not those Things which are needful to the Body; what doth it profit?* q. d. What Fruit, what *Evidence* of any true *Holiness* is there, in a *Soul* or *Life* destitute of the Fruits of *Charity*.

4. Is the *Sabbath and its Worship* Holiness to the Lord? So are *Charities and Mercies.* There is such a *Sanctity* in these, that they belong to & are a Part of the *Sanctification of the Sabbath.* Yea such Regard is had by God to an Act of Mercy to our poor Nei'bour, that He has made his own Worship to *vail* and give place thereto for the Time *. *" Go ye and learn this, I will have Mercy and not Sacrifice. Which of you having an Ox or Ass fallen into a Pit, will not straightway pull him out on the Sabbath day?* And if a good and devout Man must show this Mercy to his *Brute-Creature* on the *Sabbath* day, the *Holiness* of God directing him to to do; how much more must not Acts of Compassion and Mercy to our poor and needy *Brethren*, and to the necessitous *Members* of *Jesus* Christ, be esteemed by *the Lord of the Sabbath* to be *Holiness* to himself? The *Zeal* for God's House and Day *eat up* our Holy *Saviour*, but *more* his Zeal for an Act of *Mercy* to a poor Woman; Luke xiii. 10,—17. *He was teaching in one of the Synagogues on*

---

* Matth. xii. 7. Luke xiv. 5.

the Sabbath-day, and behold there was a Woman which had a Spirit of Infirmity eighteen Years, and was bowed together, and could in no wife lift up her Self: And when Jesus saw her, he called her to him and said to her, Woman thou art loosed of thine Infirmity! And he laid his Hands on her, and immediately she was made straight, and glorified God. Tell me now which was moſt *Holineſs to the Lord,* the *Sermon* of Chriſt on that bleſſed Sabbath, or this his Act of *Healing* the poor Woman? truly *both* alike.

Moreover, *Offerings* out of our Eſtates, and *Collections* for the poor, do both belong to the *Temple* of God and to his *Sabbaths.* St *Luke* tells us of a *Treaſury* ‖ of God in the *Temple* of old, and that on a Time as *Chriſt* was looking on the *rich Men* that caſt their *Gifts* into the Treaſury, he ſaw alſo a certain *poor Widow* who threw in *two Mites,* and ſaid, " *Of a Truth She has caſt in more than they all.* So from Heaven the *Lord Jeſus* ſtill looks with Approbation and Pleaſure, on the *free-will-Offerings* of his Worſhipers in his Houſe of Prayer, on *Lord's Days* and at other appointed Times; the *poorer* as well as the *richer.* — And ſo near *a Kin* are God's *Worſhip* and *Contributions* for the poor, that they are joyned by the *Lord* in *Affinity,* and equally declared to be *Holineſs to Him,* in that *Apoſtolical Conſtitution* and Direction *, " *Now concerning Collections for the Saints, as I have given Order to the Churches of Galatia, ſo do ye; Upon the firſt Day of the Week let every one of you lay by him in Store, as God hath proſper'd him,* &c Your *Prayers* and *Hearing* the Word this *Evening* † are not more *Holineſs to the Lord* than your *Collection* is. The

‖ Luke xxi. 1, 2, 3. * 1 Cor. xvi. 1, 2,
† At a quarter Meeting for Charity, the Lord's day Evening, March 6. 1726.

ſame

fameGod has faid to us, " *Remember the Sabbath-day
to keep it holy,* and hath alfo faid, " *to do Good and
to communicate forget not, for with fuch Sacrifices God is
well pleafed.*

5. And laftly, The *Promifes* made byGod to thofe
that are merciful and bountiful to the poor, do a-
bundantly declare that there is *Holinefs to the Lord*
in true Acts of religious Charity and Mercy. *He
that is Holy* would not be fo well pleafed with our
Charities to the poor and needy, if there were not
much *Holinefs* in them. He has therefore *bleffed* the
merciful, and faid that they *fhall find Mercy.* He is
not unrighteous to forget this Work and Labour of Love.
Not that there is any *Merit* or Defert herein, but
there is of his own *Holinefs* in it. If it were not fo,
Alms would never come up for a *Memorial* before
Him. Nor would they be fo remembred, mention'd
and rewarded in theDay of *Judgment,* as Chrift has
told us they will be ; " *Then fhall the King fay to them
on his right Hand, Come ye bleffed of my Father, inherit
the Kingdom prepared for you from the Foundation of the
World ; for I was hungry and ye gave me Meat, thirfty
and ye gave me Drink, a Stranger and ye took me in,
naked and ye clothed me,* &c. Thefe high and everlafting *Rewards* of the *Charities* of Saints, prove them
to be *Holinefs to the Lord. Bleffed and Holy is he that
has Part* in thefe Promifes *.

And thus we have feen that the *actual Ufe &* Im-
provement of our Eftates in the Service of God, in
Works of *Piety and Charity,* renders them Holinefs
to the Lord. --- But there muft be fomething added
by way of *Caution* and Limitation, and that is

---

* Matth. v. 7. Heb. vi. 10. Acts x. 4. Matth. xxv. 35.
Rev. xx. 6.

III. Always

III. Always provided that what we fo devote and ufe *is acquired honeftly and righteoufly* in the *Fear* of God and in his *Way*; and is *given* by us *with a fpiritual Mind, Heart and Affection.*

1. What we *have* and *give* muft be *gotten* in *God's Way*, which is the Way of *Holinefs*. If we go out of *that* we *fin*, and whatever we get in *finful* Ways is neceffarily *unholy* before the Lord, and abominable in his Eyes. Now that what we get may be acquired in God's holy Way,

Firft, Our *Dependence* muft be on God for his *Bleffing* to make our lawful Endeavours profperous; For it is the Bleffing of God *that makes rich*, and it is *He* that *gives us Power to get Wealth*; it is therefore *prophane and unholy* to act in our worldly Bufinefs but with a Dependance on the Governing and over-ruling Providence of a wife and Sovereign God: James iv. 14 *Go to now you that fay*, *To Day or to Morrow we will* be here or there, do this or that, and *make Gain*; *Whereas ye ought to fay, If the Lord will* we fhall do fo. Let *Jacob* teach us how to begin and go thro' the World: Gen. xxviii. 20. *If God will be with me in the Way I go, and give me Bread to eat and Raiment to put on.*

Secondly, We muft daily commit our worldly Affairs to God in *Prayer*, and more efpecially at Times our more important Concerns and Interefts. Our Lord has taught us to bring thefe before God in our Prayers: We pray for them in that *Directory* or *Form* for Prayer which he has given us, the *fourth Petition* in it. We pray " that of God's free Gift " we may receive a competent Portion of the good " Things of this Life, and enjoy his Bleffing with " them. It is greatly for the Glory of God, and for

for our temporal Interest and daily Comfort that we daily pray for God's gracious Direction to us in, and for his Blessing on our worldly Business: " *That the Lord thy God may bless Thee in all the Works of thy Hand.* So *Isaac* pray'd for his Son, " *God give Thee of the Dew of Heaven, and the Fulness of the Earth, and Plenty of Corn and Wine.* And so *Jacob* prayed for himself, " *If God will be with me in the Way I go, and give me Bread to eat.* And so *Moses* for the Tribe of *Levi*, " *Bless, Lord, his Substance*: The less it is, the more *need* to pray over it ; for the Blessing of God can make a *little* go far. The wise *Agur* has taught us *what* to pray for, " *Feed me with Food convenient for me.* He is *unholy* & prophane whose Prayer is not to God *his Heavenly Father, for these Things* *. And they are *sanctified to us by Prayer,* which makes them *Holiness to the Lord.*

Thirdly, We must keep from *every sinful & wicked Way* in our worldly Acquisitions and Enjoyments, and govern our Selves by the holy Laws of *Justice and Righteousness, Sobriety and Temperance,* and universal *Obedience* to the Divine *Law* Else all is unholy and unclean, and we forfeit God's Blessing and provoke his Curse. It is only sincere, hearty, universal and persevering *Obedience* to the holy Commandments of the Lord our God, that will render us holy and acceptable in his Sight. Deut. xxviii. 1, 2, 3. *If thou shalt hearken diligently to the Voice* " *of the Lord thy God, to observe and do all his Com-* " *mandments, all these Blessings shall come on thee,* ⸺ " *Blessed shalt thou be in the City and blessed in the Field !* " *blessed the Fruit of thy Body and the Fruit of thy Ground !* " ⸺ *blessed thy Basket and thy Store ! blessed shalt thou*

" *be when thou comeſt in, and bleſſed when thou goeſt*
" *out.*

Fourthly, In Caſe a Perſon have acquired Riches
in *any unjuſt and unrighteous Manner,* by *Deceit and
Fraud,* or by *Extortion and Oppreſſion* ; he muſt make
his Peace with God by Repentance, with deep *Humiliation* before Him for his Wickedneſs ; and if it be in
his Power. he muſt make *Reſtitution* ; which if he
cannot do to the *Perſons wronged* let him do it to the
poor, beſeeching God to *pardon* him for *Chriſt's* ſake
and accept his Oſſering ; and then his *Merchandiſe*
and his *Charities* ſhall be yet *Holineſs to the Lord,* notwithſtanding his paſt *Unrighteouſneſs* and Sin. See
the Caſe of *Zaccheus,* Luke xix. 8. *And Zaccheus
ſtood and ſaid before the Lord,* " *Behold, Lord, the half*
" *of my Goods give I to the poor; and if I have taken*
" *any Thing from any Man by falſe Accuſation, I reſtore*
" *him four-fold: And Jeſus ſaid unto him, This Day is*
" *Salvation come to this Houſe.*: " When true Faith,
Repentance and new Obedience comes to a Houſe,
Salvation comes to it, however great the Sins of it
had been before. *Zaccheus* had been a *Publican* and
an Extortioner, exacting more than was his right.
" Thoſe *Publicans* had the Ear of the *Roman Governours,* and by a falſe Account of Perſons and Things
could eaſily be injurious. This *Chief* among the
Publicans was alſo anſwerable (it is to be feared) for
many Abuſes of Power by thoſe that were under
him But he here ſtood a *Penitent* before Chriſt,
confeſſing and ſeeking Mercy. A *Change* of Heart
and Way, and *Fruits meet for Repentance,* appear
in his Words. " A very large Proportion of theſe
" ill-gotten Goods he ſet apart for Works of Piety
" and Charity. He could not refund to the Men
in *Trade* and Merchandiſe, whom he had wrong'd
in the Seat of Cuſtom : They were gone hither and
thither

thither, and he knew 'em not nor was like to ſee
ſome of 'em any more : to thoſe he could find he
reſtored *four-fold*, theReſidue he reſtored to thePoor;
and Chriſt accepted him as a humble *Believer* and
true *Penitent, a Son of Abraham.* — Thus what we
get muſt be in God's *Way*, the Way of *Holineſs.* And
then

2. We muſt *uſe it with a ſpiritual Heart and Mind.*
As, (to add unto *much* that has been already ſaid)
We muſt daily *praiſe* and *bleſs* God for *daily Bread,*
for all ourReceipts and *Increaſe* ; we muſt give Him
the *Glory* and render Him our *Thanks ;* " O God, I
*am not worthy of the leaſt of all the Mercies, and of all
the Truth, which thou haſt ſhowed unto thy Servant* ! *for
with my Staff I paſſed over this Jordan, and now I am
become two Bands.* This was *Holineſs to the Lord.* ——
We muſt earneſtly *deſire* and ſeriouſly *reſolve*, by the
Grace and Help of God, to *ſerve* Him in Righteouſneſs and Holineſs before him, and with *gladneſs of
Heart,* with all the *Good Things* that a bountifulGod
ſhall ſee fit for us, that *the Lord ſhall be our God,* and
we will live *devoted* to him, and *lay out* our ſelves
to glorify him, and make it our *Meat and Drink to do
his Will.* This will be *Holineſs* unto Him. —— The
Abundance of all Things which the Lord our God may
give us richly to enjoy muſt be ſo far from *charming* our
vain Minds and *chaining* them down to the Things
of Earth and Senſe, that we muſt indeed make *Arguments* and *Motives* of them, to *raiſe* ourHearts unto and *fix* them on theThings that are unſeen, ſpiri-
tual and heavenly. " *From Men of the World which*
" *have their Portion in this Life.*——*As for me, I will*
" *behold thy Face in Righteouſneſs* ! *I ſhall be ſatisfied*
" *when I awake in thy Likeneſs.* " *Many there be that*
" *ſay, Who will ſhew us any Good ?* Lord, *lift Thou up*
" *the Light of thy Countenance upon us* ! *Thou haſt put*

" *Gladneſs*

" *Gladness in my Heart, more than in the Time that their* " *Corn and their Wine increased* *. —— Again, We muſt be ready, thro' Grace, to *part with*, and *ſubmit to the Will of God* in the *loſs* of all worldly Things ; *learning in whatſoever State we are therewith to be content, both how to be abaſed and to abound, to be full and to be hungry*. Let this be our Frame and Temper in the Acquiſition and Uſe of our worldly Eſtate, and God will write *Holineſs* unto Himſelf on us and it.

Only it muſt be added, to the Glory of *Chriſt*, That our *Perſons* and our *Eſtate* are *Holineſs* to the Lord only *by Faith in his Holineſs and Righteouſneſs*, who is our *Great High-Prieſt* within the *Holy of Holies*, ever living to make *Interceſſion* for us, in *whom* and for whoſe *Sake* it is that repenting believing Sinners are accepted as *Holy* in the Sight of God. *Aaron* within the *Vail* was the eminent *Type* of *Jeſus entring by his own Blood*. He is *of God made to us* Holineſs, and *we the Holineſs of God in Him*. He, the *Holy One of God* was made *ſin for us*, that we Sinners may by Faith in Him become *Holineſs to the Lord*. With the Heart *Man* believeth *in Him* unto Righteouſneſs, and God is *ſanctified* therein while his Mercy *abounds unto the Chief of Sinners*. Coming to *Him*, we are built up *a ſpiritual Houſe, a holy Prieſthood*. As He went to the *Croſs*, he ſaid, " *For their Sakes I ſanctify my Self, that they may be ſanctified*. He was *ſeparate from Sin*, that we may *come boldly to the Throne of Grace* ‖. Bear *this* in Mind, That no *Saint* is Holineſs to the Lord from any *inherent* Holineſs in him, nor *for any Works of Righteouſneſs done by him*, but for the perfect and glorious *Holineſs of Chriſt* reckon'd to him.

---

* Pſalm lv. 6. xvii. ult. Phil. iv. 11. ‖ Hebrews x. 19,---22. 2 Cor. v. 21. 1 Pet. ii. 4, 5. Heb. vii. 26. Phil. iii. 9.

And

And having thus said, *When* the Traffic & Wealth of a People is *Holiness to the Lord,* I come (as was proposed) in the *third* and last place to enquire,

III. *Why* it must be so ? Why our *Merchandise and Hire* should be bro't, with *our Selves,* under a holy *Consecration* to God, and *Use* for Him.

I might easily enter into, and enlarge on, many *Reasons* of this Duty, which are also *Motives* to it, and must pray you to give 'em a just *Consideration,* and so make the *Application* of all that has been said every one to himself.

1. It is the *highest End* & *best Use* of Man and of *all* that belongs to him, his *first* and *last* End, to be *Holy to God.* " *The Earth is the Lord's, and the Fulness thereof, the World and they that dwell therein.* The *Heavens,* with all their *bright* Inhabitants, serve to no higher End. " *Angels are ministring Spirits, sent forth to minister to the Heirs of Salvation* from this Earth of ours. Those *Watchers* and *Holy Ones* on High use and *imploy* all their Powers and *Riches,* in *Bounties* to the poor and needy Children of Men, the *poor Saints* below. And can *we* do better than *They* to serve the Ends of *Holiness,* and the Glory of God ? " *Whether they be Thrones, or Dominions or Principalities,* or whether *we* be higher or lower in Rank and Estate on Earth, *all are created by Him and for Him ; to Whom be Glory for ever* *.

2. This is therefore the *prescribed, commanded Use* of our worldly Riches, that they be *holy to God.* "This is *the Will of God in Christ Jesus concerning* us, and our

---

* Psalm xxiv. 1. Heb. i. 14. Daniel iv. 13. Col. i. 16.
Sanctification.

Sanctification. God cannot *will better* concerning us, than that *we* and all that belongs to us be *holy* to Him. This is *his good and acceptable*, his *royal and perfect Will*. Let us put our *Amen* to it and say, " *Father, thy Will be done on Earth as it is in Heaven* ‖

3. It is *the greatest Honour and Dignity* put on us, and our worldly State, that we and that be *Holiness to the Lord*. " *This Honour have all the Saints*, and only They ; *praise ye the Lord*'. The Glory of God is his *Holiness*. He is the *High and Lofty One*, whose *Name is Holy* *. A *Ray* from his *excellent Glory* shines on *Angels* above, and on *Saints* on Earth, and makes them *Stars in his Firmament*. This was the peculiar Honour of *Ifrael*, " *Ye shall be a holy People unto Me*. God has not a brighter *Stone* in his own Crown than his Holiness, nor a brighter *Crown* for the Head of Creatures than to make them holy.

But it is remarkable, and the World may well wonder at the *Beaft*, That the vainest and *proudest* Creature on Earth affects this facred & *lofty* Style, *His Holiness* ! He takes the Name of God *in vain*, in the moft horrid and monftrous manner, and the Lord will not hold him *guiltlefs*. The *Man of Sin* calls himfelf *His Holiness* ! was ever any thing more *abfurd*, and yet more *natural* ? Only the Man of *Sin* durft take the moft bleffed and incommunicable Name. The *jealous God* will *confume that wicked One*. Nothing on this fide *Hell* can be *further* from the Holinefs of God. † The *Scarlet Whore, drunken with the Blood of Saints*, impudently and blafphemoufly calls herfelf *His Holiness* ! *Monstrum, informe, ingens* !

‖ 1 Thef. v. 18. iv. 3. Rom. xii. 2. Jam. ii. 8. 1 Pet. ii. 9.
* Ifai. lvii. 15. Dan. xii. 3. Deut. ii. 21. † 2 Thef. ii. 4, 8.

No,

No, the Honours of Heaven go with the *poor in Spirit*, the meek and lowly and merciful. All the Riches and Dignities of *Kings* are below thefe *poor* of Chriſt's little Flock, to Whom it is the Pleaſure of the *Father* to give the *Kingdom.*

4. Our *worldly Goods* will be vilely *abuſed* to the *Diſhonour* of God, and the *Hurt* of our Selves and others, if they be not *holy* to God. They are the *Mammon of Unrighteouſneſs* for want of this, and gender to all *Ungodlineſs.* They become a *Proviſion for the Fleſh, to fulfil the Luſts thereof*; the *Fuel* of Pride and Vanity, Gluttony and Drunkenneſs, Lewdneſs and Uncleanneſs. Or thro' *Covetouſneſs* they become *Idolatry.* The *Love of Money is the Root of all Evil,* Sin and Sorrow, to our Selves and others; ruinous to our own Families, and alſo to our Neibours, by Diſhoneſty and Unrighteouſneſs, Deceit and Fraud, Extortion and Oppreſſion. For where Charities and Mercies fail, and Works of Piety, the forenamed odious *Vices* grow up in their ſtead, offenſive to God and Man ; *Roots of Bitterneſs, bearing Gall and Wormwood,* all manner of Corruption and Iniquity, Calamity and Miſchief. But let our Merchandiſe and Hire be *holy to God,* and all this is prevented, and our *Goodneſs extendeth* to the needy and the *excellent of the Earth, in whom ſhould be all our Delight* ; and we become *Eyes to the blind, and Feet to the lame,* and *Fathers to the poor,* and abundant *Bleſſings* in our Generation *.

5. The Merchandiſe and Hire of Perſons and Places ſhould be Holineſs to the Lord, *that the Lord their God may bleſs them in all the Works of their Hands.*

---

* Pſalm xvi. 2. Job xxix. 11, 16. Philem. v. 7.

The

The Way of *Holiness* is the Way of *Blessing*. God
has promised to bless his People in *this* his required
Way. It is He that gives us *Power to get Wealth*.
Read his *Promises* to an Obedient holy People,
Deut. xxviii. " *All these Blessings shall come upon thee,*
———*Blessed shalt thou be in the City and in the Field,* &c.
He has *threatned to curse* an unholy People in the
same Instances. If he *blow* upon 'em they are *blasted*.
God justly *impoverishes* the Places that *rob* him of
his Offerings and Alms. To with-hold his *Dues*
tends to Poverty. But *prove me now, saith the Lord, if
I do not pour out a Blessing*, when you pay to Me and
mine my Part out of your Estates †. " Alas! says
" an excellent *Divine*, that Men have generally so
" little Faith in God's Providence or Promises!
" Few believe Him when he says, " *Let there be*
" *Meat in my House* that there may be eno' in your
" own ! few can *trust God* as to the *Gains* of Piety
" and Charity.

6. Our Merchandise and Hire should be holy to
God, that so *his spiritual Blessing may come on our Souls*.
This lies especially in a spiritual Mind, and heavenly Affections, and the Comforts of Grace : These
are the *perfect Gifts* from the Father of Spirits, and
are more (infinitely more) than all present *Riches*.
God gives the Power to *eat* our Bread, and use it
bolily. To him that has this Heart, he will add
more Grace. He shall increase with the *Increasings
of God*. Thus *the liberal Soul is made fat* in Spirituals,
and he that watereth is watered again. And well repaid is he that *sowes* in worldly Things, and *reaps* in
Spiritual : Like the *Woman of Samaria* who gave
Christ a little common Water, and received of Him

---

† Deut. xxviii. 15, 16, 17. Hag. i. 9. Prov. xi. 24.
Mal. iii. 8, 12.

B

a Well of living Water, within her Self, *springing up into everlasting Life.* *

7. Let your Merchandise and Hire be Holiness to the Lord, *and you shall have Riches in Heaven.* So our Lord proposed to the *young Man* that came to him. The Promise is, ' *He that soweth to the Spirit, shall of the Spirit reap Life Everlasting.* The Promises of this Nature are *multiplied* ‖ in the Book of God, because our carnal Minds are so averse to the Belief of them. But will Christ fail us in a Point that he has so *often* repeated? He has said, " *Thy Father* " *which sees in secret will reward thee openly. Thou* " *shalt be recompensed at the Resurrection of the Just,* " *Make to your selves Friends of the Mammon of Un-* " *righteousness, that when ye fail they may receive you* " *into everlasting Habitations. Provide Bags which* " *wax not old, a Treasure in Heaven that faileth not,* " *where no Thief approacheth, nor Moth corrupteth.——* These are true *Sayings* of God, *He is faithful that hath promised.* Both in our Devotions and Charities we should have *Respect unto the Recompense of Reward :* Knowing (says the Apostle) *that in Heaven ye have a better and more enduring Substance ; Cast not away therefore your Confidence which hath great Recompence of Reward.*

You must be *just* to God and your Selves, and make these *Reasons* of your Duty so many *Motives* to it.

You see 1. That the *meanest Things* may be of *good and great Use* to the *Glory of God* ; and the most *contrary Things* be made to turn to our Salvation. We may so serve God and our Selves of

---

* John iv. 14. Prov. xi. 25. Gal. vi. 8. ‖ Luke xiv. 14. xvi. 9. xii. 33. Heb. x. 24.

Mammon

Mammon, as to make it a *Friend* to Him and our
Souls. We may extract *Holiness* out of the *Dirt*
and Clay of this World, the *thick Clay* wherewith
so many load themselves and bury themselves. God
sits as a *Refiner* and does this for us. *Grace* turns all
it touches into *Gold*. It is a *Stone* that attracts and
fixes the very *Iron* to its *Pole*, which is *Holiness*,
Heaven and God. As *Phylosophy* has found out the
richest Virtues in the meanest Herbs and Plants, so
Divinity teaches us how to improve and use the
mean Things of this World to the most spiritual
and heavenly Ends: And when we serve God and
our Souls of earthly Things, then are they indeed
wisely and rightly used.

2. Let us be *humbled for the ill Use we have made
of our worldly Business and Gains*, our *Abuse* of them
unto *Unholiness and Sin*. What is more *Enmity* to
God and our Selves than this? Mens worldly Affairs *engross* and *eat them up*! eat out *the Heart* of that
little Religion they profess. *The Cares of the World
and the Deceitfulness of Riches choke the Word.* Men
go, one to his Farm and another to his Merchandise. God,
and the poor, and their own Souls are forgotten
and neglected by them. They *trust in uncertain
Riches*, and renounce the *living God.* They fall into *Temptations*, and *Snares*, and *many foolish and hurtful Lusts, which drown them in Destruction and Perdition.
They are filled*, and they fill the World, *with all Un-
righteousness, Fornication, Wickedness, Covetousness* †
What a shameful Abuse is this of the Bounties of
Providence! and *a turning his Glory into Shame!*

3. See *the Honour and Happiness of a religious People.*
They and all that belongs to them are *Holiness to the*

---

† Luke viii. 14. Matth. xxii. 5. ‡ Tim. vi. 9, 17. Rom. i. 29.
                                                        Lord.

Lord. Blessed & holy is He that hath part in *this*. They are in God's Church here in the *Image of Jesus*, the great *High Priest* of their Profession. They are a *holy Priesthood*, a *spiritual House*, *the Houshold of Faith*. What can *Angels* be, and what can *Heaven* be more than *this*, *Holiness to the Lord*? *Jesus* is *this*, within the *Holy of Holies*, at the right Hand of God. He calls his chosen into *Fellowship with Him*, and with his *Angels*. His People are a *Kingdom of Priests*, *a holy Nation*. There are *Garments of Glory and Beauty* provided for them, wherein shortly to enter *the Holiest of all*. So the *Apostle* salutes and superscribes; —— * " *To the Church of God* " *which is at Corinth, sanctified in Jesus Christ, called* " *to be Saints; with all that in every Place call upon the* " *Name of Jesus Christ our Lord, both theirs and ours!* " *I thank my God always on your behalf, for the Grace of* " *God that is given you by Jesus Christ.*

4. and lastly, I beseech you *Brethren*, by the Mercies of God, that you present *your Selves*, *Children*, *Families*, *Substance*, *Gifts*, *Talents*, all you are and have, as *living Offerings* to God, *holy and acceptable thro' Jesus Christ*. How should an *unholy Person* offer to God in a holy manner? The Person is more than his Estate. Christ *seeks not yours but you.* The *Soul* is *his*, and *all* Souls are so. There are the *Riches* of Souls, their noble Faculties and *Powers* with every natural and acquired *Gift* ; and what should be thy Gift to *God* but *These*! thy whole Self ; *Body*, *Soul and Spirit*, which is your *reasonable Service.* Prov. xxiii. 26. *My Son, give me thy Heart.*

Next to thy *Self* are thy *Children* : Give *these* to God as thy best *Riches*, thy richest *Jewels*. They are *holy* to Him by *Covenant*, as the Family of *Abra-*

' 1 Cor. i. 2. 1 Pet. ii. 5, 9. Exod. xix. 6.

ham

ham was. This *Bleffing* is come upon us *Gentiles, thro' Faith* in that *Bleffed-Seed, in Whom the Families of the Earth are bleffed*: and thro' Whom *the Offerings of the Gentiles* are *acceptable to God, being fanctified by the Holy Ghoft*. What can a Man give to God in *Exchange for his Soul* and the Souls of his Houfe? will he give his *Eftate*, and think it will be accepted ? I trow not.

God values our *Hearts and Spirits* above all our Silver or Gold, our Herds and Flocks. *If a Man would give all the Subftance of his Houfe inftead of Love*, the Loves of his Soul and the Souls of his Houfe, *it would be contemned*. Thoufands of *Rams* were a *dogs-neck* in lieu of the *Love* of one Soul.

We owe the firft and greateft *Piety and Charity* to our *Selves* and at *Home*. We and ours are *made* for ever, if we are *holy* to the Lord : But we are profane and miferable without it.

The *rich* and the *poor* equally *owe Themfelves* to God, and are equally *able* to render it. *The Lord is the Maker of them both*, and they are alike acceptable to Him. The *one* muft be *rich in good Works, ready to diftribute, willing to communicate* ; and the *other* muft be *rich in Faith, Heirs of the Kingdom*.

It is a *holy* Thing to *give* unto *fuch* as thefe, *from Faith and Love which is in Chrift Jefus*.

I will read you, the *beft Offering* that any Man can make to God! *read* it and *make* it, and I have done: Gen. xviii. 19. *I know Abraham, that he will command his Children and his Houfhold after him, and they fhall keep the Way of the Lord ; —— that the Lord may bring upon Abraham that which He hath fpoken of him.*

F I N I S.

E R R A T U M.
Page 10. line 20. for *Accidentally* read *Occafionally*.

Dr. *Colman's*

SERMON

ON THE

Unspeakable Gift.

February 1. 1739

THE
Unfpeakable Gift of GOD;
A right
Charitable and Bountiful Spirit
TO THE
Poor and Needy Members
OF
JESUS CHRIST.
A
SERMON

Preached at the publick *Lecture* in *Bofton*,
February 1. 1739.

By *Benjamin Colman*, D. D.

Prov. xxii. 9. *He that hath a bountiful Eye fhall be
  bleffed, for he giveth of his Bread to the Poor.*
Rom. v. 17. *They which receive Abundance of Grace and
  of the Gift of Righteoufnefs, fhall reign in Life by
  Jefus Chrift.*

BOSTON:

Printed by J. DRAPER for H. FOSTER in *Cornhil.* 1739.

THE

Unspeakable Gift.

II. CORINTHIANS, ix. 15.

Thanks be to GOD *for his unspeakable Gift.*

HANKS is the *leaſt* that can be render'd for any *Gift*; and *unſpeakable* Thanks the leaſt for a Gift that is unſpeakable. Let us conſider the particular *Gift* here ſpoken of, and the *Honour* here done it, the *Glory* put upon it.

Some would have it to mean CHRIST Himſelf, who is indeed the *greateſt Gift* of God to fallen Man, ineffable, inconceivable. John iv. 10. *If thou kneweſt the Gift of God!* Eph. iii. 8. *What is the Height and Depth, and Length and Breadth of the Love of Chriſt, which paſſeth Knowledge.*

Some ſay *Grace*, the *regenerating* Grace of God ; or (which is the ſame) the HOLY SPIRIT of God in all his *ſaving* Gifts, Graces and Comforts : And indeed all the

Fruits

Fruits of the Spirit (a) are unspeakable Gifts, " *Love,*
Peace, Joy, Longsuffering, Goodness, Meekness, &c. My
Context (b) speaks of this Gift, " *God is able to make*
ALL GRACE *to abound to you, that ye always having an*
Allsufficiency in all things, may abound to every good Work.

But after all, The *Grace* and the *Gift by Grace* here
spoken of, is neither more nor less than the particular
Grace of *Charity* and *Liberality* to the Poor and Needy ;
an enlarg:d Heart and open Hand to relieve and supply them in their Wants and Necessities. ---- The
whole *Chapter* is on this single *Subject* and Argument,
touching *Ministring to the Saints,* v. 1. as *a Master of*
Bounty, v. 5. *sowing bountifully,* v. 7. *giving to the Poor,*
v. 9. *supplying the Wants of Saints,* v. 12. *liberal Di-*
stribution to all Men : This is the *exceeding Grace* and
unspeakable Gift, for which *Thanks* is here given to God.

And great is the *Honour and Glory* done it, in the
Epithet UNSPEAKABLE, and in the THANKSGIVING
to God for it.

" *Who can by searching find out* GOD, or any *Gift* of
His, *unto Perfection?* Who can *shew forth all his Praise?*
All is comprehended in the one Word LOVE. Yet
my *Text* means not to dignify a Spirit of *Liberality* a-
bove the *other* Exercises of Grace, save only as the *Great-*
est of all is *Charity* (c), which is but perfected at Death
and *abides* for ever, when *Faith* and *Hope* are swallow'd
up in Vision. Nevertheless it must be added, that *Love*
in this particular *Mode* and Ministration, of which my
Text speaks, will *soon fail* ; for there are no Objects of
Charity in *Heaven,* none *poor* or *needy* there : However, *Benevolence,* the Soul and *Essence* of Charity, *reigns*
there in Glory for ever and ever.

Blessed be GOD that we have *something* and so *much*
of it on *Earth,* in our *Way* to Heaven : " *Thanks* to
Him for it, says my *Text.* The Glory is *God's,* for it is

(a) *Gal.* v. 22.   (b) Ver. 8.   (c) 1 *Cor.* xiii. 13.

his Gift, & this is the Glory of the Gift that it is *his*; this makes it the *unspeakable* thing it is : Divine, Heavenly, Infinite, in its Origine, Influence and endless Effects.

GOD is the free and bountiful *Author* of this Grace in any, He *gives* it to Those that have it ; the Ability and the Heart to do kind and liberal Things is from *Him* ; He puts it into the Heart, and he enlarges it. " Even Power to *eat* our Bread is from Him, how much more to *give* of it to *others*, to *seven* and also to *eight* (d).

The *liberal Man* is God's Gift to the World ; to the *Place* where he lives, to *distant* Places also, if he have a Hand full and *strong* eno' to scatter far and near. Some in the Churches of *Macedonia* were thus made to *differ* and excel : God ministred *seed* to them and they sowed plentifully ; God *enriched* them unto all Bountifulness, and the *Thanksgiving* was abundant to God.

The *Praise* is not to the charitable Person, who *devises* the liberal Things, but to *God* who gives him the Heart. The good Man will be *far* from taking any of the Praise to himself, but to *God's Name* he gives the Glory. " *It is not in me,* said the Princely *Joseph,* when *Pharaoh* asked him of the *unspeakable Gift* he heard was in him ; " *God shall give Pharaoh an Answer of Peace* (e) : He honour'd himself the more in the Sight of *Pharaoh* and his *Princes* by assuming nothing to himself ; " *Can we find such a Man as this* (said the *King) in whom the Spirit of God is ? for as much as God hath shewed thee all this, there is none so discreet and wise as Thou art.*

We must have a great Care not to *idolise* those whom God pleases to honour, by sacrificing to them instead of God, who alone is to be worship'd. Yet the *Man* who is God's Hand, and his *Gift*, comes in for a civil Honour and Respect, a grateful Acknowledgment of his own Goodwill in shewing the *Kindnesses of God* : Of which our *Context* is full, " For to their *Power* and beyond

---

(d) *Eccle.* iii. 13. xi. 2. (e) *Gen.* xli. 38

they

" they were *willing of themselves*, praying us to receive
" the *Gift* and take on us the *Fellowship* ; " Where-
" fore shew *before the Churches* the Proof of your Love,
" and of our *boasting* on your behalf ; for I know the
" *Forwardness* of your Mind, and your Zeal has provo-
" ked many : " As it is written, He has dispers'd abroad,
" he has given to the Poor, his *Righteousness* endureth
" for ever, his *Horn* shall be exalted with Honour (f)
" While by the *Experiment* of this Ministration they
" *glorify God* for your professed *Subjection* to the Gos-
" pel ; *longing after you for the exceeding Grace of God*
" *in you.*

Having thus set my *Text* in its true and best Light,
I shall endeavour to speak to this *Doctrine* from it,

" That a right charitable and *liberal* Frame of Spirit
to the *poor* and needy is an *unspeakable Gift of God* ; for
which great *Thankfulness* is due to his *glorious Name*, and
abundant *Thanksgiving* should be fervently render'd in
the *Churches of the Saints.*"

I am therefore to shew,
1. What we are to understand by a *right charitable*
and liberal Spirit?

2. That it is an *unspeakable Gift* of God.

3. The abundant *Thanksgivings* to be render'd for it
in the *Churches of Christ.*

I. By a right *charitable* and liberal Spirit, I understand
a Mind and Heart *prone and large*, free and ready in
Proportion to our *Ability* and the *Occasions* occurring to
us, to pity and *relieve* the Wants of the *Poor*, more e-
specially of the virtuous and *religious* Poor.

It is the *religious* Exercise of the *Grace* of Charity,
which we are to *preach* to you from the *Gospel* of Christ ;

and my *Context* confines me to *this* Confideration of it, " as the *Grace of God bestowed on the Churches*, and the *Fellowship of ministring to the Saints*. So that a *Principle* of *Grace* in the Heart, and the *Exercise* of it in the Life, are here fuppofed ; That is to fay, a giving to the poor and needy from *Faith in Christ* and his *Word*, from *Love* to Him and his *People*, upon the *Commandment* and *Promises* of the Gofpel ; in *Obedience* to the one, and *Hope* in the other.

It is not therefore meerly a *humane*, tender, generous *natural Temper*, or *acquired* Difpofition towards a neceffitous or compaffionable Object ; and yet *this* is a diftinguifhing *Gift* of Providence to fome more than others, which renders 'em more *lovely* and of a fuperior Spirit ; but we muft fuppofe a Soul of this Difpofition *fanctified*, and acting upon religious *Principles and Motives* ; or one of *another* Difpofition *changed* by the Power of Divine Grace into *this* ; and then what rais'd and *enobled* Souls do the one and other become ? *all their Things being done with Charity !* from a reigning Love to God and Goodnefs as fuch, as there is Opportunity unto *all Men*, but efpecially unto the *Houshold of Faith*, proving their Love before the *Churches*.

In this Cafe a fpecial Exercife of proper Evangelical *Faith* with *Love* is fuppofed, as in the *Frame* of Spirit, fo in the chofen *Objects*, poor *Saints* and Members of *Jefus Chrift*, for *His* fake, and as unto *Him*, and as He will accept and reward another Day ; " *Ye did it unto Me*. This is *Chrift form'd in us*, his Spirit ruling in us, a *new Nature* given to us, acting in new Manner, on new Principles, Ends and Motives ; fuch as the meer *natural* Man perceives not, in equal or greater Benefactions ; a *Sacrifice holy and acceptable to God*.

It is *eafy* to the *Power* of God and *worthy* of his *Mercy*, fo to change the Heart of the naturally *Niggard* & grudging, into this *Riches* of Benignity and Beneficence, whereof there feem to have been *many Inftances* in the *firft Days* of the Gofpel, upon the *pouring* out of the *Spirit* ; when the *Multitude* of them that believed were of *one* Heart and Soul ; neither said *any* of them, that ought of the things they poſſeſſed were their *own*, but they had all things *common*, Acts iv. *ult*. An *extraordinary* Spirit of *Love*, at an extraordinary Time and Occaſion ! a wonderful Effuſion of the HOLY GHOST, from the late crucified and aſcended JESUS. The like therefore has not been known in *ordinary* Times, nor is it the *ſtanding* Exerciſe of the *Spirit* in the ſanctified. But the *Want* of what ſhould be *common* among Chriſtians at *all* Times, is a ſad and *dark* Teſtimony of the *Poverty* of Grace ; for there certainly are among us People of *high Profeſſion*, who have *no* Heart to do almoſt any thing at all, in a way of *Diſtribution* to the Poor, or for pious Uſes ; no not a known Inſtance for Years together ; while God is liberally giving to them, and they can lay up and lay out and make Purchaſes ! but if you ſpeak of *giving*, they *hide themſelves from their own Fleſh*, even tho' they be eſteemed *Members of Chriſt* alſo.

Let us always ſee to it, that our *Principle and End* be right before God, genuine and truly *Chriſtian* ; that neither *Vanity*, Affectation or Oſtentation, nor yet meer *Humanity* and good Nature, be *paſs'd on God* for gracious *Charity*, on Whom it cannot ; nor yet on *Men*, nor on *our ſelves*, which alſo is next to impoſſible under our Illuminations by the Goſpel. Wherefore our *Lord*, according to the infinite Wiſdom and Sanctity of God in Him, has warned us to *take heed how we do our Alms*, leſt we have no Reward from *our Father in Heaven*. Matth. vi.

II. I am now to ſhow, that this Evangelical Chriſtian *charitable Frame* of Spirit is an *unſpeakable Gift of God*.

And here,
1. Literally true it is, that *no Tongue* of Man can duely ſpeak of it, or enough praiſe and *celebrate* it. It is above all our Thoughts and Words, we can neither think or ſpeak of it as it merits. Such is every *Work* and Gift of God in the Kingdom of *Nature* and *Providence*.
" See

" See that thou *magnify* these visible Works, which *Eyes of Flesh* behold. " *His Work is honourable and glorious, and his Praise endureth for Ever.* How much more his *Spiritual Work*, the *Gift by Grace* within thy Self and Others. The *Angels* of God *pry* silently into *this*, and we need *their* Eyes and Tongues to look into it and speak of it. " Bless the Lord ye his *Angels* that excel in Strength ! and *" awake up our Glory* too, though we be but *Babes and Sucklings* in comparison of Them ; for from *our* Mind and Mouth God has *ordained* Strength.----We *lisp* and stammer at a proper Word, and poorly apprehend many of the Great Words put into our Mouth. " Let Him *teach* us what we shall say ! and shall it be *told* Him that we speak ! who can *utter* his mighty Acts, or shew forth all his Praise ! ----Accordingly the Apostle *labours* in my *Context*, to speak of the *Gift* of God ; seems at a *loss*, speaks abundantly, over and over, and knows not when he has said enough of the excellent Grace : " *Inriched,* says he, *in every " thing,* to all *Bountifulness,* which is *abundant* by many " Thankfgivings to God, from those that *long* after " you for the *exceeding* Grace of God in you."---- If a Man wou'd speak of a thing *unspeakable,* it must be just after *this manner* ; it being literally true, that *no Tongue* of Man can fully speak the Praises of Christian *Charity.*

2. *Unspeakable* is the *Good done* in the World by a right *charitable* Frame of Spirit. Unspeakable are the *Needs* which Sin has brought upon us, not only on the *poor and low* of the World, but also on *others,* even on the richest and highest. We unspeakably need one anothers *Help* and Service, and unspeakable are the *Benefits* we receive from others in our Necessities. The *poor* serve the *rich* abundantly, more especially in their *Sicknesses* ; and very often do it *gratis,* for nothing, out of pure Humanity, Respect and Compassion, and are never requited : Sometimes from *Gratitude* for Favours received, and as often (I would wish) from a Principle of *Grace* within them, it being all the Way they have to express a *pious Love* to God & their Neighbours.--Others to whom God has given Riches, and *Largeness* of Heart

to do Good with it, give *Portions* to the Poor by sevens and eights, and by scores and hundreds ; *devising* liberal things, and casting their *Bread* upon the Waters. " The *Bowels* of the poor are refreshed by them, they " are Eyes to the *blind* and Feet to the *lame,* Parents to " the *Fatherless,* and they cause the *Widow's* Heart to " sing ; the Blessing of them that are ready to *perish* " comes on them, and of him that is *helpless.* They are as the Heat and Rain to a thirsty and cold Earth, as the *Light* of the Morning and the *Dews* of the Evening to those among whom they dwell, who pass their *Days and Nights* the better for their Neighbourhood. " Their Glory is *fresh* in them, and their *Bow* is re- " newed in their Hand." They live not to *Themselves,* but others *glean* by handfuls of what they plentifully sowe. God *multiply* their Seed sown, and *increase* the Fruits of their Righteousness ; while the *Loyns* of the Poor bless them, warm'd with the *Fleece* of their Flock. These are the Men of whom we shall *hear well* another Day, but how will they be able to *bear the Joy* of the blessed Words ! " *I was hungry and ye gave me Meat,* " *thirsty and ye gave me Drink, naked and ye clothed me,* " *a Stranger and ye took me in* ". Unspeakable (you see) is the *Good done* in this needy World, and *Heaven* acknowledges it to be so, and accordingly *rates the Gift* in the Book of Account.

3. Unspeakable is *the Glory redounding to* GOD from a right Christian *charitable* Frame of Spirit, in the noble humble Exercise of it thro' the Earth, and therefore is it an *unspeakable Gift.* This is a *Reason* or Argument that rises much higher than the former ; for if it be a good and great Thing to do much Good to our Fellow-Creatures, how much more is it to be any Ways Instrumental in any *Glory and Honour* to the Name of GOD ? Yet HE *is glorified* (says my Context) by *Others,* on the Account of the Acts of *Bounty* done them by their merciful Neighbour.

The Great and bountiful *God* makes *much,* makes the *most* of our *little Alms* and Offerings to Him : As our *Saviour* did of the *Widow's two Mites* ; they were

a

a *rich* Offering in his Eye, and he *magnify'd* it and her. So God *shines on his own Works* wrought in us and by us, and puts great *Honour* on 'em, makes great *Account* of 'em. And so in the last Day he will glorify *Himself* in glorifying his *Elect*, " *In as much as ye have done it* " *to the least of these my Brethren, ye have done it unto* " *me.*

We are bid to " let our Lights *shine before Men,* " that they *seeing* our good Works may *glorify our Fa-* " *ther* which is in Heaven. The *liberal Man* does so, but *not* to be seen of Men. There is that is *manifest,* and cannot be *bid.* Men do not light a *Candle* and put it under a *Bushel.* A good Man blesses God for the Light that shines on *others,* as well as on Himself. If *one* is inriched to all Bountifulness, it causes in *others* Thanksgiving to God ; yea is abundant by *many* Thanksgivings to Him, says my *Context* : " They *glorify* God for your professed Subjection to the Gospel, and *pray* unto God for you.

Now the *least* Glory to God is an *unspeakable* thing. What is *Man,* and what the *World* he lives in, and what the *Riches* thereof, and you will say what the *poor* of it, that GOD should have *Glory* from them ! " *Behold He putteth no Trust in his Saints, and the Heavens are not clean in his Sight ! how much less Man that is a Worm !* What then can *Man* think or speak of, ask or pray for, like to *this* ! *Father in Heaven, thy Name be hallowed* !--- *for Thine is the Kingdom and Power and Glory for ever* ! Well is it made the *Alpha* and *Omega,* the *first* and the *last,* in our Prayers. It must be the *everlasting Law and Motive* to us, respecting giving and receiving ; 1 Peter iv. 11. *If any Man minister, of the Ability which God giveth, that God in all things may be glorified through Jesus Christ ; to whom be Praise and Dominion for ever and ever. Amen.*

4. The *Good to our selves* is unspeakable, in a *liberal* and bountiful Spirit, and therefore it is an *unspeakable Gift* to us and in us. Unspeakable is the *present Comfort*
to

to a good Man by this *Gift*, and unspeakable is the *future and eternal Reward* of it in the Life to come.

1. If we consider only the *Pleasure* and Comfort of it to a Man in *this Life*, to be of a merciful and *bountiful Eye*, it is to him an unspeakable Gift. He is *satisfied in Himself*, God answers him in *the Joy of his Heart*. The greatest Pleasure of Life is to *be good* and *do good*. The Words of our *Lord Jesus* are to be had in everlasting Remembrance, " *It is more blessed to give than to receive.* The Man's *State* and *Frame* is more blessed ; unless it be when the *poor* Man exceeds in *Grace* in the *manner* of his receiving ; and then the *Tide* turns on his Side.

Job tells us the *Pleasure* he found in Acts of *Munificence* in the Days of his Prosperity ; and it was unspeakable : " When the *Ear* heard me, it *blessed* me ! when
" the *Eye* saw me it gave *witness* to me ! then said I,
" I shall *die in my Nest*, or *multiply my Days* as the Sand !
" my *Root* was *spread out* by the Waters, and the *Dew*
" lay all Night upon my *Branch* ! my *Glory* was fresh
" in me, and my *Bow* was renewed in my Hand ! they
" waited for me as for the *Rain*, and opened their
" Mouth *wide* as for the latter Rain ! I chose out their
" Way and fat *Chief*, and dwelt as a *King* in his Army ;
" as *One* that comforteth the Mourners."

Even all the *bitter Sorrows of Job* could not take away the Comfort of the Remembrance of his *past Joys* in Acts of *Charity* & Mercy. "*If* (said he) *I had with-held the poor from his Desire,*"-- O the *Pleasure* of yielding them *their Desire*, when it is *pious* and just, and the *Power* be in our Hand, and our *Heart* be big enough ;---or" if I *caused*
" *the Eyes of the Widow to fail:* If I eat my *Morsel*
" *alone*, and the *Fatherless* did not share with me ! for
" from my *Youth* I was his *Father*, and Widow's *Guide.*"
---I tell you, that as the *Heart* knows its own *Bitterness*, so only the Heart of a *Job* knows the *Comfort* of a Consciousness of such a *Frame* and Exercise, as this which his own Words have spoken, and who can add to them ? How did all the *Good* he had ever done to the Poor *return* into his own *Bosom*, and *flew out* of his *Lips* from
                                                        the

the *Abundance* in his *Heart* ! The *Object* of *Charity*
were always to him *as his own Bowels,* and how were his
Bowels refresh'd hereby, at the Time and long after.
He *felt* the ruling Power of Grace, and had *Confidence*
toward God. The *Joy of Faith and Hope* accompanied
and follow'd the Exercife of *Love* and *brotherly Kindnefs.*

   2. But the Great and laft, the *infinite and eternal Rewards* of Grace, to the *charitable* and godly Man, are
in the Bleffednefs and Glories of *the World to come,* and
thefe render the *Gift* of Grace to him and in him *unfpeakable.* " *Eye* has not feen this, nor *Ear* heard it,
" nor can it enter into our *Hearts* to conceive of it.
" When *the Son of Man* fhall come in *his Glory,* and
" *fafhion* his *Elect* and Merciful Ones after *his own glori-
" ous Body,* and fay to 'em in the Hearing of all his *holy*
" *Angels,*----" Come ye *bleffed* of my Father, inherit the
" *Kingdom* prepared for you from the Foundation of the
" Word ! *for I was hungry and ye gave me Meat,* &c.
--- O with what *Rapture* will they make the *humble Anfwer,* " Lord, *when* faw we thee *hungry* and *fed* thee, or
thirfty and gave thee *Drink ?*----The *Day* muft reveal it,
what the *Joy* of the *Lord* and of his *Members* will then
be ! then they fhal be *recompenc'd,* at the *Refurrection*
of the Juft. It is worth *waiting* for the *Joys* of that
bleffed Day, which will be given in *full* Meafure, *preffed
down and running over.* " Then he that has fown *boun-
" tifully* fhall reap bountifully : Then not a *Cup of
" Water* given as to a *Difciple* of Chrift fhall be for-
" gotten. The Rewards of free Grace will be found
" nothing lefs than a *Crown* and *Kingdom,* a Crown of
Glory eternal in the Heavens. How unknown, *unfpeakable,* unfearchable is this ! it is *high as Heaven,* what
can'ft thou *know ?* Infinite as GOD *Himfelf,* who is *thy*
SHIELD and *exceeding great Reward* ; O *Seed* of generous *Abraham !* It is *a far exceeding and eternal Weight
of Glory.*----We find and *fee* many *temporal* things unfearchable, how much more thofe that are *unfeen and
eternal.*   Wherefore,

                                        III. The

III. The *highest Thanksgivings* are due from us to the *blessed God*, for this *his unspeakable Gift* to any of the Children of Men ; and should be *fervently render'd* to Him in the *Churches* of his Saints. " *Thanks be to God for his unspeakable Gift.*

But (as was said before) *what* Thanks can *we* render, when the Gift is *unspeakable?* O 'tis *above* all our Praises and Blessings ! Yet as the *Levites* said to the August Congregation, Nehem ix. 5. " *Stand up and bless the Lord your God for ever and ever! and blessed be thy glorious Name which is exalted above all Praise.*

I shall only say *two* Things here,

1. They that *receive* the Gift should be very *thankful* to God for it. The charitable Person should himself give *Thanks* to God for making him so, while yet he *abases* himself before the Lord, as an unprofitable Creature, and behaves humble and lowly before *Men.* Yet ought he to glorify God for any *Heart* to do good, and for any *Means* to do it. He must assume nothing to *himself*, but ascribe all to *God* ; of Whom and *to Whom* are all things. " For what hast *thou* which is not received ? and if received, whereof hast thou to *glory ?* The Glory belongs to Him who has given to *thee*, that *thou* may'st give to others. As, suppose a rich and charitable Person puts into my Hand a *Sum* or Sums of Money to distribute unto others in Want, it is *his* Gift and Bounty, and not mine; and *I* ought to be thankful to Him together with those to whom I distribute. In like manner if GOD give *You* Ability and a Heart to do good to others, you owe the *first* Thanks to God, and shou'd be ready to say with the *Church*, " *Not unto us, O Lord, not to us, but to thy Name be Glory.*

You, my *Brethren !* that are honoured of God to *give* unto the poor, might have been your selves, and so your Families, among the *indigent* and necessitous ! You might have been *Receivers* of the Charities of others, the Objects of their Compassion.

Or

Or yet *worſe*, You might have been amóng the nig-
gardly and *covetous* in the midſt of Riches; not able to
eat of your own Bread, and leſs to give unto others '
An *Evil* too often ſeen and felt, a Miſery too common
under the *Sun*, which yet ſhines liberally on the niggard
Soul.

Or ſtill worſe, You might have been among the *frau-*
dulent and unjuſt, the Cheat, the Theif and the Robber ;
or (which is little better) the Gripe and the Extortioner,
the Spoiler of the Widow, the motherleſs and fatherleſs !
But who has made you to *differ ?* made Thee a *Bene-*
factor and Bleſſing to the World, among theſe Plagues
and Curſes in it ? GOD, who is rich in Mercy, and *So-*
vereign in his Gifts and Grace to Men, *He* has done it !
" Who has Mercy becauſe he *will* have Mercy. He
that made *Abel Cain*'s Brother, and gave to *Abraham* and
Job and *Moſes* their *Grandeur* of Heart.

Let *free Grace* therefore have all the Glory ; as the
Apoſtle teaches us, Epheſ. 3. 18. *To me, who am leſs than*
the leaſt of all Saints is this Grace given. So thou " by
" the *Grace* of God art what thou art, and his Grace
" given thee has not been *in vain !* And if you *labour*
" more than others, yet not *you*, but the Grace of God
" in You.----So when *David* had done a *kingly* part,
and his *Princes* a very *princely* one, in way of Offerings out of their Eſtates ; then *David* ſaid before the
Lord, 1 Chron. xxix. 14. " *But who am I O Lord God,*
" *and what is my People, that we ſhould be able to offer*
" *ſo willingly after this ſort ! for all things come of Thee*
" *and of thy own have we given thee.---* Thus they that
receive the Gift, ſhould give *Thanks* for it.

2. *Others*, but eſpecially the *poor and needy*, they
ſhould be very *thankful* to God. The *Charitable* are
God's Gifts to *Men*, even to the *rebellious* ; (and indeed
ſuch themſelves among their *Brethren*) *that the Lord*
God might dwell among us. I may lawfully *transfer* theſe
Words from *Miniſters* in the Church, to the *liberal*
In the Flocks; for it is the ſame *God* and the ſame *Grace*
that forms both the one and the other, to ſerve the
C
Needs

Needs of Souls and Bodies. " We *do you to wit* therefore of the *Grace of God* beſtowed on the *Church*, in both. The ſame *Holy Spirit* that deſcended on the *Apoſtles* in Tongues of Fire, came down on the *Multitude of Believers* at that memorable Time, and they had *all things common*. And now the *ordinary* Gifts of your *Miniſters* for the Service of your Souls, and the ordinary Spirit of *Charity* in our Churches, are from the ſame Fulneſs, of *Chriſt* ; of Whom all do receive and Grace upon Grace. He puts the *earneſt Care* for Soul and Body into the one and other ; whether it be *Titus* or *Gaius*, doing faithfully for the *Brethren* or *Strangers*.

The Gifts and Graces of *others*, and the *Uſe* God p'eaſes to make of them, ſhould be *pleaſant* to us and *admired* by us ; and we ſhould rejoice in all that we ſee of God in them. We ſhould prize the good *Examples* they give us, give God the *Glory* of them, and be excited to a holy Imitation. 1. Theſſ. iii. 9. *For what Thanks can we render unto God for you ? for all the Joy wherewith we joy before our God for your ſakes.*

The *poor* eſpecially ſhould be very *thankful to God*, for his unſpeakable Gift to *them*, in all the *Charities* of the rich and bountiful. They ſhould religiouſly accept the Gift of Heaven in *thoſe* whom they muſt call their *Benefactors*. They ſhould look thro' and above *Men* unto God, who gives by their Hands. They muſt no more *idolize* Men, than they would bow down to an *Image* of Wood or Gold ; no more than they would *kiſs the Calves*, or their *Hand* to the *Sun* or *Moon* in their Brightneſs ; for this were to deny the *moſt high* and firſt Benefactor. " *Why look ye ſo earneſtly at us ?* ſaid *Peter* and *John* to the wondring and almoſt worſhipping People at the Gate of the Temple, when they had in the Name of *Jeſus* given *more* than Silver or Gold to the *Cripple*, even *Feet* to walk and leap. What is a bountiful *Donor* to us, but a *Steward* and *Almoner* of God, his kind and open Hand ! Who ſhall have the *Praiſe ?* the *King* that orders his *Medals* to be ſtrowed among the Crowd, or the *Servitor* that ſcatters 'em at his Command ? *Jacob* ſaw the Face of God in *Eſau's* Affection,

                                                              when

when he *ran* with open Arms and Eyes full of Tears to embrace him. So let the *poor* see the Face and Hand of *God*, in all the Heart and Care of *others* for them. They are what God makes 'em, and he has made 'em *such* for you.

God knows the irreligious *poor*, ungrateful to Him, *unthankful and unholy*, who receive and eat and give him not Thanks. It may be they *bow* to Men, and *treble* their Thanks to them and *bless* 'em, and yet do *not* lift their Hearts at all to God. It may be they neither *pray* for themselves or others in secret, altho' their *Dependance* is so great on Providence and its Instruments ; nor do they *bless God* when he sends 'em in Supplies --- God *value*, the Thanks of the *Poor* as much as of the Rich, and they as much *owe* it to Him. Let 'em learn the Song of *Hannah*, and sing it with her gracious Spirit, 1 Sam. 2. *init* " *My Heart rejoices in the Lord, my Horn is exalted in the Lord : He maketh poor and maketh rich ; the hungry cease, and the rich have hired out themselves for Bread.*

Having thus at large consider'd the *unspeakable Gift* of God, in a right *charitable* Frame of Spirit, and the *Thanksgiving* and Praise due from us unto God therefor, I might naturally go into a large *Compass* of Meditation on *other* the unspeakable Gifts of God to us, all of which are more or less related unto *this* that I have been speaking of ; and it may be I could not well go into a more proper and profitable *Application of the Subject*.

As,
1 Look we *within our selves*, into our own *Souls* and Bodies, fram'd as they are for *Thanksgiving* to God, and for all *Offices of Humanity and Charity* to our Neighbours ; what a *Gift of God* is this *Mind* and *Heart*, and these *Eyes* and *Hands* ; first to lift up to *God*, and then to look and reach out to *his poor* ! this *social Nature* for worshipping and communicating ! In every *Relation* and in all *Offices* of Human Life, *publick* and *private*, wherein God has plac'd us to *serve* and *bless* one another ; what Gifts of God *unspeakable* ought every One to be unto

C 2   his

his *Correlate* and therein to the *Community*! from the Confort, Parent and Child, up to the *King* on the Throne; and down again from all that *rule* under Him, to the *lowest* Subject in the State!----What a *wide Compass* of unfpeakable Bleffings wou'd every Perfon, in every Order, prefent us with? all under the *Law of Kindnefs*, and all their *Things done with Charity.*

2. What an *unfpeakable* Gift therefore is a good *Government*, good Magiftrates, wife, pious, faithful, public-fpirited Rulers; great and good *Kings, Princes, Nobles, Governours, Legiftators,* and *Judges* : Whom we are bid to *pray* for, and are bound to give *Thanks* for; while under them we are living *quiet and peaceable Lives, in all Godlinefs and Honefty.* 2 Sam. xxiii. 1,---4. *He fhall be as the Light of the Morning when the Sun arifeth, even a Morning without Clouds; and as the tender Grafs fpringing out of the Earth by clear fhining after Rain.* Such *Gifts* from Heaven were *Mofes* and *Jofhua, Samuel* and *David, Hezekiah* and *Nehemiah* to the *Ifrael* of God, in their Generation.

3. What an *unfpeakable Gift* of God to us is our *Church-State*, our *fpiritual* Relation in Chrift, our *Fellowfhip* in the Gofpel, our *Brotherhood*, the *Vocation* wherewith we are called! to be a *fpiritual Houfe*, a *Kingdom of Priefts*, a *chofen Generation*, a *peculiar People and Treafure*, to fhew forth the *Praifes* of our God and Saviour. Your *Sabbaths*, the preached *Gofpel*, the *Ordinances* of our God, and the *Minifters* of Religion; thefe are among the *Gifts* from the *Afcended Jefus.* As it is written, --- "I gave them my *Sabbaths* for a *Sign* " between Me and them that I am the Lord that doth " *fanctify* them (g): He gave his *Word* unto *Jacob*, " his *Statutes* and Judgments unto *Ifrael*, He has not " done fo by many a People : He gave *Prophets, Apo-* " *ftles, Evangelifts, Paftors* and *Teachers*, for the per- " fecting of the Saints, for the Work of the Miniftry,

---

(g) *Ezek.* xx. 12.   *Pfal.* cxlvii. 19.   *Eph.* iv. 8, 11. 3 *Cor.* iv. 7.

" for

" for the Edifying the Body of Chrift. *Enoch, Moſes*
and *Aaron, Elijah* and *Eliſha, Peter* and *John* and *Paul,*
and many after them, in their Spirit, have been inva-
luable Gifts to the Church ; a *Treaſure in Earthen Veſſels,*
that the *Excellency of the Power* may be of God and not of
Man.   Nor have there been wanting in the Churches of
Chrift, nor ever fhall be, ſuch *Gifts* from among their gracious *Members,* to and of whom we may take up the *il-
luſtrious Words* of the *Apoſtle* to the *Philippians* and the
Theſſalonians, in our Thankſgivings to God (h): " I thank
" my God upon every Remembrance of you, for your
" *Fellowſhip* in the Goſpel ! and we give Thanks always
" for you all, remembring without ceaſing your *Work of*
" *Faith,* and *Labour of Love,* and *Patience of Hope in*
" our Lord *Jeſus Chriſt* ; and ye became followers of us
" and of the *Lord,* having received the *Word* with much
" Affliction and Joy in the *Holy Ghoſt* ; becauſe your
" *Faith* groweth exceedingly, and your *Charity* one to
" another aboundeth ; ſo that we *glory* in You in the
" Churches of God for your *Patience and Faith.*   Thus
the *meaneſt and pooreſt,* on worldly Accounts, in the *vi-
ſible* Church, became *unſpeakable Gifts* of Grace to
it; and will be found ſo in the Church of the *Firſt-born,*
whoſe *Names* are written in Heaven.

But to *leave* all things here *below,* and to *aſcend up
far above all Heavens,* I add

4. and laſtly, The unſpeakable Gift of CHRIST and
of the HOLY SPIRIT, the *Saviour* and *Sanctifier* of
Souls ; which *two are one* equal in *Godhead and Glory.*
Here *triumph* with me, my *Hearers,* in the *adoring*
Contemplation of the *ineffable* Gift of God, his own
Eternal Son, the *Only-begotten of the Father,* whoſe *Glory*
was beheld in his *Miracles of Mercy* to the *Bodies* of
Men, but more in his Compaſſions to their *Souls* ; his
holy *Miniſtry, Labours* and *Sufferings* for their Salvation ;
to ſave our Souls from *ſpiritual and eternal Death,* to
cover a multitude of *Sins,* to make *Reconciliation* for

_____

(h) *Phil.* i. 3,   1 *Theſ.* i. 3. 2. i. 3.

Iniquity, to bring in an Everlasting *Righteousness* for the Justification of Sinners. The *crucified Jesus* is such a a Gift of God to the Sons of Men, as infinitely transcends the Tongues of *Angels*, when they would give Him the Glory of it. They *desire to look into it,* and give *Glory in the Highest.* The *Elders* with them prepare *new Songs* for ever, and *cast their Crowns before the Throne.*

How then shall the Tongues of *Men* below be able to speak of the *Gift* of God to us in the *Incarnation, Obedience, Death, Resurrection* and *Intercession* of CHRIST, or of his *Coming again* in Glory for the Salvation of those that believe in Him!--- Here all Words are *swallowed up,* we are struck mute, & Praise sits silent. Isai. ix. 6. *To us a Child is born, to us a Son is given, and the Government shall be upon his Shoulder: And his Name shall be called, Wonderful, Counsellor, the mighty God, the Everlasting Father, the Prince of Peace!*

This, *this* (my *Brethren*) is the *unspeakable Gift* of God unto us, to be in in *Everlasting Remembrance* with us in all our *Worship* before Him, secret, private and public; every Lord's-Day and all our Communion-Days: In every *Ordinance* of Worship He is *offer'd* to us for our thankful *Acceptance,* to be of God made unto us *Wisdom, Righteousness, Sanctification* and *Redemption!* and *we* must be making the Offering of *our Selves* to Him, as *bought with a Price, living Sacrifices, which is our reasonable Service, holy and acceptable* to God. *Grace* to do this, is an *unspeakable Gift* indeed.

Therefore we must give equal Glory to the HOLY GHOST, yielding our Selves to *Him,* as the blessed *Sanctifier, proceeding from the Father and the Son! One* with the REDEEMER in *Godhead* and everlasting *Love* to Souls. John xiv. 16. *The Comforter, whom I will send unto You from the Father, He shall receive of Mine and shew it unto you.*

This Heavenly *Gift* rested on *Moses and the Elders, Patriarchs* and *Prophets,* sanctified and inspired them.
                                                                    He

He has formed every *Saint* thro' all the Ages of the Church. But the grand *Effusion* was the Glory of the *New Testament*, and the *Promise* is still flowing down to us: Isai. xliv. 3. " I will pour *Water* upon him that is " *thirsty*, and *Floods* upon the *dry* Ground; I will pour " my SPIRIT upon your *Seed*, and my *Blessing* upon " your *Offspring*: And *one* shall say I am the Lord's, " and another shall *subscribe* with his Hand to the Lord, &c. ---- *Souls* can need nor ask more. *Christ* has no more to offer to us. John vii. 37. *In the last and great Day of the Feast Jesus stood and cried, saying*, " *If any Man thirst, let him come unto me and drink, and out of his Belly shall flow Rivers of living Water: This spake He of the* SPIRIT *which they that believe on him shall receive*

CHRIST and the HOLY GHOST are the *One*, inseperable, undivided, infinite, eternal, and therefore *unspeakable Gift of* GOD. Let us *wait* for it as for the *Rain*, and *open* our Mouth *wide* for it as for the *latter* Rain. God *fill* us with this Blessing of Blessings. Revel. xxii. 17. " *The Spirit and the Bride say, Come; and let him that heareth say, Come; and let him that is athirst come; and whosoever will let him take of the Water of Life freely.*

F I N I S.

THE
RULES
OF THE
FELLOWSHIP
SOCIETY;

ESTABLISHED

At Charles-Town, South-Carolina,

APRIL 4, 1762.

CHARLES-TOWN:

Printed by Charles Crouch, Printer to the Society.

The PREFACE.

Deu. xv. 11. *For the poor shall never cease out of the land: Therefore I command thee, saying, thou shall open thy hand wide unto thy brother, to thy poor, and unto thy needy in thy land.*

T H E great author of our being, faith and existence, from the earliest period of time, doth confirm his unchangeable providence, by foretelling the common vicissitudes of human life, as being imperfect. So the Christian religion, in general, is the most perfect institution, containing the most compleat system of moral rules and precepts, that was ever extant in the world; particularly, in the doctrines of Love and Charity.

Among the various occasions which offer, for the exercise of relief to the sick and lame poor, under the provision of an INFIRMARY, is that which lays claim to our present intention; for the frequent opportunities of observing the distress of such distempered poor, as from time to time come to *Charles-Town*, for advice and assistance; and how difficult it is for them to procure suitable lodgings, and other conveniencies, proper for their respective cases, for want whereof many must suffer greatly, and some probably perish, that might otherways be restored to health and comfort, and become useful to themselves, their families, and the public, for many years after; and considering, moreover, that even the poor inha-

bitants of this town, though they have homes, yet
are therein but badly accommodated in sickness, and
cannot be so well and so easily taken care of in their
separate habitations as they might be in one convenient house, under one inspection, and in the hands
of skilful Physicians and Surgeons.

Thus to promote the good of mankind, is the
design of the FELLOWSHIP SOCIETY, held at
Charles-Town, in *South-Carolina*; and by a small contribution from each member annually have acquired
a considerable sum of money in fund, which they are
desirous should be applied towards founding an
INFIRMARY or HOSPITAL, for the reception and relief
of lunaticks, and other distempered and sick poor in
this province.

From the bountiful hand of charity, it may be re-
marked, in behalf of those institutions, that they are
confessedly of public utility, as founded on the most
allowed principles of humanity. But some men will
say, we do good separately, in relieving the sick poor,
which certainly is commendable; but we must beg
leave further to observe, that such kind of charity is
but small, when compared with what may be done
collectively. Hence the erecting of Hospitals or In-
firmaries, has been found by experience exceedingly
beneficial, as they turn out annually great numbers
of patients perfectly cured, who might otherways
have been lost to their families, and to society; for as
we are in this world continually changing, a few years
knowledge informs us, that very often the children
of the wealthy are in want and misery, while many
of those who have but a small share of the good things
of this life, are lifted into estates. Since then our
present state, how prosperous soever, hath no stabi-
lity, but what depends on the good providence of
God, how careful should we be freely to distribute a
small

ſmall portion of our ſtewardſhip towards the diſtreſs of our fellow creatures, when objects of charity, and opportunities of relieving them, preſent themſelves.

May all therefore heartily join in this neceſſary work, by which great numbers of diſtreſſed objects will be relieved, many of whom may poſſibly one day make a part of the bleſſed company above, and there acknowledge the care that has been taken of them, in praiſing GOD, and bleſſing the bountiful contributors that have founded ſo excellent an inſtitution.

PSALM xli 1. *Bleſſed is he that conſidereth the poor, the Lord will deliver him in the time of trouble.*

RULES

OF THE

FELLOWSHIP

SOCIETY, *&c.*

PROV. iii. 27. *With-hold not good from them to whom it is due, when it is in the power of thine hand to do it.*

MONG the many duties, which man from his creation was by his very nature enjoined to observe, the moſt eſſential one next to what he owes the Supreme Being, is that whereby he is bound to contribute to the relief of all thoſe miſeries, afflictions and infirmities, which from the time of *Adam*, have been entailed on mankind : That ſovereign and diſtinguiſhing faculty reaſon, wherewith we are endowed, points out the helpleſs ſtate we all appeared in at firſt, and how far gratitude exacts a beneficent return, we cannot be inſenſible of, to our parents, as agents of our delivery ; from this ſtate, we are under the moſt ſolemn obligations of filial duty, to ourſelves reſpecting our moral conduct, we ought never to deviate from thence, and to our fellow

low creatures, as far as in us lies, where real need is known to oppress them, of what climate, nation, or religion they be, we are under the strictest ties of social duty to relieve them.

The more effectually to answer this end, we, whose names are hereunto annexed, have chearfully entered into a SOCIETY at *Charles-Town*, in *South-Carolina*, the fourth day of *April*, *Anno Domini*, one thousand seven hundred and sixty-two, and have agreed to the following RULES and REGULATIONS, for the good government of the same.

RULE I.

This Society shall be known and distinguished by the name of the FELLOWSHIP SOCIETY, and shall consist of any number of persons, nor cease to be, while there remains five members.

RULE II.

The members shall assemble at any convenient house in *Charles-Town:* First, annually on the second *Wednesday* in *April*, when the several officers shall be elected for one year, by ballot, which a majority of votes shall determine. The officers are, the President, senior and junior Wardens, Treasurer, Secretary, and two Stewards. all of whom must be residents in *Charles-Town.* Secondly, quarterly on every second *Wednesday* in *July*, *October* and *January*, of which days the members shall have public notice, with the hour of meeting. Thirdly, on every *Wednesday* weekly throughout the year, and the hours of the said respective meetings shall be these, for the annual and quarterly meetings, from the hour of eleven of the clock in the forenoon, to the hour of five in the afternoon: And for the weekly meetings, from Lady-Day

to

to Michalmas, from the hour of seven to ten in the evening, and from Michalmas to Lady-Day, from the hour of six to nine, during which time the strictest decency shall be observed.

R U L E III.

Whoever the majority of votes appoints President, senior and junior Wardens, Treasurer, Secretary, and two Stewards, and shall refuse to serve in any of the aforesaid offices, he or they so refusing, shall forfeit Five Pounds each, to the general fund; and in case also of death or removal of any officer within the year of his service, another shall be elected at the next annual, quarterly or weekly meeting, for the remaining part of the year, who shall be liable to the same forfeiture as abovesaid.

R U L E IV.

The President shall have a particular chair; preside in all meetings, and agreeable to the rules, preserve due order and decorum, and together with the Wardens, shall manage and declare all ELECTIONS, and in general, do and execute all other matters and things, as shall be apropriated to his office by the Society.

R U L E V.

The senior Warden shall officiate in the President's absence, and be assistant at all times in such matters as shall be laid before them. The junior Warden shall be assistant to the senior Warden, and supply the place of President and senior Warden, in their absence, and in case the President, senior and junior Wardens shall be absent from any of the meetings of this Society, the members present shall proceed to ballot for President

B

fident and Wardens, who fhall as foon as elected, have power to tranfact bufinefs for that meeting.

R U L E VI.

The Treafurer (at the Society's charge) fhall provide a proper Pedeftal or Box, in which fhall be lodged all the Society's CASH, as received from time to time, until the fame be let at intereft, or otherways difpofed of by the Society, and all bonds, or other fecurities for money, or any other matter or thing whatfoever, which they fhall think proper to lodge therein : He fhall alfo provide a proper book, in which he fhall enter all money received or difburfed, and keep a true ftate of the fund of this Society; he likewife, as foon as elected, fhall enter into a bond to the Prefident and Wardens, in truft for the Society, in double the value of the faid box or pedeftal, and contents then delivered to him, with condition to be accountable for and deliver the fame, with all additions to, or improvements during the time of his Treafurerfhip (fire and other unavoidable accidents excepted) to the obligees, or to the order of the Society, when required by a majority of the members, at any regular meeting.

R U L E VII.

The Prefident fhall every fecond Wednefday in April, appoint a Committee to audit the Treafurer's accounts; and fhall have two exact fchedules drawn of all the contents delivered to the care of, or remain in the cuftody of the faid Treafurer, one of which fhall be figned by the Prefident, and delivered to the Treafurer, to be kept by him, and the other figned by the Treafurer, and delivered to the Prefident, to be kept by

[5]

by him, and a true copy of the fame entered in the Society's journal.

R U L E VIII.

The Secretary fhall provide, from time to time, books at the Society's charge, in which he fhall enter all the rules which now, or hereafter fhall be agreed upon, for the good ordering of the faid Society, together with the names of the members, the times of admiffion, or otherways, all payments of money, and all donations made at any of the meetings, and in general, all other tranfactions of the Society when regularly met; he fhall alfo keep a fair and regular account of entrance money, fines, forfeitures and donations anyways belonging or appertaining to the Society, and all difburfements of any kind whatever, in confideration of (which) he fhall be exempted from his proportion of expences to the houfe at all meetings of the Society, during the time of his fervice; neverthelefs he muft comply with the tenth Rule in cafe of abfence.

R U L E IX.

The Stewards fhall attend every meeting of this Society, whofe bufinefs fhall be to call for all the liquor for the Society's ufe, and fhall keep a regular account of the fame, fo as not to exceed the members quotas who are prefent, they fhall likewife demand all fines and forfeitures, and fhall do all other bufinefs relating to the Society, as fhall be required of them by the Prefident, for the time being.

R U L E X.

That every officer thus appointed may attend more ftrictly the duties of the Society, the following fines
fhall

shall be laid on absentees, viz. The President *Fifteen Shillings*; Wardens, Treasurer, Secretary and Stewards *Ten Shillings* each, unless he or they so absenting themselves, shall, at the next meeting, make a satisfactory excuse for their so doing.

R U L E XI.

Every member that shall be appointed on any Committee whatsoever, who do not attend at the time and place appointed, such member, either refusing or neglecting, shall pay a fine of *Ten Shillings* (the Committee for the Hospital excepted) unless a satisfactory excuse, which must be approved of by the Society.

R U L E XII.

Any person desiring to become a member of this Society, shall apply for the same in writing, directed to the President, Wardens, and the rest of the Members, which the Secretary shall enter in the Society's journal, and on the next meeting the said person shall be ballotted for, and if elected by majority of votes, he shall be admitted to subscribe the rules, first paying into the hands of the Treasurer, the sum of *Five Pounds*, (which admission money, after Fifty members have subscribed the rules) shall be gradually raised by the following method, viz. the fifty first members shall pay *Ten Shillings* more than the fiftieth did, and the fifty second member shall pay *Ten Shillings* more than the fifty first did, and so to advance untill said admission money raises to *Twenty-five Pounds*. Provided nevertheless, transient persons may be ballotted for the same time they petition, upon being recommended by any two or more members present, and if elected must comply as above.

R U L E

R U L E XIII.

That if any person shall petition to become a member of this Society, whose father has been a member for the space of seven years from the date of his certificate, and paid the several contributions to the fund, for the said term, pursuant to the rules; and also in case the father of any such person so applying, died within the said time, and any other person for him paid the several contributions as aforesaid, that then such person so applying, shall be voted for according to the 12th article; and if admitted, he shall pay to the Treasurer, for the time being, a sum not under *Twenty Shillings* sterling, for the use of the Society; any thing contained in the 12th article to the contrary notwithstanding.

R U L E XIV.

The Society shall have a common SEAL, on which shall be represented a woman with three children, in adversity, with this motto, viz. *Posteri mea dona laudabunt*; i. e. *Posterity shall commend my beneficence*; and to be kept by the Treasurer for the use of the Society, and every member on his election shall attend and take out a certificate, under the hands of the President and Secretary, (with the Seal affixed) of the following form, viz.

[No.   ]

THESE *are to certify, that A. B. was, by a majority of votes, regularly admitted a member of the* FELLOWSHIP SOCIETY, *at a meeting held the day of*   Anno Domini 17

GIVEN under our hands, and the Seal of the Society.

E. F. *Secretary.*   C. D. *President.*

R U L E

R U L E XV.

In order to advance the fund of this Society, every member shall pay a sum not less than *Fifteen Pence*, on every annual, quarterly and weekly meeting; and every member who do not reside in *Charles-Town* shall, and is hereby deemed as a country member, and shall pay a further sum, not less than *Ten Shillings*, every annual and quarterly meeting; and all fines, forfeitures of what kind soever, arising by virtue of the rules and orders of this Society, as also all gifts, donations and legacies, by any of the members of this Society, or any other person or ways whatsoever, shall be appropriated to and remain one general fund, which shall be applied towards founding an Infirmary or Hospital, for the reception and relief of lunaticks and other distempered and sick poor, within this province. And as often as it shall appear, that the fund is augmented to the sum of *Fifty Pounds* sterling, the President and Wardens shall let the same at interest, taking good security for the term of one year, but no member shall be allowed to take up the said sum, or become security.

R U L E XVI.

The President and Wardens shall have power to agree for the entertainment of the Society, at each annual and quarterly meeting, the expence of which, and all other respective meetings, shall be defrayed in the manner following; first, every member in *Charles-Town*, shall be obliged to contribute the sum of *Twenty Shillings*, on every annual and quarterly meeting, whether present or absent, except those who shall give such reasons for their absence as the majority of the Society approve of; and also shall give

three

[9]

three days notice of the fame, to one or other of the officers; and fecondly, for the weekly meetings, every member in *Charles-Town*, fhall pay the fum of *Three Shillings and Nine Pence*, whether prefent or abfent; and in cafe any member neglects to contribute the refpective fums above or hereafter mentioned, for the fpace of three months, the Secretary fhall publicly read his or their names, and fums due, on three fucceffive meetings, before his three months fhall expire; and if the fame be not paid to the Treafurer on or before the third reading, he or they fo neglecting fhall be excluded from all right, title, benefit, intereft or advantage whatfoever, raifed or to be raifed, by virtue of any of the rules or orders of this Society. But it is hereby provided, that fuch perfon or perfons fo excluded as aforefaid, upon his or their difcharging, and paying into the hands of the Treafurer, for the time being, all the ordinary fums which fhall remain and be in arrears from the time of his or their admiffion, fhall hereafter be entitled unto the fame right, privileges, which any perfon or perfons who are not members of this Society, have a right to; that is to fay, to be balloted for, according to the 12th article of this Society, (and if admitted) to reap the fame benefit which otherwife he would have done before breach of the faid article.

R U L E XVII.

That a peaceable and inoffenfive behaviour fhall be obferved by all the members at the refpective meetings; and when the Prefident fhall command filence, every member fhall take his feat, upon fine of *Five Shillings*; all difputes about government affairs, fhall be excluded this Society, any member perfifting in fuch difpute, after firft admonifhed by the Prefident,

fhall

shall be subject to any fine the Society shall conclude upon ; any member that shall come to the Society disguised in liquor, shall for every such offence, pay a fine of *Ten Shillings* ; and if any such member shall disturb the peace and harmony of the Society, the President shall peremptorily command him to quit the room for that meeting, on refusing of which, his name shall be erased from the list of members, and shall lose all right or benefit of this Society.

R U L E XVIII.

If any member of this Society should die in such low and indigent circumstances, that he cannot, out of his estate and effects, be decently interred, then in every such case, the President and Wardens, for the time being, shall have power to order all things in as frugal a manner as possible, and the same shall be paid out of the fund of this Society, any rule to the contrary notwithstanding.

R U L E XIX.

In case of the death of any member, all the rest shall attend his funeral, if regularly invited by the person appointed to invite, for which purpose the Secretary shall give a list of the members, if required, and every member not attending, according to invitation, shall pay a fine of *Five Shillings*, unless he gives a satisfactory excuse, which must be approved of by the Society. And all the members that do attend, shall follow next the mourners, excepting the Stewards, who shall follow after the members, with their wands in mourning, in order to distinguish the Society from other persons that are at the funeral, and in case either of the Stewards do not attend any such funeral, shall forfeit the sum of *Ten Shillings*, unless a satisfactory excuse, approved of by the Society.

R U L E

R U L E XX.

That no part of the General Fund ſhall be diſpoſed of for the term of ſeven years from the commencement of this Society, but after the expiration of the aforeſaid term of ſeven years, the members may, with the yearly intereſt ariſing from their capital ſtock, hire any houſe or houſes, and furniſh the ſame for the reception of patients, until the ſaid Hoſpital ſhall be built, and the terms of receiving and diſcharging of patients, and all officers and ſervants belonging to the Hoſpital, ſhall be the choice of, and under the direction of the Society, who ſhall allow and order their reſpective ſalaries, and may diſplace them and appoint others, as often as they ſhall think fit.

R U L E XXI.

If any member of this Society, who has been ſuch for the ſpace of ſeven years, ſhall have occaſion for aſſiſtance, he ſhall be entitled to ſuch relief as the majority ſhall think proper ; and in caſe of the death of any member within the aforeſaid term of ſeven years, from the date of his certificate, and his heirs, executors or adminiſtrators, do pay or cauſe to be paid, the ſeveral contributions before mentioned; and provided alſo, the ſaid deceaſed member ſhall leave a widow that ſhall want the charity of the Society, then and in that caſe, his widow ſhall be entitled to ſuch relief as the majority aforeſaid ſhall think proper, and ſhall be ſubject to the articles, and under the care and direction of the committee of nine members appointed to manage the Hoſpital.

R U L E XXII.

All reports of committees appointed by the Preſident, for amending or altering any of theſe rules, or

C

making

making any additional rules, or for any other matters relating to the Society, shall be read on three succesive meetings in the Society, before the same shall be approved of, confirmed or rejected.

R U L E XXIII.

That a committee of nine members shall be appointed every six months, five of their number shall be a quorum, as managers of the Hospital, and shall meet once in every month, at the time and place appointed by the Society; any member absent from the said committee, shall pay a fine of *Twenty Shillings*, sickness, or out of town, excepted. The said committee shall visit the patients in the Hospital, as often as they think proper, and regulate all matters for their conveniency, and shall report their opinion of matters relating to the said patients, or Hospital, at the next meeting of the Society after. Whoever is thus appointed, and shall refuse to serve, shall pay a fine of *Five Pounds*, and another shall be appointed, who in like case, shall comply as above.

R U L E XXIV.

No person shall be admitted into the said Hospital, whose cases are judged incurable (lunaticks excepted) nor any whose cases do not require the particular convenience of an Hospital.

R U L E XXV.

That no person having the small-pox, or any other infectious distemper, shall be admitted, until there are proper apartments prepared for the reception of such as are thus afflicted.

R U L E

R U L E XXVI.

That all persons desirous of being admitted into the Hospital (not residents of *Charles-Town*) must before they leave their places of abode, have their cases drawn up in a plain manner, and directed to the President and Wardens, for the time being, together with a certificate from a justice of the peace, and the Church-warden or Wardens of the parish in which they reside, that they have gained a residence in such parish, and are unable to pay for medicines and attendance, to which an answer shall speedily be returned, informing whether, and when they may be admitted.

R U L E XXVII.

All persons who have obtained a letter of licence to be received into the Hospital, must be there at the time appointed for their reception, and must bring with them that letter, and must deposite in the hands of the Treasurer so much money, or give such security as shall be mentioned in their respective letters or licences, to indemnify this Society the expence of carrying them back to their several places of abode, that they may not become a charge to the parishes of *St. Philip* and *St. Michael*.

R U L E XXVIII.

Notwithstanding such letters of licence, if it shall appear by a personal examination of any of the patients, that their cases are misrepresented, and that they are improper subjects of the Hospital, the Society shall have power of refusing them admission.

R U L E

R U L E XXIX.

If several persons applying to be received, exceeding the number allowed by the Society to be entered at one time in the Hsopital, the preference will be given, when the cases are equally urgent, first to such as are recommended by one or more of the members of this Society, residing in the parish to which the poor persons belong. Secondly, to those who stand first on the list of applications, but if some cases are more urgent than others, those of the most urgent symptoms shall be preferred. That at least one bed shall be provided for accidents that require immediate relief.

R U L E XXX.

That if there shall be room in the Hospital to spare, after as many poor patients are accommodated, as the interest of the general fund can support, the Society shall take in other patients, at such reasonable rates as they can agree for; and the profits arising from boarding and nursing such patients, shall be appropriated to the same uses as the interest money of the general fund. Provided that no such persons under pretence of coming to board in the Hospital, shall be admitted unless on the first application made on their behalf, and a certificate be produced from the Church-warden or Wardens of the parish where they live, and of their having gained a residence in the said parish, and unless sufficient security be given to the President and Wardens, for the time being, to indemnify the Society from all charges and expences whatsoever, occasioned by their removing hither, or being sent back to their places of abode.

R U L E

RULE XXXI.

Those that are taken into the Hospital at a private charge, may employ any Physicians or Surgeons they please.

RULE XXXII.

That all persons shall be discharged as soon as they are cured, or after a reasonable time of trial, are judged incurable; that all patients when cured, sign certificates of their particular cases, and of the benefits they have received in the Hospital, to be either published, or otherwise disposed of, as the Society shall think proper.

RULE XXXIII.

That no patient go out of the Hospital without leave from one of the Physicians or Surgeons, first signified to the Matron; that they do not swear, get drunk, behave rudely or indecently, on pain of expulsion, after the first admonition.

RULE XXXIV.

That no patients presume to play at cards, dice or any other game, within the Hospital, or beg any where in *Charles-Town*, on pain of being discharged for irregularity.

RULE XXXV.

That such patients as are able, shall assist in nursing others, washing and ironing their linen, washing and cleaning the rooms, and such other services as the Matron shall require.

RULE

R U L E XXXVI.

That no Women having young children, fhall be received, unlefs their children are taken care of elfe-where, that the Society may not be burthened with the maintainance of fuch children, nor the patients difturbed with their noife.

R U L E XXXVII.

That the Society fhall choofe by ballot, fix practi-tioners in Phyfic and Surgery, for one year, to vifit and take care of the patients in the faid Hofpital, and the other practitioners, who are members of this Society, fhall have the privilege of attending and obferving the practice of thofe chofen for the fervice of the year.

R U L E XXXVIII.

The practitioners chofen, fhall give their attendance at fuch times, and in fuch manner, and be claffed with each other, as fhall be agreed upon by the Society and the practitioners.

R U L E XXXIX.

Upon extraordinary cafes, the practitioners in atten-dance, fhall call in two or more of the practitioners chofen for the fervice of the year, to confult with.

R U L E XLX.

In all cafes which will admit of time for delibe-ration, all the fix practitioners chofen for the fervice of the year, fhall have timely notice thereof, if any practitioner be removed for neglect of duty, or any other caufe, the Society fhall choofe another practioner (who is a member of this Society) to fupply his place.
R U L E

R U L E XLI.

Each apprentice, or other student, the practitioner shall introduce, to see the practice of the Hospital, shall pay two *English Guineas* per year, to be laid out in medicines, or in such other manner as the Society shall think proper.

R U L E XLII.

No practitioner during the term for which he is chosen to serve the Hospital, shall be appointed on the committee for regulating the patients and Hospital.

R U L E XLIII.

The practitioners shall keep a fair account (in a book provided for that purpose) of the several patients under their care, and the disorders they labour under; and shall enter in the said book, the receipts, or prescriptions they give to each of them.

R U L E XLIV.

No person shall be employed in the said Hospital as a Physician or Surgeon, until he be a member of this Society, nor then, unless he be of the age of twenty-five years, hath served a regular apprenticeship in *Charles-Town,* hath studied physic or surgery seven years, or more, and hath undergone an examination of six of the faculty, in presence of the committee for the Hospital, and is approved of by the Society, and with respect to Strangers, they shall have resided three years or more in *Charles-Town,* and shall be examined and approved of, in the manner, and under the restrictions aforesaid.

R U L E

R U L E XIV.

That a minister shall be chosen for the Society, by ballot, who shall be a member of the Church of *England*, and must perform in the Hospital morning and evening prayers, and shall compose proper and suitable Sermons for this Society, when, and as often as they shall require. And that two tin boxes shall be provided for each door or gate of the Hospital, on which shall be written in gold letters, CHARITY FOR THE HOSPITAL, each of the committee having one in open view, to receive casual benefactions, which shall be applied to the use of the said Hospital.———— LASTLY, no alteration or amendment shall be made of these rules, unless the same be committed to writing, and moved for in the Society, and seconded; then the same shall be referred to a committee, which the President shall appoint for that purpose; who shall report their opinion thereon, which shall be entered in the Society's journal, and if agreed to, shall be annexed to these rules, and become of force, and binding upon all the members of this Society, to which each of us, for himself, and not for each other, promising FAITHFULLY to perform, all and every part thereof, unto the true intent and meaning of the same. And whereas it appears by the journal of this Society, that since the 4th day of *April*, 1762, the members have made several alterations and amendments in these rules, 'tis hereby further agreed, that no alteration hereafter shall be made, but in the manner as before directed. Signed with our Hands and Seals, this 17th day of *November*, one thousand seven hundred and sixty-eight, and in the eighth year of the reign of our Sovereign King George the Third, Defender of the Faith, and so forth.

N. B. **All**

THE
PLAN of a SOCIETY

THE
PLAN of a SOCIETY
FOR

Making Provision for Widows, by Annuities
for the remainder of Life ;

AND

For granting Annuities to Persons after certain Ages,

WITH THE

Proper T A B L E S for calculating what must be
paid by the several Members, in order to secure the said advantages.

By WILLIAM GORDON.

B O S T O N :
Sold by Joseph Edwards and John Fleeming.
MDCCLXXII.

THE
PREFACE

THE painful circumstances in which numbers are involved, when aged, or deprived of that, or those, on whom their support chiefly depended, are too notorious to require a recital. But that same Divine Wisdom, which allows and orders the existence of these calamities, has mercifully, and in proof of his providence, so directed its manner, as to admit of their being greatly alleviated, by the joint endeavours of mankind. Casualties, decays and death cannot be prevented, and separately considered appear to be under no particular regulation ; and yet, when viewed collectively, are in a certain proportion, as has been confirmed by long and repeated observation ; so that many, by co-operating with each other, may secure individuals from those hardships they must otherwise experience ; and that, on terms with which a reasonable and humane person will readily comply, for the relief it must afford him to recollect, that he and his family are thereby insured, tho' in the other way they should never be benefited. An attention to these particulars has given rise to various Societies in *Great-Britain*, which within a few years have multiplied apace, chiefly in *London*. Though such Societies have been formed with a good design, yet having in general gone upon mistaken principles, they must at length, if not speedily regulated, be productive of much disappointment and calamity.

A benevolent desire of informing the public what calculations might be depended upon, and of averting that distress which was otherwise to be expected, has induced the Rev. Dr. *Price*, an eminent Mathematician, to publish Observations on Reversionary Payments

on fchemes for providing Annuities, for Widows, and
for perfons in Old Age, &c. Being poffeft of this
help, a manufcript copy of the whole Conftitution of
the *London* Annuity Society, eftablifhed by deed inrolled in 1765, to make annual provifion for widows;
and a printed Abftract of the Deed of Settlement of
the Laudable Society, for the benefit of widows, begun in 1761—underftanding, that there were no general
Societies of this nature in *America*, and that the e-
rection of fuch was wifhed for by many—and having
a defire of contributing my mite towards the happi-
nefs of the Colonifts, more efpecially fince a perfonal
acquaintance with and numerous obligations to them,
have here collected together, and do prefent to the
public, materials for forming fuch Societies, wifhing
that the fame may prove of extenfive fervice, at leaft
hoping that they will meet with a favourable reception. The *firft* part contains the plan for the erection,
continuance and government of the Society, with the
various reafons : the *fecond*, the payments to be made
by each member, according to his refpective age, and
the advantages he propofes to obtain. The fcheme is
larger than thofe of the *London* Societies, as it admits of
the purchafing annuities to be enjoyed, either by the
purchafer after fuch a period, or by another after his
death in cafe of furvivorfhip ; and, notwithftanding
difference of age, upon proper allowance—affords parents
the opportunity of purchafing for their children, brethren for their fifters and the like—does not exclude
females from becoming purchafers—nor debar military
and fea-faring perfons, from fecuring annuities to be
enjoyed by them after fuch an age, though from purchafing annuities for others after their own deceafe.
Should fuch a Society be attempted and formed,
fhall chearfully afford it what further affiftance may at

any time be in my power; and, that none may be mif-
led by errors in any fpurious edition of this pamphlet,
fhall fubfcribe my name to every copy.

Many might decline forming themfelves, notwithftanding their defires, of having fuch a Society eftablifhed, and of belonging thereto, from an apprehenfion of
their being too few. To obviate fo plaufible an objection, let it be noted, that the *London Annuity Society* when it firft formed, the beginning of 1765, confifted of no more than twenty-one members. The
beginning of this year it confifted of 335. Would not
wifh to begin fuch a Society with more than forty, or
fifty perfons at moft, as it will probably be far more
eafy for that number, than a much greater, to regulate every matter, to be concluded upon at its formation.

The honeft fears of fome, and the interefted views
of others, may lead many to affert that a Society of
this nature cannot be carried on without the immediate
affiftance of able mathematicians; efpecially as Dr.
Price thus exprefſes himfelf, p. 131, fpeaking of the
Society for equitable Affurances on Lives, viz. " I would
" obferve, that it is of great importance to the fafe-
" ty of fuch a Society, that its affairs fhould be un-
" der the infpection of able mathematicians. Me-
" lancholy experience fhews, that none but mathema-
" ticians are qualified for forming and *conducting*
" fchemes of this kind." 'Tis indifputable, that this
paffage was haftily worded, and that the Doctor had
forgot for a moment what he himfelf had been doing,
for in p. 133, he fays, " I have, with a particular
" view to this Society, given *rules*, by which may be
" formed *every* Table it can want, for fhewing the
" values of affurances on the *whole duration*, or any
" *terms*, of any *one* or *two* lives, in all poffible cafes;

" and nothing but care and attention can be neceſſary
" to enable any good arithmetician to calculate from
" them." By the Doctor's own rules any ſuch arithmetician may try the calculations in this performance, may
correct any miſtakes, may ſupply all defects, and may
adopt other terms at pleaſure.

It may be agreeable to the reader of Dr. *Price's*
work, to be told, that after its publication the laſt
year, ſeveral gentlemen of *London* were engaged in
obtaining information as to the duration of life, both
in men and women; and found that men in *London*,
of good common health and expoſed to no particular
dangers, from twenty-four to the extremity of old age,
die at the rate of one in thirty-one annually; and that,
according to the regiſters of the Million Bank, widows
may live eighteen years; according to thoſe of the
Mercer's Company (which in the year 1690 adopted a
ſcheme for paying annuities to widows) twenty-one
years on an average.

Such Societies, beſides being ſerviceable to individuals, will, after a while, prove of great public utility;
not only by encouraging matrimony, but by furniſhing
large ſums of money to be loaned out; through the
help of which, young induſtrious planters may puſh
their improvements to the further enrichment of the
community; others may be affiſted in large and profitable undertakings; and intereſt may be reduced to
a more moderate ſtate, or the exacting uſerer's
methods of increaſing it beyond what is legal, be prevented.

It being a public advantage, that there ſhould be a
full ſupply of money to loan out; and the nature of the
country (comparatively, but little ſettled) not allowing
the thought of a redundancy, it may be prudent to
extend the limits, comprehending the members of the

Society, beyond the bounds of a particular Colony, as far as an equal degree of healthiness and safety will admit, that so the cash of individuals, in those provinces where such Societies do not exist, may centre where they do.

Tho' foreign to the present purpose, yet as it may be pleasing to the generality of readers, who may have no opportunity of seeing Dr. *Price's* performance, the following particulars are added.

The Doctor writes, p. 204, 205. " The original " number of persons, who in 1643, had settled in *New-* " *England* was 21,200. Ever since it is reckoned, that " more have left them than have gone to them. In " the year 1760, they were increased to half a million. " They, have, therefore, all along doubled their own " number in twenty-five years. And if they continue " to increase in the same rate, they will, seventy years " hence, in *New-England* alone, be four millions ; and " in all *North-America*, above twice the number of " inhabitants in *Great-Britain*." The Doctor subjoins in a note, " Since writing the above—I have seen " a particular account, grounded chiefly on surveys " lately taken with a view to taxation and for other " purposes, of the number of males between 16 and " 60, in the four provinces. According to this ac- " acount, the number of such males is 218,000. The " whole number of people therefore between 16 and " 60, must be nearly 436,000. In order to be more sure " of avoiding excess, I will call them only 400,000." The Doctor proceeds, and upon a moderated calculation infers that—*the whole number of people will be* 720,000. But supposing that there was this number when the surveys were made, and that the inhabitants double in the time specified, they will be more than four millions in *New-England* in less than 60 years :

and in fifty, the Colonists of all *North-America*, what by internal population and settlers from *Europe*, will *probably* be more than double to the *then* inhabitants of *Great-Britain*. For it appears from Dr. *Price's* Supplement, lately published, that *Old-England* and *Wales* are depopulating apace, and that the inhabitants are now *a million and a half* fewer than in the year 1690, see p. 21. He further says, p. 60, " the " number of houses in the kingdom (meaning *Eng-* " *land* and *Wales*) in 1766 was 980,692. Call them " however a million, and the number of people " in *England* and *Wales* will be four millions and a " half, allowing $4\frac{1}{2}$ to a house; and five millions al- " lowing five to a house. The former is *probably* too " large an allowance; but the latter is *certainly* so. " The number of people in the kingdom may, there- " fore, be stated as *probably* not more than four milli- " ons and a half; but *certainly* not five millions."

When the Colonists shall have become thus numerous, and shall so far exceed in people the mother country, they must either be easy and happy, in the secure and confirmed enjoyment of their respective liberties; being closely united in one common cause; or be miserable in abject slavery, thro' divisions and cowar- dice; or be convulsed in dangerous struggles. The period is so nigh, that the parent may look upon his new born infant, as a future actual partaker in the hap- piness or misery thereof; and must therefore be ani- mated in exerting his several powers, that so it may be a day of joy and gladness.

Roxbury, May 20th, 1772. *William Gordon*

PART I.

Containing the Plan for the Erection, Continuance and Government of the SOCIETY, *with the various reasons.*

THE defign being to eftablifh—not a company of a few members, who fhall make a particular advantage, and enrich themfelves, by infuring fmaller benefits to others; but—a Society, where all fhall be joint proprietors, in one common ftock formed from their refpective contributions, and have equal rights, and receive their full advantage in proportion to their feveral payments: And as the Society fhould be large, that fo the cafualties, by being greatly divided, may the lefs affect its capital, and the annual contingencies may come the nearer to an equality; and yet not too large, left its good government fhould be prevented, or the greatnefs of its ftock in a diftant period, fhould induce perfons of power, having no right, to interfere in its concerns: And that it may be the more extenfively ufeful, let it be agreed by

ARTICLE I.

The Society may confift of, but not more than, two thoufand perfons; and each to be admitted fhall by himfelf or agent, fubfcribe one common deed, upon that commence a member, and be bound by the agreements and covenants therein mentioned. The members fhall form two claffes, the firft of which fhall compre-

A

hend thofe who propofe fecuring annuities, after their
own deceafe, to wives or others, in cafe of furvivorfhip; the fecond, thofe who are for purchafing to themfelves an annuity after a certain age, for the remainder of life.

All perfons, at admiffion, fhould, in point of age, be
clear of either extreme, and inhabit within certain limits. Prudence and equity require, that they of the
firft clafs fhould not be expofed, from their refidence,
calling or manner of life, to peculiar dangers, beyond
what belong to mankind in general; and yet, that no
objection fhould arife from ferving in the militia, that
being the conftitutional defence of the whole community, and fo implying the fafety of the fmaller focieties. No danger arifes to the Society, from any in-
creafed hazards to which they of the fecond clafs
may be expofed; and therefore thofe, who cannot with
fafety be admitted into the firft, may with advantage
be taken into the fecond. A perfon admitted into the
firft clafs, may be allowed, when not too far advanced
in life, to hold alfo under the fecond. And therefore
let it be

ARTICLE II.

Every perfon at admiffion fhall not be younger than
twenty-one, nor older than fixty years; and fhall re-
fide within the limits of— [*Here the limits to be fpeci-
fied, as may be concluded on, after mature deliberation,
by the firft members.*] No one of the firft clafs fhall
follow a fea-faring life, or be engaged in the land fervice as an officer, foldier or otherwife, by reafon of
the fuperior rifk of his employment; but may belong

to, and ferve in the militia. One, who cannot be of the
firft clafs, on account of his calling and manner of life;
or, whom the directors may refufe admitting into it,
becaufe of bad health or other threatning circumftances; may become a member in the fecond. A perfon
admitted into the firft, may at any time, when not too
aged, join himfelf alfo to the fecond, fubject to the limitation of acting only as a fingle member, in all the
management of the Society's affairs.

That the Society, may be fecured from frauds and
impofitions, let it be

ARTICLE III.

Every perfon, propofing to be a member, fhall give
in his name, refidence, age, title or profeffion; and
mention whether married or fingle ; if married and in-
tending to fecure the benefit of a furvivorfhip to his
wife, her age, chriftian and former name—and where-
ever fuch benefit is intended, the age, chriftian and fur-
name, and refidence of the party for whom it is defigned
—to the directors at one of their meetings, and at fome
fubfequent one, fhall, if refiding within twenty miles,
appear perfonally to be examined by them, as to the ftate
of his health, readinefs to conform to and be bound by
the rules of the Society, and the like ; and upon their
having obtained all needful fatisfaction and agreed upon his admiffion, he fhall upon paying the ftipulated
premium become a member, and, upon figning the
deed by himfelf or agent, receive, without any farther
charge, a policy fetting forth, that he the holder thereof, in confideration of his complying with the terms
therein mentioned, fhall himfelf receive, or fecure to

another the propofed benefits, in cafe he fhall have lived one whole calendar year from the time of his admiffion, but that otherwife all he may have paid fhall
be forfeited, and go to the Society's capital. Should
the perfon propofed live at a greater diftance than
twenty miles, then the directors may be fatisfied in a-
ny other way that fhall be agreed upon. The policy
fhall be invalidated where obtained by fraud, deceit, and
Impofition.

To counteract any partiality by which directors
may be induced to reject a proper candidate : to
rid the Society of fuch as may become offenfive and
fcandalous : and to fecure it from being burthened with
payments, before the natural courfe of things require
them; and from paying improper perfons, it may be
ftipulated by

A R T I C L E   IV.

Any perfon rejected by the directors may appeal to
the Society when affembled at any general meeting,
and upon the majority's voting for his admiffion, he
fhall be put up again at the next general meeting, and
upon then having the votes of the majority fhall be
forthwith admitted, upon his complying with the ufual
requirements. Should it happen that a member becomes injurious, difgraceful, or obnoxious to the generality, the expulfion of fuch perfon fhall be lawful,
provided that the orders for the fame be made at a general meeting of the fociety and confirmed at the next
fucceffive one, either affembled of courfe or called on
purpofe, and at each, by the unanimous confent of all
prefent, or, in cafe of a divifion, of three fourths; but

upon such expulsion the party shall receive back all the net principal monies paid by him, upon his peaceably agreeing to surrender up his policy; and on his refusing to do it shall forfeit both. Was the person expelled entitled to, or an actual receiver of, an annuity, in consequence of his having been a member of the second class, the full time required, he shall not be deprived of his annuity, which shall be paid, notwithstanding his expulsion. Should a member become a felon, die or have his death occasioned in or by a duel; or feloniously make away with himself; or should he make a voyage exceeding twenty English leagues from port to port, without licenfe first obtained from the directors, and die in such voyage; or should he go beyond the limits agreed upon without a licenfe, and there die; or should he betake himself to a sea-faring life; or engage in the land service, as an officer, soldier or otherwise; in any such case the benefit of survivorship intended to have been secured to another by his policy shall be forfeited. Should the wife be divorced for adultery, or in any other way have her relation dissolved; or should the receiver of an annuity live in an unlawful cohabitation, or be guilty of felony, the right to the annuity shall cease.

That persons may have ample encouragement for becoming members, and still the society be secured against any unfair practices; and that none of either sex may be unnecessarily excluded, let it be

ARTICLE V.

A bachelor or widower may become a member for the benefit of a future wife; but, in that case, to pre-

∧ and the monies received from him be retained.

ferve the fociety from being injured by marriages of de-
figning perfons in a dying condition, or deceived by any
one's pretending to be the widow of fuch member after
his deceafe, and to afcertain the certainty of the members being legally married, be it agreed, that no perfon claiming as the widow of fuch member fhall be entitled to any annuity, unlefs fuch member, whofe widow
fhe claims to be, fhall, at leaft three months before his
death, have delivered in to the directors, or fome one
of them, a fatisfactory certificate of his marriage with
fuch perfon, together with her true age ; and they
fhall have approved thereof, and fettled for the fame.
Women way be admitted into either clafs, under fi-
mular reftrictions with thofe already, or hereafter to
be mentioned, and be allowed to vote in all the Society's affairs either in perfon or by proxy.

Where the individual intended to be benefited by a
future annuity, dies before the time of it's becoming due,
the member purchafing the fame may poffibly think,
that, without paying afrefh as though newly admitted,
he fhould have a right of fubftituting another in the
place of the deceafed, in confequence of what he may
have already paid ; but as the deceafe of fuch perfons
is one of the chances the fociety muft avail itfelf of,
in order to its paying the propofed annuities where
they become due, it is needful that the member fhould
pay afrefh, as though newly admitted, on his propofing to fecure an annuity to another individual : however, if he has accomplifhed, or upon his accomplifhing,
his probation year, the renewal of that may be difpenfed
with ; he may have the right of continuing a member,

and the payments he may make after the deceafe of
one individual till he fettles for another, may be difcounted in fuch future fettlement; and it may be

ARTICLE VI.

Upon the deceafe of the party, for whom the annuity propofed in the policy was defigned, the member forfeits the monies paid, to the ufe of the Society; and muft fettle as a new admitted member, for a-
ny frefh perfon propofed as a future annuity-receiver,
and take out another policy; but, having accomplifhed, or upon accomplifhing, the probation-year, the renewal of that fhall be difpenfed with: he fhall alfo
have the right of continuing a member, and all the
neat principal monies paid by him, in the intermediate
fpace, between the deceafe of one individual and his
fettling for another, fhall be difcounted in fuch fettlement.

It's effential to the exiftence of the Society, that
the payments fhould be both fully and regularly made;
but, as experience abundantly proves, that, whatever
time is allowed, many will delay performance to the laft
period, and if not compelled by a forfeit, exceed; and
yet, fhould the time allowed be very fhort, or the forfeiture large, there will be a perpetual litigation; and
as, after repeated refufal or neglect upon notice given,
an abfolute exclufion fhould take place, it may be the
purport of

ARTICLE VII.

The member fhall pay what annual fum he has ftipulated for, in half yearly payments, reckoning from the
time of his admiffion, within thirty days after becom-

ing due; on penalty of fix-pence for every day he exceeds the thirty ; and in cafe he fhall not pay the half yearly fum with the forfeitures due thereon, within two calendar months from the day of its becoming due, notice in writing or print fhall be delivered to each perfon fo making default, or left for him at his laft place of abode, or if that cannot be conveniently done, then an advertifement fhall be inferted in fome one of the public papers requiring payment of the fame, on pain of forfeiting his policy, and being excluded by a limited time, not lefs than twenty days from the date of fuch advertifement, and in cafe the fame fhall not be paid together with the forfeitures and all charges attending fuch default, within the fpace of three calendar months from the time when the fame became due, or within the time advertifed, his policy fhall be forfeited, and he be totally excluded, and all his former payments go to the ufe of the Society: but fhould a member who has neglected paying, happen to die before the end of the three calendar months, or the time appointed by fuch notice or advertifement, fo as not to be at his deceafe actually excluded, in fuch cafe the perfon to be benefited by his policy fhall receive all the advantages of it, upon paying the monies due to the Society, with all the forfeitures and charges attending the fame.

The Society is fuppofed to be actuated by principles of honefty, honor, and humanity, and to have no defign, of inducing perfons to fecure advantages to themfelves or relations, by coming into it at the expence of creditors ; or, of obtaining benefits to itfelf from the misfortunes of its members; therefore let it be

ARTICLE VIII.

The party who was to have received an annuity, but, which has been forfeited from a failure of payment, through the late member's becoming a bankrupt or public infolvent, may, in cafe fuch perfon was a member and made his payments for the fpace of three years and upwards, have paid to him or her, in lieu of fuch annuity, at the rate of ten per cent; for all the net principal monies received from him: and fhould it happen, that any individual member, or propofed, or actual receiver of an annuity, fhould, by the operation of the Society's general rules, fuftain any particular hard-fhip, fuch perfon may apply to the body when affembled, who fhall have power to grant what relief fhall be judged reafonable and confiftent with the true intereft of the Society, and the ability thereof.

The deaths of the members fhould be timely and fatisfactorily notified, and the lives of the annuity-receivers properly afcertained, that the Society may guard againft frauds, and proceed regularly in its accounts; let it be provided for, in

ARTICLE IX.

Notice of the death and burial of every deceafed member, fhall be left with the fecretary or directors of the Society, one month next after his deceafe, under the penalty of five fhillings, to be deducted out of the firft payment of the annuity to be received, and the annuity-receiver fhall by oath, affirmation, or in fome other way that may be thought fufficient, give proof to the directors of the time and place of fuch members deceafe, and of the caufe of his death, or of the dif-

B

temper of which he died ; and fatisfaction fhall be given, when required, of the annuity-receiver's being living, and not having forfeited the annuity, at the time the payment applied for became due.

Let

ARTICLE X, contain,

The fubftance of 2d pt. fpecifying the confiderations to be made by the members, and the benefits to be fecured, and that the annuities fhall be paid half yearly, and begin upon the fecond of the four ufual quarter days, that fhall happen next after the annuity-receiver becomes intitled thereto, on his having complyed with what is required by the other articles. Here it may be provided, in order to accommodate all, that a perfon upon making an half payment, a full payment and an half, or a double payment, though it may not be prudent to admit more, fhall fecure a proportionable annuity; as alfo that a member may, with the allowance of the directors, take out a frefh policy, till his whole right amounts to a double annuity, but no further.

To guard againft all poffible events, however improbable and unexpected, and to prevent the Society or annuity-receiver's being greatly or unfairly injured thereby, let

ARTICLE XI, exprefs, that,

If, in cafe of an unufual mortality among the members, any heavy loffes, or calamities that may befal the

Society, the directors shall find upon inquiry, that the capital with the half yearly payments is not sufficient to answer the present annuities and also to secure the like for future annuity-receivers; they shall then be empowered to call upon the members for an additional sum, not amounting in the whole to more than at the rate of two shillings for the half year on every pound to be paid; nor from the members who paid the wh le consideration money at entrance, more than at the rate of five shillings half yearly on a future thirty pound purchased annuity: Should not this call fully answer, then the annuities shall be gradually reduced in equal proportions, till such reduction together with the call, shall have balanced for the deficiency, occasioned by the calamity with which the Society may have been overtaken, when the annuities shall be raised again to their first height.

Should the Society by the utmost improvement of its monies, and remarkable prosperity, be found, after a trial of twenty years, upon the strictest examination, made by persons appointed thereto, to have a surplus capital beyond what is needful, it may be agreed by

ARTICLE XII.

The interest of the surplus shall be appropriated annually for raising the annuities, where the annuity-receivers shall be fifty years old or upwards, and the persons through whom they became intitled had been twenty and one years members before the commencement of such title.

The neceffity and advantage of fecuring the annuities unalienable to the intended receivers named in the
policies, are very apparent; by that means the beneficial defigns of the plan are more fecure of taking
place, and the fociety itfelf is guarded againft litigi-
ous claims by virtue of affignments; let it therefore be
refolved by

ARTICLE XIII.

For the better fecuring the feveral annuities, to the
proper ufe of the intended receivers named on the policies, no annuity fhall be transferable, or affignable,
or liable to be charged, either by the member holding
the policy, or the propofed annuity-receiver, fo
as to convey away the benefit defigned to be fecured
to fuch receiver: fuch affignment, transfer or incum-
brance fhall be in itfelf void; and whenever made by
the intended or actual annuity-receiver, the Society
fhall have power, at a general meeting, either of declaring the annuity forfeited, or of appointing the payment of it, by order of the directors, as thefe may
conclude upon, to one or more, for the fole benefit of
the annuity-receiver named in the policy.

That the annuity-receiver may be fubject to no un-
neceffary trouble, and yet the Society be fafe, let it be
fettled by

ARTICLE XIV.

The policy fhall be brought to the place appointed
for payment, and the annuity be received, by the perfon therein named and intended to be benefited thereby; but in cafe of ficknefs, infirmities, diftant refidence, or any other fufficient obftacle, the annuity

may and shall be paid to such person whom the annuity-receiver may depute; which person shall be approved of by the directors, and shall bring the policy, together with an order signed by the annuity-receiver, and a certificate from two credible witnesses inhabiting the place of the annuity-receiver's residence, declaring that such annuity-receiver signed such order, and was then living.

Whereas every member is equally concerned in the affairs of the Society, though the policies may be of different value, the lowest being (it must be supposed) of like importance, with the highest, to the respective holders; and that the baneful influence of ambition, superiority, dependance, connections, assurance and impetuosity, may not lessen the freedom of individuals, engross the management to a certain set, and exclude others however qualified and desired by the generality, let it be stipulated by

ARTICLE XV.

Every person shall have one vote, and no more, be the value of his policy what it will: the admission of members, and the choice of individuals to fill up the different offices shall be always by ballot; and the determination of all questions, whether at a general meeting, or among the directors, when not unanimous, shall be also by ballot, if demanded by any two present. Fifteen directors and a treasurer shall be chosen at the general meeting appointed for that purpose, any or all of whom shall be liable to a removal at the pleasure of the Society, duely called or regularly coming together in a general meeting. The treasurer may be continued from year to year without being changed;

but the directors shall not any of them be continued longer than three years successively ; five shall go out every year, and five new ones, who shall not have been in the direction for full three years back, shall be chosen in their room. Should the increase of the Society and other circumstances require it, their number may be enlarged to twenty four, and eight, old ones go out, and new be chosen in, annually.

Should the legislature of any particular government, in which such a Society may be formed, concur in promoting a scheme, confined to no party, and calculated for public as well as private utility, and bestow upon it an incorporation, there will be no call for trustees ; but should any motives of mistaken policy prevent their doing it, let it be concluded on by

ARTICLE XVI.

Till an incorporation can be obtained, five trustees shall be chosen annually, to hold in their joint names the Society's effects and monies, such only excepted as may be in the hands of the treasurer for current use ; the number or sets of whom may be increased as the stock of the Society enlarges, that so no set may hold too great a value. These trustees shall be continued removed or changed at the pleasure of the Society : and every policy shall be signed by three of them. No person shall be a trustee, who has any of the Society's money on interest.

N. B. Societies are not illegal for want of incorporation : such societies are very common in *London*, and are allowed to form themselves by deed of settlement, which are inrolled in the highest courts of the king-

dom. The deed of fettlement of the Laudable Society,
for the benefit of Widows, was inrolled in the High
Court of Chancery, bearing date the 18th of March,
1761. That of the London Annuity Society, in the Court
of Common Pleas by order of Lord *Cambden*, bearing
date the 1ft of January, 1765. Some of the firft public focieties in *London* are unincorporated, and though
poffeft of very large capitals hold them fafely, and
without fear, by the help of faithful truftees.

Let it be
ARTICLE XVII.

The truftees and treafurer fhall from time to time
execute to the directors, proper and fufficient declara-
tions of truft, to evidence that the feveral fums in their
hands, and fecurities by them taken, and purchafes
made, are for the ufe and benefit of the Society, and to be
difpofed of according to the rules and orders thereof,
and from time to time made concerning the fame.
They fhall alfo refpectively enter into and give that
fecurity which fhall be reafonably required of them,
for the due execution of the trufts in them repofed ;
which fecurity fhall be given to fuch perfon or perfons
as fhall be nominated by the members at a general
meeting.

That the rights of the body may not be encroached
upon, and at length furreptitioufly leffened, by thofe
elected for and entrufted with the management of its
affairs ; that every individual in his private capacity
may have his full fhare of power, and may receive

all due information of what has been done or is doing,
and that the executive part may have the opinion of
the whole when wanted, and may be under a proper
check, let it be declared in

ARTICLE XVIII.

There shall be two stated annual general meetings,
half a years distance from each other; the first to be
as near as convenient after the Society's having been
formed six calendar months, at which, vacancies occasioned by death, absence, neglect or resignation, shall
be filled up for the remainder of the year; and five
members, being neither trustee, treasurer nor direct-
or, shall be chosen for auditors to examine and audit
the Society's accounts, as near down to the next stated general meeting as possible; at which, being the
second, to be held soon after the anniversary of the
Society's formation, the, or the major part of the, auditors shall report to the body the state of its accounts,
and of the capital stock, and the directors, treasurer
and trustees for the year ensuing shall be chose agreeable to what has been before mentioned. At these
stated general meetings, no matter of consequence,
and only business of course or necessity shall be trans-
acted, unless notice of the same shall have been given
full three weeks before, in the summonses advising of
such meeting. The directors may and shall at their
discretion summon general meetings, as often as affairs require it, and also whenever any nine members
shall request the same in writing; and in case of the directors neglecting to comply with such request for the
space of one calendar month, then the said nine members may, by letters and public advertisements signed
by themselves, summon within three weeks a general
meeting, which shall be equally valid as though called

by the directors. The particular bufinefs, to be tranfacted at thofe general meetings which are not ftated,
fhall be mentioned in the fummonfes and advertife-
ments, and no one thing fhall be finally concluded upon relative thereto, unlefs abfolutely neceffary for faving the being, liberty, or property of the Society, at
a firft general meeting, but fhall ftand over for confirmation to a fecond, diftant at leaft one calendar
month. At every general meeting, the minutes of
the former, together with the proceedings of the directors, fhall be read over, the laft for the information
of the body, the others for their confirmation amendment or rejection.

The difpofal of the capital is an affair of too much
confequence, and too effential, to be lodged with any
other than the whole body met in a general affembly.
Should it be faid, that the directors muft be beft acquainted with the Society's affairs, and therefore muft
be beft judges ; granting it to be true, the directors
make a part of the whole, the body in their general
affembly can avail themfelves of their knowledge, and
at the fame time form fome judgement, whether other
motives than public good have influenced their opinion ; befides, the directors, from their fuperior knowledge, and the refpect the Society is likely to have for
the perfons whom they have chofen to conduct their
affairs, can fcarce fail of fupporting any fcheme relative thereto, which they may form, unlefs manifeftly
improper, let it therefore be

ARTICLE XIX.

So much of the monies of the Society, as fhall be

C

judged neceffary by the directors to anfwer the current demands thereof, fhall be kept in the hands of the
treafurer; the reft fhall be paid at their order into the
hands of the truftees, to be by them vefted in, or fecured upon or by, government or other public or real fecurities, or laid out in the purchafe of lands, tenements or hereditaments in their names; in fuch manner as fhall be directed, by order made and confirmed
at two general meetings of the Society.

The reafonablenefs and juftice of the fubfequent article are felf-evident.

ARTICLE XX.

The directors, treafurer and truftees, and all acting
under them, fhall be indemnified in performing all lawful acts in purfuance of thefe prefents, and of the rules
and regulations made concerning the fame, out of the
ftock of the Society, which is in the firft place charged
therewith, and the reimburfement of all cofts that they,
their heirs, executors and adminiftrators may have
fuftained, by the legal performance of their refpective
offices, provided that in cafe of caufes and fuits relative thereto, the fame are carried on and defended, by
the confent and under the direction and approbation of
the directors, until there is a general meeting of the
Society, to the controul or direction of which the fame
fhall be fubject. The directors, treafurer, truftees and
all acting under them, their refpective heirs, executors or adminiftrators, fhall be anfwerable for no more
monies or effects than what were actually received by
them refpectively, or by another on their exprefs order without the direction, confent or licenfe of the di-

rectors ; nor fhall any of them be anfwerable for the default, or neglect, or mifdoings of the other or others of them, but only each one for his own refpective acts and conduct.

Let the power and bufinefs of the directors be exprefled in

ARTICLE XXI.

The directors for the time being fhall have the care and management of all the Society's affairs, according to the rules and orders contained in the deed, and hereafter to be made by the body ; fhall admit members ; iffue orders for the figning of policies, the lending calling in or paying of monies ; fhall appoint, and vary as needful, the time and place of their own meetings, the choice, fufpenfion, removal and government of the Society's fervants, together with the falaries and wages and all difputes or doubts concerning the fame ; fhall meet at leaft once in every fix weeks ; fhall compofe a legal board for the tranfacting all bufinefs, when and while amounting to feven ; fhall declare a vacancy among themfelves, when any one has been abfent from their meetings for four fucceffive months, without affigning a fatisfactory reafon for the fame ; fhall grant licenfes for going and abiding beyond the limits allowed by the deed ; fhall receive the furrender of policies of perfons quitting the Society ; fhall examine claims and determine the fame ; fhall compound, adjuft and fettle difputes relating to the policies and the annuities intended to be fecured thereby ; fhall fee that the accounts be carefully kept and all proceedings regularly entered in proper books, all which books, excepting what contain the loans of money to private persons, and the ages of the members and annuity receivers, wherein secrefy ought to be obferved, may be infpected by the feveral members at proper feafonable times ; and fhall give all needful directions for accommodating themfelves and the Society at their refpective meetings, and for fecuring their deeds, books of accounts, &c. and fhall take care of the regular and punctual payments of the annuities ; and every director, who fhall diffent from the proceedings of the Society or of the directors, may have his diffent with his reafon for the fame entered in the minute book of the Society,

'Tis to be hoped, that there will, for a long time to come, be members fufficiently qualified, whofe circumftances will allow it, and whofe public fpirit will incline them, to ferve the Society as truftees, treafurer and directors, without requiring any pecuniary confideration, though fuch in fome future period may be highly reafonable. Servants muft be paid, but they fhould be allowed no fees, which in too many inftances have proved introductory to various abufes and abominable impofitions, let it be then

ARTICLE XXII.

No truftee, treafurer or director fhall receive any falary, fee or reward, for his fervices or attendance on the Society or their affairs, unlefs hereafter it fhall be found requifite to appoint any fum of money for fuch purpofe, and the fame fhall have been agreed upon and confirmed at two general meetings. No clerk, agent or fervant of the Society fhall take any fee or reward, from any perſon tranſacting buſineſs with the Society, or receiving annuities from it, under penalty of being immediately diſcharged for ſo doing.

Human foreſight like human knowledge is confined within narrow bounds, and when united are very incapable of forming regulations ſuitable to the ſeveral exigences future time may produce, ſo that it ſhould be concluded by

ARTICLE XXIII.

For the more effectual completing the benevolent intention of the Society, and to provide for all exigences, a general meeting may make ſuch orders and rules, for the better executing the agreements herein contained, for ſupporting the Society and extending the plan and rendering it more uſeful, as may be deemed proper, provided that ſuch rules and orders ſhall, before they become binding, be confirmed by a ſubſequent meeting, called for that purpoſe and held at the diſtance of one calendar month, and are not repugnant to the fundamental rules of the Society, but conſonant to their true intents and meaning.

PART II.

TABLE I,

Shewing what a person must pay in purchasing a twenty pound annuity, to be enjoyed, in case of survivorship, by another for life, the latter not being younger than the former,

Age.	In present payment without an annual one, interest being at			Where there is an annual payment of 5£. subject to failure on either of their deaths, interest being at			Would he secure an additional £10, so as to make the annuity £30, upon living 10 years after admission, and paying annually £5 as before, he must add to the sum in the immediately preceding column, Interest being at		
	4prCt.	4½prC	5prCt.	4prCt.	4½prC	5prCt.	4prCt.	4½perC.	5prCt.
21	71	62 13	56 12	4 17	- -	- - - .	18 2	15 4	10 4
25	70 12	62 14	56 18	6 14	1 14	- - - .	17 10	15 2	12 1
30	70	62 13	57 2	9 2	4 8	1 8	16 11	14 8	12 14
35	68 1	62 4	56 19	11 6	6 17	4	15 8	13 10	12
40	67 8	61 6	56 9	13 5	9 4	6 8	13 19	12 8	11 1
45	65 3	59 16	55 8	14 17	11 4	8 12	12 6	11	9 18
50	62 3	57 12	53 15	16	12	17 10	10 6	9 6	8 10
55	58 6	54 10	51 5	16 13	14	11 18	8 2	7 8	6 15
60	53 6	50 7	47 15	16 11	14 9	12 15	5 12	5 4	4 16

From the above table it appears, that, money yielding an uninterrupted compound interest of $4\frac{1}{2}$ per. cent. a person of 35, in order to secure an annuity of 20 *l.* for the life of another of the same age, in case of survivorship, must give in present payment 62*l.* 4*s.*

but should he chuse to make an annual payment of 5*l.* subject to a failure at his own death or that of the intended annuity-receiver, then he will have to pay down only 6*l.* 17*s.* the value of such annual payment being the difference between 62*l.* 4*s.* and 6*l.* 17*s.* or 55*l.* 7*s.* But would he secure an additional 10 *l.* so making the annuity 30 *l.* in case he should live ten years after admission, besides the annual payment of 5 *l.* he muſt pay down 13*l.* 10*s.* more than the 6*l.* 17*s.* or in all 20*l.* 7*s.* Does he prefer paying at once the whole value of the increasing annuity, he muſt to 62*l.* 4*s.* add 13*l.* 10*s.* that being the worth of an additional 10 *l.* annuity after ten years. N. B. The worth of an annual payment of 5 *l.* for the life of a person, subject to the above mentioned failure, is, the difference between the sum to be paid at admission when there is no such payment, and the sum to be paid when there is: And the value of an additional 10*l.* after ten years is the sum mentioned in the laſt set of columns. An attendance to this observation may help a Society in varying its terms to accomodate different persons: and thus, a member may be admitted to secure a 10 *l.* annuity after ten years, when he is 35 years old, to one of the like age in case of survivorship, on his paying down only 13*l.* 10*s.* or a 20 *l.* annuity after the said term of ten years on paying 27 *l.* but in this case should he die *before* the ten years, the intended annuity-receiver reaps no benefit from what has been paid, which goes to the use of the Society.

TABLE II.

Shewing what a purchaser must pay, more than in the the preceding table, upon every year he is older than the intended annuity-receiver, supposing interest to be at 4½ per cent.

Age of the person to be benefited.	Age of the purchaser.	For the 20 £. annuity where the payment is made at once.			For the 20 £. annuity where there is an annual payment of 5 £			For the 30 £. annuity after ten years, where there is an annual payment of 5 £.		
		£.	s.	d.	J.	s.	d.	£.	s.	d.
15	21	0	18	0	0	12	0	1	13	0
20	25	1	0	0	0	15	0	1	2	6
15	25	0	19	6	0	15	0	1	2	0
25	30	1	3	0	0	18	0	1	6	0
15	30	1	2	0	0	17	0	1	4	6
30	35	1	7	0	1	1	0	1	10	6
20	35	1	5	0	1	0	0	1	9	0
15	35	1	4	6	1	0	0	1	8	6
35	40	1	11	0	1	5	0	1	15	0
30	40	1	10	6	1	5	0	1	15	0
20	40	1	8	0	1	3	6	1	13	6
15	40	1	7	0	1	3	0	1	12	6
40	45	1	16	0	1	9	6	2	1	0
35	45	1	15	0	1	9	6	2	1	0
30	45	1	14	0	1	9	0	2	0	0
25	45	1	13	0	1	8	0	1	19	0
20	45	1	12	0	1	7	0	1	18	0
15	45	1	10	6	1	6	6	1	17	0
45	50	2	2	0	1	15	0	2	7	6
40	50	2	1	0	1	15	0	2	7	6
30	50	1	18	6	1	13	6	2	6	0
20	50	1	16	0	1	11	6	2	3	0
40	55	2	7	0	2	1	0	2	15	0
30	55	2	4	0	1	19	0	2	12	0
20	55	2	0	6	1	16	6	2	9	0
55	60	2	18	0	2	10	0	3	4	0
50	60	2	17	6	2	10	6	3	5	0
40	60	2	14	0	2	8	6	3	3	0
30	60	2	10	0	2	5	6	2	19	6
20	60	2	6	0	2	2	6	2	15	6

TABLE III.

*Shewing what annuity the purchafer may become enti-
tled to, after a certain period, for the remainder of
life, upon a given fum.*

Age.	Annuity.	When arrived at.	Upon paying, intereft being at					
			4 perCt.		4½ p rCt		5 perCt.	
21	30		90	19	77		65	7
25	20	45	75	11	65	4	56	9
30	20		100	3	88	11	78	9
21	40		80	11	66	18	55	13
25	40		100	8	85		72	2
30	30		99	16	86	11	75	4
35	20		88	18	78	19	70	5
36	20	50	94	6	84	3	75	5
37	20		100	1	89	15	80	12
38	20		106	5	95	15	86	8
39	20		112	17	102	3	92	13
40	20		119	18	109	2	99	8
40	20		76	13	68	9	61	3
41	20		81	10	73	2	65	13
42	20	55	86	14	78	2	70	10
43	20		92	5	83	11	75	15
44	20		98	4	89	7	81	8
45	20		104	13	95	14	87	12
40	30		69	15	61	2	53	12
41	30		74	3	65	5	57	10
42	30		78	18	69	15	61	15
43	30		83	19	74	12	66	7
44	20		59	12	53	4	47	11
45	20	60	63	10	56	19	51	3
46	20		67	13	61		55	1
47	20		72	3	65	8	59	6
48	20		77	1	70	2	63	18
49	20		82	6	75	5	68	18
50	20		87	19	80	17	74	7

D

T A B L E IV.

Shewing what the purchaser must give down, besides making a payment annually of 5 £. till he becomes entitled to the annuity.

Age.	An-nui-ty.	When arrived at.	4 per Ct.		4½ per Ct.		5 per Ct.	
21	30	45	27	4	16	3	7	4
25	20		17	17	9	17	3	4
30	20		51	15	41	15	33	2
21	50						7	10
21	40		11	14	1	11		
25	40		36	8	23	19	13	16
30	30		43		32		22	15
35	20	50	41	4	32	16	25	11
36	20		48	15	40		32	8
37	20		56	14	47	12	39	14
38	20		65	4	55	16	47	11
39	20		74	5	64	11	56	
40	20		83	18	73	19	65	2
40	20		29	17	23	2	17	5
41	20		36	15	29	14	23	10
42	20	55	44	2	36	14	30	5
43	20		51	18	44	6	37	10
44	20		60	5	52	7	45	6
45	20		69	4	61	1	53	15
40	30		15	8	8	17	3	6
41	30		21	7	14	9	8	12
42	30		27	15	22	10	14	4
43	30		34	10	26	18	20	5
44	20		11	19	7	3	3	8
45	20	60	17	15	12	13	8	5
46	20		23	18	18	11	13	17
47	20		30	10	24	18	19	19
48	20		37	11	31	14	26	10
49	20		45	2	39		33	11
50	20		53	4	46	18	41	4

Let it be noted that the purchasers only become entitled to their annuities at the respective ages of 45, 50, 55 and 60, and are not to begin receiving them in half yearly payments, till half a year after.

☞ Though the preceding Tables are in Sterling money, they may be changed into any currency whatsoever.

In forming the preceding tables, the calculations have been made down to the fourth decimal inclusive, and all needful exactnefs been attended to; fo that they may be fafely depended upon, for the folution of other queftions, than thofe to which they are direct anfwers.

In working the probabilities of the given lives, the procefs has been carried on according to Mr. *De Moivre*'s Hypothefis, as recommended by Dr. *Price*, note. p. 23. which is probably the reafon of the difference in the value of the annuities (intereft at 4 per cent) as in Table III, and as given by Dr. *Price*, p. 109.

According to the Doctor.				By Table III.	
Annuities of	to be enjoyed after	by perfons aged	amount to	to	
40		21	85 12	80	11
40		25	103 15	100	8
30	50	80	101 1	99	16
20		35	88 18	88	18
20		40	119 1	119	18
20	55	40	74 12	76	13
20		45	101 15	104	13
30		40	67	69	15
20	60	45	60 17	63	10
20		50	85 2	87	19

The Doctor calculated on the probabilities of the duration of life, as deduced by Dr. *Halley*, and given in the appendix p. 316.

The purchafer of an annuity, to be enjoyed, after his deceafe, by another in cafe of furvivorfhip, being a year upon probation, wherein he hazards all he has advanced, the calculation for the annual payments gives him fome credit for the fame, by reckoning as though they began to be made on his commencing a member, inftead of a year after.

In calculating the value of the additional 10*l.* the reckoning goes upon nine years inftead of ten, as it will be but nine years after the 20*l.* has been fecured, before the right to that addition will be obtained; by this means the purchafer is charged fomewhat more than had it went upon ten years; but far lefs than is allowed for, by reckoning the annual payment as tho' made when he becomes a member. Should it be thought that in juftice the calculation fhould have gone upon ten inftead of nine years, it is only determining that he fhall not pay for the additional 10*l.* till he has paffed through his probation year; which may be more agreeable than the paying for the whole together.

The tables fuppofe that the money is put out immediately, accumulates continually by an uninterrupted compound intereft, is never loft, nor diminifhed in value; now, as in fact it muft often lie by, cannot accumulate at that rate, and will be fubject to a diminution through loffes, failure of intereft and the like, it may be moft advifeable to reckon upon no more than 4$\frac{1}{2}$ per cent, certain compound continued intereft, and therefore Table II. goes only upon that eftimate. They, who are otherwife minded from confidering the height of legal intereft, may be convinced upon reading the following quotations from Dr. *Price, viz.* p. 8. " In equal ages the mortality of males has been " found to be greater than the mortality of females. " P. 271, 272, *the greater mortality of males* appears " on the whole to be a fact well eftablifhed. P. 106. " The iffue of the beft fchemes of this kind muft be in

" fome degree uncertain. For want of proper obfer-
" vations, it is not poffible to determine what allow-
" ances ought to be made, on account of the higher
" probabilities of life among females than males. No
" prudence can prevent all loffes in the improvement
" of monies; nor can any care guard againft the in-
" conveniencies to fuch fchemes, which muft arife
" from thofe perfons being moft ready to fly to them,
" who, by reafon of concealed diforders, feel them-
" felves moft likely to want the benefit of them. 'Tis
" vain to form fuch eftablifhments with the expecta-
" tion of feeing their fate determined foon by experi-
" ence. P. 107. No experiments of this fort fhould
" be tried haftily. An unfuccefsful one muft be pro-
" ductive of very pernicious effects. All inadequate
" fchemes lay the foundation of *prefent* relief on *fu-*
" *ture* calamity, and afford affiftance to a *few* by dif-
" appointing and oppreffing *multitudes*. P. 111. Cer-
" tainly a Society that means to be a permanent ad-
" vantage to the public, ought always to take higher
" rather than lower values, for the fake of rendering it-
" felf more fecure, and gaining fome *profits* to balance
" *loffes* and expences. P. 129. In matters of chance,
" it is impoffible to fay, that an unfavourable run of
" events will not come, which may hurt the beft con-
" trived fcheme. The calculations only determine
" probabilities; and, agreeably to thefe, it may be
" depended on, that events will happen on the whole.
" But at particular periods, and in particular inftances,
" great deviations will often happen; and thefe devi-
" ations at the commencement of a fcheme, muft
" prove either very favourable, or very unfavoura-
" ble."

Should a better intereft then be made of the mo-

ney than allowed for, the advantages arifing from it
will tend to give eftablifhment to the Society, fecurity againft unexpected ills, befides an ample fupply for
all neceffary expences.

'Tis of importance, in calculating annuities, to determine whether the lives of females are *univerfally*
better than thofe of males ; and *how much* better :
And his Honour, the Lieutenant Governor, having very obligingly communicated to me, fome manufcripts
containing an account of the number of inhabitants,
&c. in *Maffachufett's-Bay*, taken by order in 1764,
the refult was fuch as induced me at firft fight to conclude, that in this colony, as in many other places,
the lives of females were better than thofe of males :
For it appeared from them, that there were 33438
houfes ; 41110 families ; 59090 white males above 16
years old, and 64755 females, making together 123845 ;
—and that there were 58390 white males under 16,
and 55945 females, in all 114335. The whole number of males and females was 238180. Though the
males under 16 exceeded the females by 2445, yet the
females above 16 exceeded the males by 5665. The
number of towns that fent in accounts was 196 :
fome few declined, or neglected doing it. In 46
of thefe towns the males above, as well as under
16, exceeded the females. In 47 of them the females
exceeded the males under as well as above 16. In 18
of them the males above 16 exceeded the females, and
the females under 16 exceeded the males. In the remainder the males under 16 exceeded the females, and
the females above 16 exceeded the males. But notwithftanding this appearance in fupport of the better
lives of females *here* as well as elfewhere, when information had been obtained—that the order appeared

...rious, occasioned an alarm in many places, was disagreeable to multitudes, was not enforced by any penalty, and was not carefully complied with—that different towns purposely took such loose accounts, as should prevent its being known how numerous they were—that it was highly probable that the return of the males was lower than the truth, and that all who were at sea, amounting to some hundreds from various ports, were left out of the account—and that the colony had lost full five, if not near ten thousand men by the war immediately preceding—could not but conclude, on further thought, that the full number of the white inhabitants was not to be determined from the return, and that the males in the *Massachusett's* were not only more, but better lives, * than those of the fe-

---

* Since writing the above, have been confirmed in my conclusion, by what Dr. *Price* mentions in his *Supplement*, p. 15, 16, 17. "There is a difference between the mortality of "males and females.—I must however observe, that it may "be doubted, whether this difference so unfavourable to "males, is *natural*; and the following facts will prove, that "I have reason for such doubts.

"It appears, from several registers in *Susmilch's* works, that "this difference is much less in the *country parishes* and *villa-* "*ges* of BRANDENBURGH, than in the *towns*: And agreeable "to this, it appears likewise, from the accounts of the same "curious writer, that the number of males in the country "comes much nearer to the number of females.

"At the time the accounts were taken of the inhabitants "in the province of NEW-JERSEY in AMERICA, they were "distinguished particularly into *males* and females under "and above sixteen.

"In 1738, the number of *males* under 16 was, 10639; females. The number of negroes returned, was, males 3020, females 2226; the disproportion between the sexes may be accounted for, upon the far greater import of males. The Indians were 728 males, 953 females; but nothing decisive can be gathered from hence, unless it could be known, whether any, and how many males had perished by the war; whether numbers might not be absent upon hunting, fishing or other engagements, who were not in the account; and what was the disproportion between the sexes, of those that had perished by the excessive drinking of that artificial American poison—Rum. There was no taking the ages of either Negroes or Indians.

Much exactness, and an attention to every circumstance, are requisite in communicating accounts, that may be used by other's as a foundation for calculations; or the whole may be extremely erroneous. Thus Dr. *Price* concludes, p. 198, that, " at *Boston* " the inhabitants would decrease were there no sup- " ply from the country; if the account given in the " *Gentleman's Magazine* of 1753, p. 413, from 1731 " to 1752, of births and burials in the town was just; " seeing that the burials all along exceeded the births." Have examined the *Magazine*, and observe, that it is not an account of *births* and burials, but of *baptisms*

" males 9700 : males above 16—11631; females 10725. In " 1745,these numbers were, males under 16—14523 ; females " 13754: males above 16—15087 ; females 13704.

" The inference is obvious ; that human life in males is " more brittle than in females, only in consequence of ad- " ventitious causes, or of some particular debility, that " takes place in polished and luxurious Societies, and especi- " ally in great towns."

and burials—that the number of burials in the time
specified was 13384; of *baptisms* 11850;—that the
baptisms were therefore less than the burials by 1534
—and that in the burials were included 2011 blacks,
so that the number of whites buried was only 11373.
Now it must be noted, that these accounts of burials
and baptisms were most probably taken from the
news-papers—that little stress is to be laid upon their
authority in this matter, as it's notorious to the ministers, that their lists, especially in the article of baptism, are very imperfect and below the truth, though
likely to be much more correct in the other—that
great numbers are born, who from various causes are
not *baptized*—and that the marriages and births a-
mong the negroes, cannot, by reason of their peculiar
circumstances, bear the same proportion with their burials to those of the inhabitants. Nothing positive
concerning the decrease of the inhabitants at *Boston*,
can then be concluded upon, from the accounts given
in the *Gentleman's Magazine*.

Would gentlemen who have time and opportunity
communicate by the help of news-papers, or any o-
ther way, the proper intelligence, calculators might
be at a much greater certainty; especially, were they
to observe the like exactness with what appears in the
following letter, *viz.*

Rowley, March 12, 1772.

Messi'rs FLEETS,

" B Y one of your late Boston Evening Posts, we had
intelligence of a remarkable instance of the shortness
of human life; of 100 persons born the same year,
one only remained alive the 76th year after. And by
far the greater part of them died many years before.

E

" Be pleafed, therefore, on the contrary, to take this account of longevity from the records of the firft Church in Rowley ; wherein, from September 10, 1682, until January 25, 1691, the fpace of eight years and nearly five months, there were 246 perfons baptized. And February 4, 1771, there were twenty four of them living.

" Now, divide 246 by 24, and you will find that more than one of ten lived to be between 80 and 89 years old.

" Of the faid 24, males and females being in number equal, three were baptized Anno 1682, turned there-fore into their 89th year, four in 84, one in 85, one in 86, two in 87, two in 88, two in 89, eight in 90, and one in 1691. And there being but thirty two baptiz-ed in 1690, and eight of them living February 1771, fhews that one of four baptized that year, have lived to be turned into their 81ft year. A rare inftance in-deed !

" And there is a perfon now living in a neighbouring town, baptized in this, October, 1681, Æt. 91. And there are now living, in the firft parifh in the town, nine perfons between 80 and 90 years of age, and pro-bably about fo many more in the other parts of the town.

" And there have died in the town, the two laft years, eleven aged people, including but three of the faid 24 (which three died a few months paft) one Æt. 81, three 83, one 87, four 88, one 90, one 93.

" It may be added, that there lived in the place now called the firft parifh in Rowley, four perfons, the firft of whom died Anno 1716, and the laft 1729, and each of the four, by the beft accounts that could be had, died an 100 years old and upwards.

" There were but about 220 perfons buried there between thefe four, and fcarce 1000 fince the firft of them unto this time.

" It has been a common remark, that people in New-England do not live fo long as in Old. Judge how juft an one. You will rarely find in accounts from thence, that more than one of 1000 live to be 100 years old or upwards. Here are four in lefs than 1000.

" You may depend upon the above account as genuine and certain, unavoidable human errors excepted."

F I N I S.

AN

ORATION,

DELIVERED AT THE

ORPHAN-HOUSE OF CHARLESTON,

SOUTH-CAROLINA,

OCTOBER 18, 1797,

BEING THE EIGHTH ANNIVERSARY OF THE

INSTITUTION.

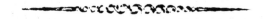

By the Rev. WILLIAM HOLLINSHEAD, D.D.

ONE OF THE MINISTERS OF THE INDEPENDENT, OR CONGREGATIONAL, CHURCH, IN CHARLESTON.

Published at the request of the Commissioners of the
Orphan-House.

Printed by W. P. YOUNG, No. 43, Broad-Street,
CHARLESTON.
1797

TO

THE HONORABLE

HENRY-WILLIAM DESAUSSURE, Esquire

INTENDANT;

AND

ADAM GILCHRIST,   JOHN C. MARTIN,
THOMAS H. M°CALLA,   ROBERT HOWARD,
SETH LOTHROP,   THOMAS R. SMITH,
WM. ALLEN DEAS,   SIMON M'INTOSH,
WM. ROBERTSON,   JAMES LOWNDES,
JOSEPH PEACE,   AND
JOHN WARD,   JOHN C. FOLKER, ESQ'S.

WARDENS OF THE CITY OF CHARLESTON,

AND TO

JOHN DEE HOLMES,   JOHN EDWARDS,
PHILIP GADSDEN,   DANIEL HALL,
WM. SOMARSALL,   WM. JOHNSON, ...
JOHN ALEXANDER,   AND
JOHN PARKER, JUN.   THO. SIMONS, ESQ'S.

COMMISSIONERS OF THE ORPHAN-HOUSE,

AS A TESTIMONY OF HIS ESTEEM OF THEIR PERSON-
AL WORTH, AND RESPECT FOR THEIR PUBLIC
CHARACTERS,

THIS ORATION

IS INSCRIBED

BY THEIR,

OBED'T HBLE SERV'T,

THE AUTHOR.

Oration.

Fellow-Citizens,

CUSTOM hath dignified the obſerving of anniverſaries, on all occaſions, either of real, or imaginary, importance. The eſtabliſhment of empires, the founding of cities, the birth of heroes, and ſtateſmen, and benefactors of mankind, victories and revolutions have been admitted to this honorable diſtinction.

The day conſecrated to humanity and benevolence; the day that ſhines to relieve the diſtreſſed, to enlighten the ſteps of the wanderer, to give protection to the helpleſs, and revive the orphan's hope, hath a much ſuperior claim to our attention.

On ſuch an occaſion, ſolicited by the commiſſioners of this benevolent inſtitution, I need no apology for attempting to addreſs to you a few ſentiments to animate your virtue, and to encourage your already fervent zeal, in favor of this aſylum of the unfortunate.

B

And, I flatter myself, I need not great powers of eloquence to gain access to the hearts of an audience, who are accustomed to sympathize, both in the joys and sorrows of human nature, and ever have shewn a promptitude to aid the designs of benevolence and utility.

On former anniversaries, "The superior importance of this charitable institution in the community, its title to your future patronage, its excellent nature, the reasons we have to expect its continual prosperity, and the measures that appear best calculated to promote that desirable end," have been ably pointed out.

Difficult it would be to find any thing new or interesting on these topics to add; but the nature, the expressions, and the advantages of BENEVOLENCE, that most amiable of the human virtues, which gave birth to this useful establishment, still deserve our consideration, and may properly be made the subject of the present address.

I describe that noble principle as the law of kindness impressed on the heart of man, to man, in his first formation, in the image of his Creator. It is the disposition in the human mind that most assimilates it to the nature of the Deity, raises it nearest to the perfection of the heavenly state, and is its best qualification for usefulness on the present theatre of action, and for the enjoyment of a future immortality. It is that something within us, that interests our feelings in all the prosperity or adversity of mankind; that infpires the foul with a pleafing fympathy in all the joys of human nature, and draws forth the commiferating tear in all its woes; that prompts to generous difinterefted works of kindnefs; and often is the fpring of the nobleft enterprifes of public fpirit.

It is not contended, that in the prefent imperfect ftate, this, or any other of the virtues of the human mind, can be found in that pure, unmixed exercife, which would raife it above the influence of the felfifh paffions. That fad cataftrophe which hath introduced diforder and confufion into the whole terreftrial creation, it muft be confeffed, hath occafioned diforder in the moral difpofitions of our nature. Our beft affections now require the government of reafon, and the ftimulating influence and powerful motives of religion to excite them to action. But ftill there exifts in every heart, not debafed to the loweft degree of turpitude, a generofity and tendernefs of nature, which takes a part in all the viciffitudes to which man is fubject, in this changeful life. And, abftracted from all confiderations of felf, without any perceptible act of the will, without reflection, we rejoice with the profperous, and fuffer with the unfortunate, and experience pleafure or pain, before we have time to reafon on the circumftance that occafions it. Even the tale of imaginary wo, or of the long paft fcenes of forrow and affliction, awakens an involuntary compaffion in the heart, excites the tear of pity, and raifes thofe tender emotions, which, if we even are difpofed, we are unable to refift. Much more when we witnefs prefent mifery and diftrefs, when we fee virtue injured and oppreffed, and helplefs innocence caft out and expofed to the fufferings of poverty, without aid or protection, our foul fprings forward to the relief of the fufferers, and before we are aware, we become partners in their diftrefs.

Thus godlike, difinterefted, almoft infeparable from our nature, and prompt in its exertions is that amiable principle, which is the fubject of our prefent confideration. Have I faid too much in afferting that, in its firft emotions, it waits not the determinations of the will; nor ftops to reafon on the propriety of its exertions? Is benevolence the lefs a virtue becaufe it is an effential in the original conftitution of human nature; becaufe it is impreffed by the hand of the Creator on our hearts? No: The want of it is vicious and unnatural. The man that is divefted of it, muft be fubject to fome unreafonable and improper bias; to fome difgraceful felfifhnefs of temper, that narrows and contracts his heart, and forbids the generous, difinterefted exertions, which the voice of nature, of reafon, and religion invariably demands.

O Benevolence! Let me never become unyielding to thy perfuafive, charming influence! Sooner may I fink down into the humbleft ftate of poverty and fuffering, and be denied the confolation of a friend to fympathize in my

affliction, than ever be incapable of the generofity and tendernefs thou infpireft.

Benevolence is among the foremoft of the
moral virtues: Aided, improved, and confirmed by reafon and religion, it becomes an eftablifhed principle in the foul, ever prepared
for expreffion, when occafion and opportunity prefent. Such being the nature of benevolence, how great and noble may we expect it
to be in its expreffions! But, like every other
difpofition of human nature, it is limited in
its operations, and, in the poffeffion of an individual, extends its beneficial effects but to a
few, comparatively, of the human race. In
refpect to thefe few, however, it is forward
in promoting works of patriotifm and public
fpirit; feeks and feizes the opportunity of adding to the felicity of the profperous, and be-
friending the unfortunate; and lays itfelf
open to the approaches of the indigent and neceffitous, that it may bind up the heart that is
wounded with forrow, give bread to the hungry, clothe the naked, and bring the deftitute
under the fhelter of hofpitality.

'Though other, and moft ungodlike paffions
may contribute to form a hero, or a ftatefman;
though pride and felfifhnefs may prompt to
good and ufeful undertakings, and fhine in the
borrowed robes of virtue; though it is not
every fplendid action, that originates in that
goodnefs of heart, which entitles the perform-
er of it to the thanks and approbation of mankind, it is not the lefs; the property of benevolence to exert itfelf in fuch important

6

works as are of general utility. That disinterested virtue that animates the soul of the
benevolent man, and extends his views to the
universal happiness of mankind, glows with
a peculiar ardor in the love of his country,
and rises with eagerness to promote her interest. As he feels himself a son of Adam; a
brother of mankind: He feels by a tie more
exquisitely endearing a son, a brother, a
citizen of that nation which gave him birth,
or affords him protection: Whatever affects
her interest, lies near his heart: When she is
wounded he bleeds: He rejoices in her prosperity; and spares not his exertions, within the limits of propriety and justice, for her honor and improvement. If the sphere in which
he moves does not permit him to shine amongst
the most conspicuous patriots, yet, while his
philanthropy hath full exercise, in discharging
the cares and duties of his own domestic circle, he bears a cheerful part, in promoting
useful public institutions, and gives his time
and abilities, and pecuniary aid, with liberality for their support: He esteems it a duty, and
a privilege, to give his proportion of assistance
in the public provision for advancing the interests of piety and virtue; for diffusing light
and knowledge among the ignorant; for supplying the necessitous, and opening a retreat
for the indigent and infirm; for promoting the
habits of industry and usefulness among the
rising generations of the poor; and, in fine,
for the correction of vice and folly, and the
encouragement of general piety and goodness.

But he confines not his views to the cold limits of duty and obligation—He extends his exertions with a generous hand, and embraces every opportunity for aiding in the enterprises of virtue, for the promotion of the public welfare.

I shall not say so much on the influence of a benevolent temper, in the more private circles of friendship. Every one knows, in a greater or less degree, what it is to enjoy the sweet sensibility of affection, that springs from an unison of hearts, and a similarity of aims, pursuits, and inclinations. This may exist, in some measure, where the heart is cold to that generous philanthropy, which hath all mankind for its object. Many interfering passions may prevent its operating beyond the selfish expectation of reciprocal advantage. In such a case it seldom extends further than the limits of its own circle, and often admits of discord and dissention even there. But where mutual benevolence strengthens the bonds of union, it softens and refines the affections of the heart, and adds a delicacy to friendship, which greatly enhances the value of its enjoyments. The presence of the benevolent man, with his friend, encreases the pleasure of his satisfactions. His looks, his actions, and expressions speak the noble effusions of a soul that delights in the happiness of others; that participates in their joys; and knows how to impart its own. He is equally delicate and sympathetic in the season of sorrow and distress. The silent involuntary tear that falls from his eye, and the gentle tenderness of his behaviour on such an occasion, impart a consolation superior to the most refined eloquence of compliment and form.

It is impossible to say how much a benevolence of heart contributes, in this view, to facilitate the performance of the common duties of social intercourse: It is a source from which flow innumerable good offices, which tend to smooth the rugged paths of life, to enlighten the darkness of our afflicted moments, to enlarge the sphere of knowledge, and to improve a taste for truly rational and virtuous enjoyments.

To complete the character of benevolence, it is easy of access to all the sons of affliction, poverty, and want; and stands prepared, if possible, to succour their distresses, and dissipate their woes. Some classes of sufferers are, by the uncertain lot of human nature, beyond the reach of the regular plans of systematic charity. Unknown to the directors of public institutions, for the relief of persons in their condition, unacquainted with the modes of application for the benefit of such relief, or unwilling, from a recollection of better fortune, to subject themselves to the humiliating condition of pensioners on the public, and to be obliged to mix with the vulgar and licentious, who are sometimes the most numerous sharers in the public bounty; they become more particularly the objects of private beneficence. For the sake of such, a well-directed benevolence will both have its contingent funds to refort to for their relief; and be ever ready to attend to their petitions; and often, unfolicited, will feek opportunities to diftribute to their neceffities.

It would be eafy to infer, from the above hints, how many advantages muft arife from cultivating a benevolent temper, in promoting both the general interefts of fociety, and the improvement, and virtue, and fatiffaction of him who poffeffes it. Of thefe I ought now to fpeak; but I find that I have incorporated feveral important obfervations on this head, with what hath already been faid, and thereby anticipated the tafk I had propofed to myfelf here. I fhall therefore only make thefe few remarks on the advantages of benevolence to its poffeffor.

Whatever purfuit a man may be engaged in, this amiable temper will be found generally to contribute much to his fuccefs; it will ingratiate him into the efteem and goodwill of all men: It will gain him their confidence as well as refpect: And while the turbulent and unfeeling, excite againft themfelves a general refentment and difguft, and by their ungracious manners, create an oppofition to their undertakings, which obftructs their wifhes and fruftrates their defigns, the man of benevolence and philanthropy enjoys the friendfhip and affiftance of all: Such a man hath the bleffing of heaven promifed to his enterprifes, will attain to the objects of his defire,

almoſt without difficulty, and enjoy them
without envy.

But whatever effect the exerciſe of benevolence may have upon our outward condition,
it hath a certain efficacy in enlarging the ſoul,
and improving our internal character in virtue
and goodneſs. The frequent exertions of every
virtuous diſpoſition help to confirm its habits,
and heighten its aſcendency over the oppoſite
vices of our nature. By every act of benignity, therefore, a good man is ſtrengthened, at
leaſt, in the habits of this virtue: And, at the
ſame time, by theſe means he corrects the remaining roughneſs of his nature, and, by
cultivating the humane and ſocial affections,
acquires a facility in bringing into exerciſe the
amiable diſpoſitions of his heart.

Benevolence is further, a ſource of pleaſing and grateful reflexions. As every human virtue promotes an inward peace of mind
in its poſſeſſor, this, in a peculiar manner,
arms the ſoul againſt thoſe turbulent, unruly,
or fretful paſſions, which are ſometimes provoked by little imaginary wrongs, and are
always unfriendly to the tranquility of the
heart. And while moſt of our other plea-
ſures are ſoon diſſipated and gone, and many
of them leave behind them an unpleaſant recollection; the pleaſure of a benevolent action is always encreaſed by reflection, and contributes much to heighten every other pleaſure and enjoyment of life. There cannot
be a more exquiſite ſatisfaction, than a good
man enjoys, when he hath been enabled to

add to the happiness, or relieve the sorrows of a fellow creature; it expands his soul with a delight unknown to you, ye sons of gaiety and mirth, in the highest glee of those sprightly scenes in which ye love to revel.

But I must not omit to mention that highest advantage of benevolence to the individual, which arises from its connexion with piety and religion: It is only, as it is a christian virtue, that it can be carried to its highest measure of improvement. And as the precepts of the gospel direct and regulate its exercise, and propose the most illustrious examples of it for our imitation; the divine doctrines of christianity teach us to look for its final rewards, in a future state. There, the cup of cold water given to a saint, to one of those little ones, who are considered, as proper objects of the care, and kindness of the Son of God: There, those small expressions of generous tenderness to the widow and the orphan, which a good man performs with exquisite pleasure, shall be acknowledged, as done to Christ himself; and again rewarded, with the smiles of his everlasting approbation, with the inheritance of a kingdom prepared from before the foundation of the world, for those whom he condescends to call his good and faithful servants.

The advantages derived to society from a benevolent disposition, brought into exercise, are too obvious to require, and too many to admit, of a particular enumeration. One of the moſt important, and which correſponds moſt with our preſent deſign, hath been formerly mentioned: I mean its influence in promoting works of public beneficence and utility. A moſt pleaſing inſtance of this is preſented to our eye, in this inſtitution:—A handſome building, erected on the foundation of your charity, the aſylum of ſo many helpleſs children, who, but for this aſſiſtance, might have been expoſed, deſtitute and friendleſs, to the ſufferings of poverty and the ſnares of vice, now comfortably provided for, inſtructed in their duty to God and man, training to a fitneſs for learning ſome uſeful employment, and affording promiſing hopes of their becoming valuable members of ſociety, is a ſpectacle that muſt excite a ſingular ſatisfaction in every benevolent mind.

With ſuch an object before you, need I to ſolicit the continuance of your benefactions to ſo intereſting a charity? With ſuch a proſpect of benefit to individuals, and of advantage to the community, need I ſuggeſt the propriety of your contributing, on this occaſion, with liberality? The ſmiles of Divine Providence on the eſtabliſhment, the care, the diligence, and attention of the perſons employed in the ſuperintendency of the children, the general effect of this attention, with as few exceptions as could be expected, on their morals, with the decency of their appearance, furniſh ſtrong inducements for you to add to the munificence you have ſo well expreſſed in the paſt years. Till ſubſtantial funds can be

annexed to the inftitution, fuch continual benefactions are neceffary; efpecially while fo
much is to be done with the monies that can
be raifed. That fo much hath been done is
highly to the honor of the contributors to this
ufeful charity, and much to the credit of the
commiffioners, entrufted with its particular
direction. But ftill the annual expenfes go on,
and create new demands upon your benevolent exertions.

If additional arguments are neceffary; remember, I befeech you, that you are the ftew-
ards of God, to lay out as much of his bounty
as you can fpare from yourfelves, for the needy
part of his houfehold. The poor, and efpecially the more helplefs of them, are in a peculiar manner, recommended to your care and
compaffion: And by a fpecial authority from
heaven, have a particular demand upon you,
for affiftance and relief: And your improvement of the talents, entrufted in your hands,
will either be required or rewarded, in that
day when the fons of affluence and the needy
will ftand on equal ground, at the tribunal of
heaven, to give an account of their fteward-
fhip.

Confider, alfo, the extent of the benefit
you will confer by continuing your contributions:—You will be inftrumental in delivering
many from the depths of poverty and diftrefs;
in laying a foundation for their obtaining an
honorable livelihood and becoming ufeful members of the community. You may fee the day
when thefe tender plants, nurtured under the

sunshine of your benignity, shall have grown up to maturity, and in their turn become a blessing to society. Perhaps you may have the honor, having rescued them from the snares of vice, to save their souls from destruction; and you "shall surely have your reward." Should you retrench from some unnecessary expense, or deny yourselves some costly gratification, which you well may spare, that you may contribute more largely to this work of beneficence, you will be amply repaid, in the pleasure that arises from the recollection of so amiable and virtuous an act.

Children of Prosperity! Permit me to remind you, that heaven hath blessed you with the riches of his goodness, to enable you to do good to your fellow-creatures; And while you shine in a higher sphere than others, let it teach you, like the sun, to send forth your light and influence in every direction, to cheer the dark abodes of poverty and distress. Let it teach you to "be ready to distribute, willing to communicate, dealing your bread to the hungry, covering the naked, and providing a habitation for the poor that are cast out." Such pursuits will adorn you with a character almost divine: For you will thereby become God's substitutes on earth, relieving the calamities of the wretched, and spreading joy and gladness all around you.

You who stand on a more equal level with the generality of your fellow-citizens! Tho' Providence hath not given you a profuse abundance; yet from what you have, you have some to spare, to promote the designs of charity, of virtue, and religion. If you are not wealthy, yet you have a sensibility of heart, which interests you in the happiness of others: And you are capable of as refined a pleasure in doing good, as those in the most elevated stations. Your good works, if not quite so great in measure, as theirs, who are better able, yet if done in the spirit of the gospel, will as soon obtain the approbation of him, who accepteth the humble sacrifice of the lowly and sincere, as the most splendid offerings of the opulent and great.

A disinterested philanthropy, a generous pursuit of works of beneficence, particularly as expressed in care and attention to the poor, are strongly recommended in the precepts of our holy religion, and enforced by the sublime example of our divine master. Love, according to the christian system, is the fulfilling of the law:—Love to brethren, to friends, to enemies, to the houshold of the faithful, to the whole family of mankind; all which is urged with great energy, in the life and miracles of him who went about doing good, administering to the consolation of mankind, freeing their bodies from painful maladies, dispelling their errors, and communicating all necessary useful instructions.

Daughters of Carolina! I need say but little to interest your feelings, in favor of the benevolent work we are endeavoring to recommend.* Your gentle natures are peculiarly qualified, for the tender offices of humanity; and you have many inducements to difpofe you to encourage the object of this inftitution—Mothers, who by the bleffing of heaven have brought your children fafely through the perilous ftages of childhood and youth; and fee them profperous and flourifhing, in the ftation allotted to them by Providence: Or you whofe little prattlers are yet but tottering around your feet; when you prefs them to your bofom, and indulge the pleafing expectation, of feeing them hereafter a bleffing to their country; thank God that they are not orphans, caft upon the care and bounty of ftrangers, bound to them by no ftronger a tie than charity: And while in your houfes "there is bread enough, and to fpare," impart of your fuperfluity to thefe children of neceffity, and lay up for your own offspring, a fund in the treafury of heaven, which fhall be reftored to them an hundred fold, fhould they ever fee the day of adverfity and want.

A fairer opportunity of gratifying a benevolent difpofition cannot be, than this which now folicits your attention; nor one that promifes more to be highly and laftingly benefi-

---

* The public virtue of the Ladies of South-Carolina hath furnifhed one of the moft refplendent pages in the hiftory of their country: But the attention of numbers of them to works of charity, and their fenfibility to the woes of human nature, does an honor to the female character, not to be equalled by the fineft eulogium.

cial. Other charities, for the moſt part, terminate in the objects to whom they are immedi-
atly applied; this is a good felt by every
member of the community: Its effects will
become more diffuſive, as its little penſioners
arrive at an age to enter on the active ſtage of
life: Its bleſſings will be handed down to poſterity; and in reſpect to many, I hope, will
be remembered as among the firſt means of
bringing them to the knowledge of ſalvation,
in that world where infinite grace condeſcends
to acknowledge what is done for the humble
poor, as done unto the Lord.

It is with pleaſure I remark, that what is
given to this eſtabliſhment promiſes certain
utility; as it is committed to gentlemen whoſe
humanity and good ſenſe, in the opinion of
their fellow-citizens, eminently qualify them
for the diſcharge of ſuch a truſt: And it is
with ſingular ſatisfaction, that I now tender
it on the thanks of all the humane and benevolent of the community, for their judicious,
faithful, and compaſſionate attention to the
management and application of the public
benefactions.

Gentlemen of the City Council! Raiſed as
you are, by public ſuffrage, to high and honorable office, and entruſted with the government and guardianſhip of the city; protectors
of the lives and properties, of the rights and
privileges of your conſtituents; it is not for
me to point out to you, the duties for which
the public voice hath declared you ſufficient.

It was an honor to some of your predecessors in office, which will never be effaced from the memory of the good and virtuous of the community, that they projected this design of a provision for orphan, outcast, and necessitous children; and by their exertions, encouraged by the countenance of the citizens at large, brought it into effect and operation. More brilliant undertakings might have procured them a more splendid applause: But none could better express the benevolence of their hearts. It is an honor devolved on you, to continue, to foster, and cherish their design and bring it forward to maturity. The peace, the prosperity, and good order of the city will be promoted by your common acts of government; but in no one respect do you contribute so much to either, as in your attention and countenance to this institution: And while you are framing just and beneficial regulations, in the administration of your office, in every other view, your known humanity, your wisdom, and your respect for whatever is truly amiable and interesting to the human heart, afford the best assurance to your fellow-citizens, that you will continue your particular attention to these adopted children of the public. Your own heart-felt satisfaction, in promoting a work of so much beneficence and public advantage, will be a reward superior to the highest popular applause. And at the same time, the work which so deservedly entitles you to the satisfaction of a self-approving mind, will ensure to you the esteem and approbation of the wise and good; and "upon you shall come the blessing of them that were ready to perish."

Gentlemen, Commissioners of the Orphan House! I am confident of the full approbation of my fellow-citizens, in saying, that in conducting this institution you have merited their sincerest thanks. It does honor to your feelings, that you have so cheerfully undertaken, and so diligently attended to this work of piety and labor of love. The effects of your attention appear in the order and regularity, visible in the management of this house; in the proficiency of the children, in those branches of learning, in which they are instructed; and, may I not say, in the general decency of their behavior. It does honor to your understanding, that you have incorporated into your plan for their education, an attention to the christian religion, on liberal principles, and particularly that it constitutes a part of their exercises to read the scriptures. By these means, you contribute to fortify them against the influence of those corrupt sentiments which spoil the morals, and destroy the comfort of so many poor, who by a negligent and loose education, are left ignorant of the bible, till they are turned out into the world to procure a subsistence for themselves. By these means you furnish them with a store of the most useful knowledge, acquaint them with a perfect system of morality, lay a rational foundation for their being actuated by worthy principles, when they grow up to maturity, and prepare them for meeting, with fortitude, the adversities they may have to contend with. The pleasure you must enjoy in contemplating these little dependents on your patronage, growing up to a qualification for useful employments, and the hope you entertain of seeing them, hereafter, acting an interesting part in society, must afford a satisfaction more easily conceived of than described. Proceed in your delightful task, and heaven will bless your labors, and give you your reward.

Children of this institution! Your patrons will indulge me in endeavoring to speak to you, according to your years and understanding. I look upon you with pleasure, when I consider you as children of the public care, comfortably provided for, and instructed; and more especially when I consider you as preparing to become good and useful members of society. I rejoice to think of that day, when you shall be grown up to years of discretion and manhood, when you shall make to the community the most pleasing and grateful return for their kindness to you, by living a life of industry and goodness. This will indeed be your own advantage; and you ought to consider, that it is for this purpose, among others, that God hath disposed the hearts of good people to take care of you and provide for you. Let me, therefore, put you in mind, that you are brought to this house to make you fit for some business, by which you may obtain a livelihood

for yourfelves, and in which you may be enabled to do good to others. The end will not
be anfwered, except you attend, with diligence,
to the inftructions you receive, and endeavor
to learn the habits of induftry here, while you
are young. I am forry when I think of thofe
of you who are without father and mother;
but God, who is the father of the fatherlefs
children, hath raifed up friends for you, who
are determined to watch over you, and do
you good; who are determined to do all that
can be done for you, to make you happy in
this world, and to prepare you for the world to
come. You ought to endeavor, in your turn,
to learn all that you can, that your teachers
and benefactors may be rejoiced when they fee
that you are making good progrefs, and that
their care of you is not in vain. Particularly,
let me requeft you to attend to what may be
taught you of the great things of religion.
" Remember your Creator in the days of your
youth." Strive to be acquainted with whatever you ought to know, in order to falvation.
Learn, and beg of God to help you to underftand the truths of his holy word. Read your
bibles with diligence, and forget not to pray
every night and morning, for the divine
blefling upon yourfelves, and upon thofe who
have the care of you. And, above all, remember that though you are children, you are fin-
ners, and muft be faved, if ever you get to
heaven, by Jefus Chrift, who loved little children, and had them brought to him that he
might blefs them. Pray to him, to help you

to come to him, that you may receive his
blefling, and be made the children of his
heavenly kingdom. Endeavor to love one
another, like children of the fame family.
Abftain from all falfehood and difhonefty,
from all differing and quarreling, and walk together in unity and peace. Strive to behave
well when you go abroad, that you may not
difhonor your teachers, nor be a reproach to
one another; and, that you may be beloved by
all good people, who wifh you well. And I
fervently pray that God may blefs you, in the
prefent life, and make you everlaftingly happy,
in the life to come.

END.

Orphanotrophium.

OR,

Orphans Well-provided for.

An ESSAY,

On the CARE taken in the
Divine PROVIDENCE
For CHILDREN when their
PARENTS *forsake* them.

With Proper ADVICE to both
𝕻arents and 𝕮hildren, that
the CARE of Heaven may be the
more Conspicuously & Comfortably obtained for them.

Offered in a SERMON, on a Day
of 𝕻rayer, kept with a Religious
Family, [28. d 1. m. 1711.] whose
Honourable PARENTS were lately by Mortality taken from them

By 𝕮otton 𝕸ather, D.D.

Pfal. xxxvii. 25. *I have not seen the Righteous
forsaken, nor his Seed, when asking for Bread*

𝕭ofton: Printed by *B. Green.* 1711

Preface.

IT was taken into Consideration, which among the Tribes of our Israel, had not yet been Considered in the Essayes to do Good, whereof we are Debtors to all the World. That of our Orphans presently appeared, and brought their Enquiry, What shall we do? Who were Agents for them, and what Providence of God it was that made them so, will be soon understood, by all that Peruse the Maxims and Reliefs here Provided for them. A Legacy for Orphans, to befriend them in their Temporal Interests, is to be had from a Doctor Godolphin. Behold here, A Legacy for Orphans, to befriend their Temporal Interests, and their Eternal too. Some Children that were made Orphans, caused me to Prepare it; and it may be more Parents, who See themselves Likely to leave Orphans, will Dispense it. Some will, it may be, leave it with other Tokens of their Love and Care, unto such as these, for whom it is intended as a Monitor and a Comforter. And it is not amiß, that wherever the Composure comes, the Occasion of it be Remembred; the Persons that Occasion'd it Live

in

Preface.

in this *Memorial*. In the *Mean time, the Writer* most heartily runs into the Opinion of the *Excellent* **Alting** ; Majus est in Ecclesia aliquid dixisse quod ad ejus ædificationem pertinet, quam Summa inter homines Gloria et Potestate gavisum esse.

If the Servants of GOD *could write as many Instruments of Piety, as the Hyperbolizing* Jews *tell us* R. Jochanan *did ; So many, that* if the Heavens were Paper, and all the Trees of the Forrest were so many Pens, they would hardly Suffice to Write them all ; *Truly, the Condition of this Miserable World would bespeak them all.*

For my own Part, the Little I have done this way, is but Little to what should have been done, if my want of Industry *and of* Capacity *were not, what it is.* But yet, if God will give me *Life and Leave, I will* hold *on my way, and in this Way of Serving the best Interests* Wax Stronger and Stronger. *And the Words of* Jerom, *shall give me as much Consolation as ever they gave unto* Hiltenius. Nunquam meum, juvante CHRISTO, Silebit Eloquium. Legant, qui volunt ; Qui nolunt, Abjiciant. Magis vestra Charitate Provocabor ad Studium, quam Malorum Detractione et Odio deterrebor.

The

The Orphans Patrimony.

Exhibited,

On a Day of PRAYER,

Kept in a Religious FAMILY,

With the Neighbourhood ;

Upon the DEATH of an Honourable FATHER, [*John Foster* Efqr.] Who Expired 9. *d.* 12. *m.* 1710, 11. And a Valuable MOTHER, [Mrs. *Abigail Foster*,] Who Departed, 5. *d.* 1. *m.* 1710, 11.

PSALM XXVII. 10.

When my Father and my Mother forfake me, then the LORD will take me up.

IN the Oracles of God, the Diftrefled Chriftian has that *Motto* provided for him ; *Not Forfaken.* Behold, A Bereaved Orphan challenging that Glorious *Motto* : *Not Forfaken.*

faken.   O Child of God, Thy Beſt *Father*
allows thy challenge ; And thou ſhalt not
be *Alone,* while thou haſt that *Father with
thee* !

Some of *My Neighbours,* who do me the
Honour, to reckon themſelves among *My
Children,* being lately *Forſaken* by a very
valuable *Father* and *Mother* within Three
Weeks of One another, have deſired that
You, My Hearers, may ſhare with *them,* in
the Entertainments of a Diſcourſe upon a
Text which they have wiſely choſen, as,
The Orphans Patrimony.

If One of the Ancients, would call our
Book of Pſalms, *A Divine Treaſury* ; and
another of the Ancients would call it, *A
Divine Armoury* ; Our *Orphans* will very
particularly find ſuch a *Supply* there, and
ſuch a *Defence,* as will juſtify the Appel-
lation.   Our *Orphans* are ſome of thoſe,
who like other *Children of Sorrow,* will
find the admirable Book, ſo agreeable to
their circumſtances, that they may well
apprehend it ſpeaking, as One of the *Fathers* tells us, every man may do, *Deſe in
re Sua loqui themſelves,* and very directly to their condition.   I am ſure, The
Scri-

Sentence now before us, will be notably found so !

The Illustrious *David*, being to direct the Fabrick of a *Temple* for God among His Chosen People, God gave Him a Vision of His Glorious *Temple* in the *Heavenly World*; Yea, in his Vision, there was One thing relating to that Glorious Temple, more clearly Exhibited unto *David*, than it had been unto *Moses* before him; namely, *The Throne of the Majesty of the Lord*, which is by *David* called, *The Chariot of the Cherubims.* The Servant of God hereupon gave order for a *Temple*, and a *Worship*, that should be agreeable to the *Patterns* he had Seen *in the Heavens* ; and Things that should *Serve as the Shadow of the Heavenly things.* Among the rest, he ordered an Office of *Singers* ; that so by *Singing* the Praises of GOD, and the Maxims of Truth, continually, a charming Imitation of the *Heavenly World*, might be carried on ; Yea, he not only appointed the *Officers*, but he also furnished them with *Materials*, with *Instruments* ; Under the Inspirations of God, he composed the *Songs*, wherein *Earth* was dignified with the *Echo's* of *Heaven.* The

The *Pfalm* now before us, is **One of** them ; and it was put into the Hands of the Church, after the Deliverance of this *Hero*, from Some terrible Diftreffes, which his Adverfaries (doubtlefs in the *Sauline* Perfecution,) had brought upon him. *Wicked Men* were his *Adverfaries*, tho' he were fo Good a Man ; Yea, for that cáufe they were fo ! They came upon him with a formidable Fury. Tell us, O *Pfalm of Triumphs*, Tell us, how he Encountred them. We have here a Commemoration of his Difpofitions in the Time of his Dif-treffes ; By which he would have the Church to underftand, (as MOLLER Ex-preffes it,) *Quibus rebus Munitus, tantam Hoftium multitudinem, et tantam Periculo-rum Magnitudinem, Suftinere ac Superare Potuerit* ; How he got fo well thro them all. From the Notes of *Thanksgiving* on the Harp of *David* here, the Judicious *Calvin* concludes, *The Pfalm was compofed after the Storm was over.*

Tis a *Singular Happineß* enjoy'd Some-times by Eminent Men of God ; No *Singu-lar Affliction* befals them, without Some excellent *Fruits of Righteoufneß* brought forth

forth unto the Church of God, on the occasion thereof. Perhaps they can *Contrive*, that it may be so ; they can *Foresee*, that it will be so. How easy, how welcome, is the most *Grievous Affliction* made unto them, from this consideration ! Oh ! their Glorious *Triumphs over Troubles* ! The *Life* which they find in the *Deaths* of their dearest *Relatives* ! The *Friends* which the Fiercest of their *Enemies* prove, in the *Kindnesses* of God, thro' their Enmity done unto them ! The *Honours* which *Libels* and *Slanders* heap upon them ! Happy *David* ! The whole Church of God fares the better for thy *Troubles.* The Incomparable *Songs of Zion*, were produced by thy *Troubles.* O *Happy Troubles* ! In this Issue of them, they cease to be *Troubles.* O *Joyful Sorrows* ! *Useful* Ones are so.

Contiguous to my Text, there is, First, A *Prayer* of the Psalmist. *Leave me not, neither forsake me, O God of my Salvation.* Truly, 'Tis a Sad Thing to be *Forsaken* of God. All Wretchedness is contained in that One word; *I will Forsake them,* saith the Lord. That Person is dreadfully *Forsaken* of God already, who does not

B   reckon

reckon this *Word of the Lord,* the moſt heavy *Burden* that ever a Sinner had laid upon him. *Wo unto them, when I depart from them,* ſayes the Good GOD. No *Evil* comparable to this ; In all the *Wo-Trumpets,* nothing, nothing ſo formidable ! Nothing to be ſo vehemently deprecated. *Orphans,* You above any in the World, have cauſe to make this Prayer inceſſantly, *O Great God, Leave me not !*

But I take notice of a clauſe accompanying this Deprecation, which is a Little obſervable. *Put not thy Servant away in Anger ;* I will not Propound the Interpretation which the Hebrew Writers have upon it : *q. d.* ' Don't leave thy Servant un-
' to the Sinful Cares of this World, which
' cauſe a continual *Wrath* and *Rage* in the
' Minds of Men. This indeed is a thing,
which *Orphans* may do well to be afraid of.
But I will think it worth the while to
mention a Gloſs, which one of the beſt Ex-
poſitors in the World, has upon it. *q. d.*
' Leave me not unto an *Angry* Impatience,
' under the Indignities which my Adverſa-
' ries heap upon me. One *Forſaken by God,* will be given up to *Anger* and Impatience,

ence, under Oppreſſions. But if an op-
preſſed man, *Ceaſe from Anger, and Forſake
Wrath*, and be a very Patient One ; *The
Lord is with thee, Thou mighty man of Patience.* And yet this Excellent Author, than
whom no man had more *Occaſion* for that
Expoſition, or more ſweet *Experience* of it,
returns to the more common Gloſs ; which
Suppoſes the *Anger of God* here Pray'd a-
gainſt. But then with his uſual Penetra-
tion he notes upon it ; That there is a Ta-
cit Confeſſion of *Sin*, in this Term of *Anger* : The Holy Soul, confeſſes, That he
had by *Sin* procured & incurred the *Anger*
of God ; made himſelf worthy to be rejected in His deſerved *Anger.*

Orphans, Theſe Hints may be of no little uſe to *You* ; otherwiſe I would not have
made a Pauſe upon them.

And now, in my Text ; Secondly, The
Prayer grows up into a *Faith* ; which indeed it ought to do ! One who *Prayes*
much to God, is *with God* ; and may *Believe*, that God will not *Forſake* him.

Our Pſalmiſt *Believes* this, and *therefore he Speaks*, as now he does.

Behold, the Memorable circumſtances,

in which this Faith is Exercised; *When my Father and my Mother forsake me.*

Some take this in the largest Sense imaginable; That under the Name of *Parents,* (*Omnia Consilia et Præsidia intelligit,*) he means all the *Humane Helps,* which the Children of Men, can have any Expectation from.   Tis very sure, A Religious Person left wholly destitute of all *Humane Helps,* may still hope in God.   1 know, The Word, *Asuppi,* which comes from what is here used in that clause, *The Lord will take me up,* does in the *Lexicons* of the Jewish Law signify, *An Exposititious Child:* Or One, *Qui tollitur de Platea, neque novit Patrem Suum, aut Matrem Suam.* How humbly, how meanly, does our Saint think of his own feeble Condition, when he looks on himself, as no less *Helpless,* than an *Exposititious Child,* cast out in the *Day that it is born* !

But we may very well Suppose our Psalmist Speaking of his *Natural Parents* ; take him *Literally.*   Be sure his *Parents* had now *Forsaken* him, as to any *Capacity* to do for him.   If they were *Living,* yet it was his Turn to do now for *them* ; they were

capable

capable to do no more for *him*. Thus *Geierus* upon it ; *Ipsi mecum Exules facti, ipse Eorum curam gerere cogor.* But it is also Probable, they had *Forsaken* him, as to their *continuance* with him.　Probably, they were *Dead* ; and he was become an *Orphan*.

But now the *Lively Faith* of the *Orphan*, when both his *Parents* were *Dead*! *The Lord will take me up.* If it be an Allusion to the Action of Tender *Parents*, who *Take up* the Weeping *Infant*, and Set it on their Knee ; the Intention of it, is ; *The Lord will make a better Provision for me, than ever my Parents could.*

But I Imagine that we have here an Elegant Allusion unto the Passage of the *Israelites* thro' the *Wilderness.* When the *Three* Squadrons of the *Hosts of the Lord,* had Passed on before, it was the Business of the *Fourth*, to *gather up*, the Sick, and the Weak, & the Lame, and Such as had been *Left behind* by them that Passed on before. I entertain this Tradition, tho' I do not *that* of the Four Images in their *Banners* ; which *Bochart* has well confuted.　Now, sayes our Psalmist ; ' *My Father & my Mo-*
　　　　　　　　　　　　　　　　　　　' *ther*

' *ther* are Paſſed on, towards the Degree
' of Bleſſedneſs in the Heavenly World,
' which is as yet attaineable by the Dead
' Servants of God.   They are got thro' the
' horrible *Wilderneß*, where they have Left
' me, in a Land of *Pits*, and of *Droughts*,
' and *fiery flying Serpents*.   But the God of
' my *Parents* is my God.   He will do
' more for me, than ever my *Parents* could.
' I ſhall have his Gracious Eye upon me,
' in this *Howling Wilderneß*, and He will
' not let me Miſcarry in the Difficulties of
' it.   He will do for me, as much as He
' has done for them ; and I ſhall get Safe
' to Bleſſedneſs after them.

   This then is the *Legacy* which in my
Adminiſtration, I am now to diſpenſe unto
our *Orphans*.

It ſhould be the Prayer of all Children, and it
   may be Peculiarly the Faith of Some Chil-
   dren, to be by the Mercies of the Lord
   comfortably Taken up ; when their
   Parents, yea, both of their Parents, do
   Forſake them.

                              I. The

I. The Firſt Propoſition, before us, and One that I don't care to Inſiſt upon, [For a cauſe you may well apprehend, in a Favour of God continued unto me, and a Part of the preſent Auditory, like what *Nazianzen* enjoy'd when he made his Funeral Oration on his Brother *Cæſarius* :] it is Qne of a Melancholy aſpect ; *That our Parents in the courſe of Nature muſt Shortly Forſake us.* The *Parents* between whom and us, there are thoſe Endearments, that they cannot *caſt us off*, yet muſt be *gone from us.* What *Benignity* would not let them do, *Mortality* will make them do ; & ſo to have *done with us.* What can hinder our *Parents* from, *Going the Way of all the Earth* ?

Indeed, Many Children do in this way *Forſake* their *Parents.* Tis a Frequent Thing for Parents to bury their *Children* ; Elſe we could not ſee, as they ſay we do, at leaſt Half the Children of Men dying Short of Twenty. The Two Sons of *Aaron*, are not the only Ones, of whom that Report may be given, which was of them ; 1 Chron. XXIV. 2. *Theſe dyed be-*
fore

fore their Father. Parents, Be not *Surpri-
fed* at this Calamity, but be *Prepared* for it.
God may call you to *Sacrifices* ; If you
are the *Priests* of the Lord, your *Lives*
must be full of *Sacrifices* ; In the *Deaths*
of your Children, Endured with a due Sub-
miffion, to the *Father of Spirits*, you offer
up fome of your Fatteft *Sacrifices.* Now,
My Friend, *I know that thou fearest God*,
if thou withold not thy *Ifaac*, but Sub-
miffively part with him, and yield him up,
when God fays, *I will have him out of thy
Hands.* If the Poor *Pagans*, could *Sacrifice* their Children, in cruel and horrid Fires
unto a curfed *Moloch*, O dear *Chriftians*,
how can you refufe to prefent yours in a
Flame of Love, unto the God, whofe they
are ; who does but remand *His Own* ; who
*Spared not His own Son, but delivered Him
up for us all!*

But that which is moft *Natural*, is for
the *Parents* to *Forfake* the *Children*, and *Go
First* ; go out of the World before them.
Thus we read ; Eccl. 1. 4 *One Generation,*
[or, that of the Parents,] *Paffeth away,
and Another Generation,* [Even, that of the
Children,] *Cometh on.* The *Parents* muft
make

make Room for the *Children.* There is the Glorious *Wisdom* of God expressed in such a *Recession* of the *Passing,* and *Succession* of the *Coming Generation* : *Destruction and Death,* or, the *Destruction* of Generations by *Death,* found the *Fame* of this *Wisdom of God* in our *Ears.* Thus the *Wisdom of God,* brings on a vast Number of Subjects, for Numberless Displayes of His *Glories* upon them. There is a Tradition among the *Egyptians,* That the *Salome,* of whom we read in the Gospels, in Some of her Discourses with our Saviour, asked Him ; *How long Mortality, should continue in the World* ? And He made that Answer, Μεχρις αν τικτωσιν αι γυναικες. *As long as Parents brought forth Children.* Most agreeably answered ! *Propagation* in a Sinful World, must make work for *Mortality.* [compare *Luk.* XX. 35, 36.]

If we could Prolong the Lives of our *Parents,* we would, Oh ! how gladly do it, and make them our glad Parents, unto more than the *Nestorean* years. And even when they come to ly more *Bed-rid* than the Patriarch *Jacob,* we would count their *Presence* with us, and the Opportunity it

C   gives

gives us to wait upon them, the *Bleſſing* and *Honour* of our Families. But had we never ſuch a *Multitude of Riches*, None of *us can by any Means Redeem* his Father, or his Mother, *that they ſhould Live for ever, and not ſee Corruption.*

However, we will *Sweeten* their *Lives*, it we can't *Prolong* them ; and by *Sweetning* them, as far as ever we can, *Prolong* them. We will make their *Lives* as comfortable as we can ; We will very often Study and Invent the moſt *Exquiſite wayes* we can to do ſo ; think, *What will make their Old Age moſt Eaſy to them ?* and bring it unto them. Tis what we Owe to them, to whom under God, we owe our *Lives*, and the *Principal Benefits* of our Lives.

But we can't alwayes keep off the Stroke of *Death* from our Parents. No, tho' with an Agony equal to what brought a Speech to the Dumb Son of *Cræſus*, we cry out unto the Deſtroyer, *Oh ! don't kill my Parent !* Nor, if we ſhould make a Tender, even of our own Lives, (as ſome have bravely done,) to ward off the Blow. This *King of Terrors* is the truly *Catholick King*. *Death* does Invade Mankind, as *David* once

once did the *Geshurites* ; *He smites the Land, and Leaves neither Man or Woman alive.* Be our *Parents* never so *Wise*, never so *Rich*, never so *Good*, nothing will keep off their *Mortality.* A *Solomon* himself must be a Practical commentary on his own Text ; *Man goes to his Long Home.* Tho' *Money* be the *Monarch* of this World, still *Death* has a greater Monarchy, and can't be bought out. Tho' the *Fear of God prolongeth Dayes*, yet the best of men may say, *I must shortly put off this Earthly Tabernacle*; and the Better they grow, the more they *groan* to do so. *Death*, like *Cæsar*, will *tax all the World*; and will not spare *Cæsar* himself. Even *Rulers* themselves, and they that have the *Power of Life and Death* over other Men, must themselves fall under the *Power of Death.* They that are called, *Gods*, must nevertheless *Dy like Men* ; and with wounded *Alexander*, disclaim their Titles. The *Shields of the Earth* are but *Earthen Shields. Death* is a *Wolf*, that will Sieze, even on the *Shepherds of the People.*

We must then look on our *Parents* as *Mortal*; with *Fear*, with *Grief*, so look up-
C 2   on

on them : *Cursed* the *Monster* that shall do it, with an Heart wishing of it ! But since they are *Mortal*, we will Hearken to them. The Charges of *Dying Persons* are weighty Things ; Those of *Dying Parents* have a Weight beyond that of Mountains. We will *Converse* with them as *Mortals* ; And especially, when things concur to render it more *Suspicious*, in every Converlation with them, we will have some Noble, and Holy Passage or other, which may be worthy of being Thought upon, if it should happen to be the *Last Time* of our being with them ; -- to think, *The Last Time I was with my Parent, this was the Thing we talked of* ! What if we should likewile put thole *Books* into their Hands, as well as discourle often with them on the *Points*, by which a *Meetneß for the Inheritance of the Saints in Light*, a Ripenels for the Heavenly World, may be most of all befriended in them ? We will also render their Expiring Lives, which *we* lo much delire, as *delireable* to *them* as we can ; Multiply the *Tokens* of our *Affection* to them. Our Apostle reckoning up Tranlgreßions against the Ten Commandments, the Tranl-
greffors

greſſors of the Fifth, he calls, *Murderers of Fathers, and Murderers of Mothers.* Children, If you don't *Honour* your *Mortal Parents*, you *Murder* them ; If you don't *Comfort* them, you anticipate, and precipitate their *Mortality. Why do ye ſuch things ? Nay, My Sons, Tis no good Report.*

I have only this to add. Since our *Parents* are *Mortal*, certainly, my Brethren, we ſhall conclude our ſelves to be as *Mortal* as they. Certainly, our Conſtitution differs not from theirs; we are of the ſame Original with them ; *Who can bring an Immortal thing, out of a Mortal ?* Our *Clay* can be no Stronger than theirs. This Intimation comes in the more Eaſily ; Becauſe it may be my Text will countenance it. Says our Pſalmiſt, *The Lord will take me up.* Whither ? Some Gloſſators add ; *Unto Himſelf.* Truly, If the Lord has *taken up our Parents*, out of this, into the Upper World, we may Expect, that we ſhall be *taken* after them. *Nos te Sequemur* ; was the *Farewel*, which the Old Romans took of their *Dead*; We take no other Farewel of our *Departing Parents* than this ; *We ſhall follow.*

Such

Such a sense of their own *Mortality*, will be very Particularly Seasonable and Serviceable, unto *Orphans*, who step into fair Estates on the Death of their *Parents*. T will help to *mortify*, the Lusts of a Proud, and a Vain, and a Worldly Mind, which may be too ready to stir, when much Wealth flows in at once upon the *Heirs* thereof. Children. *If Riches increase, O Set not your Hearts upon them. The Riches your Dead Parents have left you, O Remember, tis to Dying Children they have left them.*

II. I will proceed now unto a Proposition, which I can with much more Pleasure insist upon : [And you may be sure, with not the less, for having of my *Own Children*, in the Auditory !] Tis this ; *There are Children, whom God will Take up, when their Parents do Forsake them.* Tis what a Good God will do for *Orphans* ; *He will Take them up.* It implies, in one Word, a Kind *Providence* of Heaven, doing for the *Children* all that their *Parents* could have done, if they had Liv'd ; Yea, Perhaps all that they would have to be done. *Orphans* are in a *Pupillage*, wherein
GOD

GOD is their *Guardian.* A *Pupil* is one, who, *Caret Patre, sed non præsidio paterno.* He wants a *Father,* but in GOD, He has an Alsufficient *Father.* There is a Providence of God always at work every where in the World ; Yea, a *Special Providence* at Work about the Children of Men , More especially, about *Orphan Children.* There are Few Things in which the Providence of God is more conspicuous, than the *Care of Orphans.* Thus we read ; Psal LXVIII. ; *A Father of the Fatherless, is God in His Holy Habitation.* There is a wonderful Providence of God, at work for many Children, when their *Father,* and their *Mother* do *Forsake* them : and *Children* are wonderfully Provided for ! The Scarce miss their Parents, tho' the Departed Parents had a most unspeakable Fondness for them. *Gods Providence my Inheritance ;* 'tis a Motto very strangely Verified unto them. In that *Family* Particularly with which we are now Humbling our selves before the Lord, there has been an Experiment of it, never to be forgotten.

The Concern of Parents to provide for their *Children,* is One

Things in the World; *Nature* knows not a greater Paffion. I need not quote *Euripides* to tell you, αρ' ω ψυχη τεκια. *To all men Living, their Children are as dear as their very Lives.* But this dear word, *The Lord will take me up*: Oh! it carries the Tenderneſs of the Divine *Providence*, vaſtly beyond the Paffion of any Earthly Parents for their *Orphans.* The God of Heaven, will do for them far *beyond all they could ask or think*, of any Earthly Parents. It ſets the Great God, where, as my *Calvin* ſweetly ſayes, *Ipſe qui ſons eſt omnis Bonitatis, Longe ſupra cunctos mortales emineat* : He that is the *Fountain of all Goodneß*, will be better than the Beſt of Mortal Parents. God will go beyond meer *Nature*, yea, a thouſand times over turn the very *courſe of Nature*, ſooner than be wanting to our *Orphans*, whom He has *Taken up.*

Firſt; The *Orphans* are *fed*, are *cloath'd*, have a competent Relief of their *Neceſſities.* As our Saviour ſaid unto His Diſciples, whom He had ſent into a Wide World, with Nothing to Support them ; *Lacked ye any thing ? And they ſaid, Nothing*: This Teſtimony to the Faithfulneſs of God, may

may be brought in by very many *Orphans*; *We have had Nothing, and yet we have lack'd Nothing.* Of our God, we read, Pfal. CXLVIII. 9. *He gives Food unto the Young Ravens, which Cry.* The *Ravens*; A Fowl, for whofe Prefervation *Men* would as little concern themfelves, as for any of all the Feathered Tribe : The *Ravens* ; A *Fowl*, whofe Dams defert it almoft immediately ; Yea, do even expel it, and compel it to wander *for Lack of Meat* : The Cryes of thefe Young *Ravens* are conftrued by Heaven, as an Expoftulation upon the *Aftorgie* of the *Old* ones. God interpofes, He fhows them where to find their Nourifhment : Some fay much of it is bred in their very *Nefts*, before they leave 'em. None of them are Starved. The Word of our Saviour Places the *Sparrows*, as well as the *Ravens*, under the care of Provi..ence. And are not our Little Birds, when left *Orphans*, as much cared for ? Our & Their Saviour fays unto them ; Matth. VI. 31, 32. *Take no Thought, Saying, What fhall we Eat? or, what fhall we Drink? or, wherewithal fhall we be Clothed? For your Heavenly Father knows that Te have need of all thefe things.*

D   My

My Quotation is from *The Orphans Chapter* ; A *Chapter* which the Poorest Orphans may make a Living on. Orphans, Read over that *Chapter* more than an Hundred times !

Secondly. God so *Takes* up the *Orphans,* that they are *Brought up.* Their *Education* is provided for. God puts it into the Hearts of those the Law calls *Foster-Fathers,* or Mothers, [From the Old Saxon, *Festrian,* or Danish, *Fosterer,* whereof Perhaps the Latin, *Pascere,* may be the Original ; which signifies, *To Nourish* :] To *Foster* them, & Furnish them, & Cherish them. Such an one the Spanish Tongue well styles, *El Amo que cria* ; from the Hebrew, *Aman, To nourish.* The *Orphans* have a *Nurture* from such Friends. They are the *Foster-children* of Providence, in their Education ; *Alumni, qui ab aliquo velut a patre aluntur, sive victu, sive moribus, sive Doctrina* ; if you'l accept a Legal Definition of them. They have *Parents in Law,* which are *Parents in Love* ; and Redeem the too often Obnoxious Reputation of the *Step-father,* and the *Step-mother.* The *Pupils* have *Tutors,* and flourish under their careful

ful and skilful *Tuition.* Some of the moſt
Learned, and Famous Men, ſome of the
moſt accompliſhed Children in the World,
never had any thing done by their *Parents*
towards their *Education* ; Perhaps never
Saw them.

Laſtly. He *Takes them up* at laſt, into
the ſame *Heavenly World,* with their Godly
Parents. There is an Anguiſh in the
Minds of Godly Parents, leſt their Children *fall ſhort of Entring into the Reſt of
God.* They are in a *Travailing Anguiſh* for
their Children all their **Dayes,** to ſee a
Chriſt formed in them. It may be, their
cryes for the Grace of Heaven, to take hold
on the Hearts of theſe Children, were not
anſwered while they *Lived.* But, *There
is Light ſown for the Righteous.* Tis as yet
unſeen, under the *Clods.* But when the
Children are become *Orphans,* and the Parents are themſelves laid *Aſleep* under the
Clods of the Valley ; Providence all this
while is not *Aſleep.* Then the *Succeſs* appears ;
then the *Harveſt* arrives ; Then the Orphans are Savingly Awakened, & brought
home unto God their Saviour. And ere
long, they come in ſafe, to the *Fair Haven*

where their Parents are got in before them.

You will not wonder, if here I make a Pause, & Recommend it unto ORPHANS, To *Stand still & consider the wondrous works of God.* Orphans, Perhaps while you were yet *Infants* (even in the proper Etymology of the Term,) and *could not Speak* for your selves, your very *Infancy* did *speak* for you, and *bespeak* that Providence of God, which did very Kind Things for you. Now you *can Speak*, Oh! Let your *Mouth Speak the Praise of the Lord, and bless His Holy Name for ever, and ever.* Yea, Let all of you Reflect on the more than *Parental care*, which the Gracious and Marvellous Providence of God has hitherto taken of you. Make your Thankful Reflections on, and Confessions of the Providence, which has constantly watched over you for Good; Supplyed your *Wants*, Prevented your *Fears*, Raised you up obliging *friends*, dealt most Mercifully with you. Orphans whom God has *taken up*, Go over the Story of your Lives hitherto; and say, " O God, Thou hast taught me from my " Youth, yea, kept me from my Birth, and " hitherto I have seen thy wondrous
" works

" works ; Now alfo Forfake me not, O
" God, until I am Old, nor when I fhall
" be fo !

But that which I will pafs over to, fhall
be, An *Encouragement* unto *Dying Parents*,
[in which Number, what caufe have I to
reckon *my felf* !] concerning their *Orphans*.
There are fome Servants of God, fo Sick of
the World, that they could fcarce be any
other than *Unwilling to Live*, if it were not
for a Dread of what may befal their *Orphans* ; Be fure, nothing renders them fo
Unwilling to Dy, as their Sollicitude for
Thefe. Tis a moft frequent and Pungent
Uneafinefs on the Minds of *Dying Parents* ;
*What will become of my defolate Family ; and
how will my Forfaken Orphans be difpofed of ?*
But, Let us not be difcouraged. Thefe
Orphans, when *their Father and their Mother forfake them, God will take them up.*
Never be afraid. Caft them on the Providence of an *Heavenly Father.* Yea, *Caft
all your care* of them upon Him, for *He car-
eth for them.* Hear the *Father of Mercies,*
from Heaven making you that Invitation ;
Jer. XLIX. 11. *Leave thy Fatherlefs Children, I will preferve them, alive* ; and I will
deal

deal well with them. Our *Caryl* quoting that word, makes this very due Acclamation upon it; *A word from God, is a better, and a bigger Portion, than all the Wealth of this World!* At once, I would leave my *Orphans,* with such a *Faith* as this concerning them; "*When I received my Children, it* "*was with this Consolation,* That the King-"dom of my Saviour was Enlarged by their "coming into the World. I have given "them up to my Saviour; I have been de-"sirous and studious that they may know "my Saviour, and Serve my Saviour, "and be the Subjects of that Glorious "LORD. I now commit them into the "Precious Hands of my Saviour. I Be-"lieve that the whole World is under His "Government; the Earth is the Lords, "and the Fulness thereof. I am well af-"sured, that He does Govern the World, "very much by the Ministry of His An-"gels; and my Children shall have His "Angels to be their Guardians. And "now, Be not thou cast down, O my Soul, "nor be thou disquieted within me; Hope "in thy Saviour, for He will give thy Or-"phans cause to Praise Him: to Sing His "Praises.

III.

III. By the grasp of a Third Proposition, we shall take in all that we designed. It is, *That as it should be the Prayer of all Children, so it may be the peculiar Faith of Some Children, to be so favourably dealt withal.*

First ; You will easily grant me my First Assertion ; It should be the *Prayer* of *all* Orphans, That God would Mercifully *Take them up.* There is Argument enough, in the Quality of the World, wherein the Orphans find themselves. Orphans, You are left in an *Evil World* ; An Ungrateful, Abusive, Uncharitable *World* ; A *World* wherein *Iniquity abounds*, and the *Love of many waxes cold* ; and the Children of Men are *Wolves* to one another. Finding your selves in such a *World*, how can you do any other than Pray most Importunately ; *O Great God, Be thou my God, and do thou Take me up!* Tis a *Friendless World.* In such a World, *Orphans*, How can you Live without Multiplyed Repetitions of that *Prayer* ; *Lord, Be thou a Friend, and a Father to me!* Our Lord said unto those whom He had made His Children, Joh. XVI. 5, 6. *I go my way ; Because I have said so, Sorrow has filled your Heart.   But the Comforter will come.*   Truly, when your *Parents* are gone away from you, *Sorrow* may justly *fill your Hearts,* if you have not this to *Comfort* you, *My God will take me up* !

Secondly.   I carry the Point further than this, in a Second Assertion.   This may be the *Peculiar Faith* of *Some Orphans.* Indeed, it is *a Faith* to be countenanced in *All* Orphans whatsoever ; *God will take me up.*   God would not have any Orphans give way to *Unbelief.*   The Voice of God unto all Orphans is, *Trust in the Lord, and do Good, and Verily, thou shalt be fed.*   I will direct my Orphans to a Word, which every One of them all, are to lay hold upon : A Word worth more than the Richest Mine in *Brasile* !   Tis that ; Hos. XIV. 3. *In thee, the Fatherless findeth Mercy.   Hearken,* O all ye *Orphans, every* One *of you* ; Fall down before the Lord, and Profess unto Him, *O Great God, I rely upon thee, for thy Mercy to the Orphan.*

But yet, the *Faith* of *Some Orphans,* for the Divine *Favours,* may have peculiar Animations.   I will say, Of whom.

First

First. Such *Orphans* as have been singularly *Dutiful* unto their *Parents* ; these have singular cause to hope, That *God will take them up.* *Dutifulneß* unto Parents, is a Thing very usually and signally Recompensed unto the Children which have been Mindful of their Duty ; even *Recompensed in the Earth* : And when the Children become *Orphans,* Then particularly they reap some of the *Recompense.* Of the *Fifth Commandment* we read, Eph. VI 2 *It is the First Commandment, with Promise.* I agree with *Marckius* ; That the clause, *with Promise,* must be joyned, not with, *First,* but with, *Commandment.* It should be read ; *Which is the First Commandment, and with a Promise.* It may be called, *The First Commandment* ; because tis not only a *Principal* One, but also the very *First* in that Table of the Decalogue, which requires the Things our Apostle was now inculcating. The *Promise* annexed unto it, contains Blessings for *Orphans* in it. The *Parents* which have been gratified by the Dutiful and Obliging Behaviour of their *Children,* do Bless them in the Name of God, and Pronounce *Blessings* for them, which

F. they

they shall be left as *Orphans.* They say, *O my God, Be thou the God of these Children, and when I forsake them, do thou take up the Orphans!* There is an *Efficacy,* I had almost said, an *Authority,* in the *Blessings* of such *Parents.* I may the rather make this Remark, in that our *David* was a very *Dutiful Son.* One Instance of it, we read, 1 Sam. XXII.3. *He said to the King of Moab, Let my Father and my Mother, I pray thee, come forth and be with you.* He could never trust his *Parents* to the Mercy of *Saul,* whose *Tender Mercy* the *Priests of the Lord* had found to be *Cruelty.* It is likely the King of *Moab* had an Aversion for *Saul,* because of the Destruction he had brought upon the *Ammonites,* who were Brethren to the *Moabites.* Yea, *David* himself was by the Mothers side, akin to the *Moabites;* being descended from *Ruth* a *Moabitess.* Now he that had procured the King of *Moab,* to *Take up* his *Father* and his *Mother,* might well say, *The Lord will take me up, when I am forsaken by my Father and my Mother.*

Secondly, It may be peculiarly hoped, by *Orphans* whose *Parents* have *laid up a*
Good

Good Stock for them : ---- Dont miſtake me ; Leſt you do ſo, I will not finiſh the Sentence, without that clauſe, ---- *in the Remunerations of God.* Parents may lay up a *Stock* of *Wealth* for their Children, and lay up a *Curſe* with it : the *Providence* of **God** thereby but rendred an Enemy to the Orphans. If the *Wealth* were not honeſtly gotten, there is a *Blaſt* from God upon it, and upon them whom it falls unto ; the *next Heir* at furtheſt is the *Laſt.* There is an *Engliſh Proverb,* that Speaks very raſhly and rudely concerning the Happineſs of thoſe who are deſcended from ſuch *Hoarding Parents.* I will not pay ſo much Regard unto it, as to Recite it. But I will tell you how ſome underſtand that *Proverb of Iſrael ; Tho' hand joyn in hand, the wicked ſhall not be unpuniſhed;* Tho' the *hand* of the Father deliver over his Eſtate into the *hand* of his Offspring, yet the Puniſhment of *getting Riches & not by Right,* will cleave unto it. And I can tell of another *Sacred Proverb* that ſayes, *A juſt man walks in his Integrity* (and is a Righteous Dealer;) *his Children are bleſſed after him.* Whereas If there have been a notorious Injuſtice in

E 2

getting the Estate, there will be *Entailed* upon it, a Necessity of RESTITUTION, which the Enriched *Orphans* do so seldom Trouble themselves about, that an unavoidable wrath of God Pursues it ; The *Treasures of Snow* are melted before it. Or, if the *Successors* be of a Vitious Inclination, then all the Wealth Left unto them, serves only as a *Fuel* for their Vices. It had been better for the Wretches that their *Fathers* had left them no better than *Beggars.* *Poverty* with *Industry* left unto the *Orphans,* would have been a much greater kindness unto them. Whereas Now, they *receive a Sop,* and *Satan Enters into them.* The more *Enriched* they are, the more *Extravagant,* the more *Exorbitant* ; and the *Fork* Succeeds the *Rake.*

But now there are *Orphans,* whose Parents have laid up for them a *Stock* of *Better Things* ; even of *such Things as Accompany* a most *Remunerating Providence* of God. And in this case, the *Orphans* are dealt withal, as was one of their Brethren, of whom we read, Gen. XXV.11. *It came to pass after the Death of Abraham, that God blessed his Son Isaac.*

Firſt.

First. There are *Orphans*, whose *Parents* have laid up a *Stock of Prayers* for them. They were *Parents*, who, as *Job*, Chap. I. 5. *Continually offered up Offerings for his Children, according to the Number of them all*; So, have every Day mention'd every one of their Children by Name unto the Lord, in their *Continual Supplications*; and particularly inserted this Petition for them, *When their Father and their Mother does Forsake them, Lord, Let thy Fatherly care of them take them up*: *Parents* who have often Set apart *whole Dayes*, to Pray and Fast and Weep unto the Lord, for His Mercies unto their Children; and Perhaps *One Day* sometimes more especially for *One* of them, and then *Another* for *Another*; *Parents* who would carry their Children alone with them, into *Secret Chambers*, & there first of all Speak the most Heart-breaking Things unto them, and then cause them to kneel down by them, and be the Witnesses of the *Prayers* and the *Tears* which they poured out before the Lord, on their behalf. The *Abraham* has kept crying unto the Lord, *Oh! That my Son may Live in thy Sight*! The *David* has kept crying, unto the Lord; *Oh*!

Ob! Give to my Son a Perfect Heart! The *Monica* has Pursued the matter with such a Restless Vehemency, that it must be said unto her; *Tis impossible a Child of so many Prayers and Tears should perish after all.* When these *Parents* are *Dead,* their *Prayers,* in the Fruits of them, *Live* after their *Death.* *Orphans* of such Parents, You are they who above others may believe, *The Lord will take me up!*

Secondly. There are *Orphans,* whose *Parents* have laid up a *Stock of Alms* for them. They were Parents who *devised Liberal Things;* Their *Alms went up as a Memorial before God,* and will be *Remembred;* Even with a Requital to their Orphans. *Parents* they were that laid up a *Portion* for their Orphans in *Bags that wax not old;* in a *Chamber* that no Potent and Shameless *Robber* can Prey upon ; and, *Casting their Seedcorn into the moist Ground,* it is found *after many Dayes,* even by those who do come after them. It is among the *Songs of Zion,* which we Sing in the *Strange Land,* where we leave our *Orphans* ; Psal. CXII. 2, 3, 9. *His Seed shall be Mighty on the Earth; the Generation of the Upright shall be be blessed ; Wealth and Riches shall be in his House.* Whence all of this ? *He hath dispersed, he hath given to the Poor, his Righteousness endureth for ever.* The Children of such *Parents,* Let them not *hang their Harps upon the Willows. Orphans,* You may above others believe, *The Lord will take me up* !

Thirdly. There are *Orphans,* whose *Parents* have laid up for them, a *Stock of Services* to the Kingdom of God. An *Obed-Edom* does Good Offices for the *Ark* of God ; and we read, *God Blessed the House of Obed-Edom.* He had a Numerous Progeny ; All of them Employ'd in the House of God ; Laudably discharging their Employment ; yea, Advanced unto considerable Dignity, being *made Rulers thro' the House of their Father. Jehojadah* does Good Offices for the *House* of God. He had a *Son* that proved an Eminent Man. Parents are at work for their own *Families,* when they are at work for the *Church* of God. Let them *Do Good in Israel* ; and they will *Do Good* for their Orphans. We read ; Prov. XIV. 26. *In the Fear of the Lord, is Strong Confidence, and his Children shall*

shall have a place of Refuge. The Jewish Rabbi s, take, *His Children,* to mean, *The Children of the Man who has the Fear of the Lord.* The *Fear of God* will inspire a Man with courage to do all possible Services for the *Church of God.* Such a Servant of Christ may be *Confident,* his *Children* shall be under a special *Protection* of the Lord. *Orphans,* You may now believe above others, *The Lord will take me up!*

And yet Even to the *Orphans* of *such Parents,* there must be given this awful Admonition. Children, By *Impiety,* You may *Forfeit* all of these Consolations. The Character of your Parents, will but aggravate your confusion, if you take to the courses of *Impiety.* The Holy God, will He *Take you up,* O wicked Orphans ? No, you may fear, He will *Throw you down;* yea, cast you down to the Place of *Dragons.* By *Impiety* you may cut off the Entail of *Blessings.* You may, *Because of Unbelief be broken off.* And unto such Orphans, *Ye are as the Children of Ethiopians unto me, saith the Lord.*

In my Passage to the mainly intended APPLICATION of these things, I am stop'd

stop'd by Some Objects of Compassion,
standing in the way, and looking to be a
little Spoken to.

My Doctrine must Perform that Act of
Pure and Undefiled Religion, Jam. I. 27. *To
Visit the Widows in their Affliction,* as well
as the *Orphans.* We read, *There were many
Widows in Israel.* We see, there are so a-
mong our People. The GreatGOD joyns
the *Widows* with the *Orphans* in His *Comforts.* We will not Separate them in our
Speaking Comfortably to them. Oh ! Let
not the *Forsaken* Handmaids of the Lord,
give way to hopeless Dejections, to sinking
Despondencies. The compassionate God,
who *Takes up* the *Orphan,* will not *Cast off*
the *Widow.* Our Great Saviour on His
Cross, was Mindful of a Poor *Widow,* and
said unto her *Nephew, Behold, Thy Mother !*
Nor is He now on His *Throne* become un-
mindful of the *Widow;* *A Judge of the Widows,* is HE in *His Holy Habitation.* Indeed, You have a Dark Time of it ; it may
be the *Hour and Power of Darkness* with
you : You are *Afraid of all your Sorrows.*
Your Moans are, *The Almighty has dealt
very bitterly with me.* And, *The Lord hath*

F   *made*

made me desolate and faint all the Day!
But One Burden that now appears unto
you of all the most Insupportable, is ; *How
shall I and mine be provided for !*   Now,
Be comforted, O *Forsaken* Ones ; and, *Cast
your Burden on the Lord* ; *He will sustain
you!*   The *Providence* of God will have a
Special Eye upon you ; You shall be *Provided for.*   I bring you this Day, a Word,
which will fully come up, to all your Distresses.   Tis that ; Ha. LIV. 5. *Thy Maker
is thy Husband*; *The Lord of Hosts is His
Name* ; *And thy Redeemer, the God of the
whole Earth.*   We see Things done
for a Multitude of Poor *Widows* every
day before our Eyes ; They are not
Miracles ; But they are very little Short
of *Miraculous.*   There will be such Things
done for *You* also, by the LORD, whose
Mercy Endureth for ever.   Only be prepared withal, to do the Part of, *The Widow
indeed*; which, You know, is, *To abound
in Supplications night and day* : Therein
feeding on, and Pleading of that Precious
Word ; Psal. XXXIV. 10. *They that seek
the Lord, shall not want any Good Thing.*
The best of your *Earthly Friends* has Forsaken

saken you. Now, do not you *Forsake* that
Friend that is Infinitely Better than him.
Go to your Glorious LORD in the Heavens, who has *betrothed you unto Himself*
in His *Covenant*. Mention to Him, all
your Temptations. Tell Him of all the
Afflicts you. *Pour out your Souls before Him*
There was a Vertuous *Woman*, who was
one of a *Sorrowful Spirit* But you read,
She Poured out her Soul unto the Lord, and
then she was *no more sad*. Unto the Vertuous *Widow*, we will commend Our Relief; Psal. XCIV.19. *In the Multitude of my
Thoughts within me, thy Comforts delight my
Soul.*

But there is now nothing to detain us
from the Two Applicatory Articles,
which you are waiting for.

I begin with,

I. An Advice to PARENTS.

Let PARENTS now be much Appre-
hensive of this; That they are to Look to
Forsake their *Children*, and leave them Or-
phans. When you look on your Children,
Oh, how often be watch'd with Rebukes!
Thou dying, shalt in a point from them
Soul, *I know not how soon I shall be gone*

them. Therefore *Seasonably,* Therefore *Immediately,* Do those Things for them, to which you must be Reasonably awakened by such Thoughts as these. Leave nothing undone, that you may do before you Dy, for the Welfare of your Children after you are *Dead.*

Make a *Testamentary Provision* for them. Let your *Wills* be made, and in a Good order always Lying by you. You will not, I assure you, *Dy the Sooner* for it; you will the *Easier.* Perhaps, it may be a Discretion in you also to find out *Patrons* for each of the *Children.* Find out a Prudent, Charitable, Affectionate Person, who shall wish well to you & yours, and either by an Engaging Discourse with such an One, or by a Letter to be delivered after your Decease, to him, Request him, to become a Sort of a *Ward* unto the *Orphan,* and use a Kind Inspection on the Childs conduct and condition. What the *Civil Law* of old, mentioned about, *Curatores* for Children, till they were Twenty five years of Age, may lead Parents, to a well-contrived Provision, that none of their Children may in their Non-age want Fatherly *Overseers* and *Counsellors.* But

But that which is yet more to be Endeavoured, is, That the Children may have such an *Education* as may render them *Acceptable* to God and Man ; such as may render them *Serviceable* in their Generation. The more you accomplish them with *Arts*, that may Enable them to *Support themselves*, when they are left unto themselves ; the more accomplish'd they are with *Beneficial Arts* and *Sciences* ; the more *Faithful Parents* are you. Among the *Jews* of old, Let the Children have never so *Polite* an *Education*, still their Parents would have them taught some *Opificial* and *Beneficial Mystery*, by which they might Support themselves among Mankind, if *Hard Times* ever shall force them to it. Certainly, If *Paul the Tent-maker* were hearken'd to, he would say some Things to *Parents* on this head, that would be worth hearkning to. In this affair, *Wisdom* would find out, *Witty Inventions* !

But that which most of all calls for your Endeavours, is ; That they may be *Effectually called* into the Actions of a *Believing* and *Repenting* Soul ; and into confirmed Resolutions of a *Godly*, and *Sober*, and
Righ-

Righteous Life ; and into such a consent unto the *Covenant of Grace,* as will *bind their Souls up in the Bundle of Life.* To this purpose, *Quickly,* and *often* call upon them ; and *Call upon GOD* for them. With all possible Solemnity and Inculcation, lay upon them the *Charges* of God ; 1 Chron. XXVIII 9. *Know thou the God of thy Father, and Serve Him with a Perfect Heart, and a Willing Mind* Or, what the *Mother* should say to the *Child of her Vows.* And it may not be amiss for you, to Prepare in Writing for them, those *Lessons & Counsils,* by which you would have them to Regulate their Lives, after you are departed from them. How *Forcible* will the *Right Words* of the *Parents,* be upon the *Children,* when they are Left unto them under the Advantage of being their *Dying Charges!* The most Eloquent Orators of old, going to Write *wholesome Things* for Young Persons, have with an Ingenious *Fiction* put their *Pens* into the Hands of the *Dead Parents* to the Young Person. Truly, the *Pens* of *Dead Parents,* when *Ready,* without any *Fiction* such, are as Lively and as Cogent and as proper Engines

gines to lay the *Bonds of Piety* on the *Orphans* as any that can be thought upon. Or, if you judge your selves not able to Write so Pertinently or Pungently with your own *Pens*, you may Bequeath such and such *Books* unto your *Orphans*, as may most fully Speak, what you would have Spoken to them. In these things, *Your selves being Dead, will yet Speak* unto your *Orphans*.

Having done all this, *Now* by an Act of a Glorious *Faith*, chearfully *Commit* your *Children*, unto the care of your Great *Saviour*; Beg of Him, Trust in Him, to *Take them up.* And say for *Them*, as well as for your selves; *O my Saviour, I know whom I have Believed, that He is Able.* [An, Lord, Thou art Able!] *to keep what I have committed unto Him.*

This is all that I can think of doing for them.

There must now follow,

II. An Advice to ORPHANS.

But now, Let ORPHANS make sure of it, that when their *Parents* do *Forsake* them, the *Lord will take them up.* O Forsaken Children, Tremble, Tremble, at being

For-

Forsaken of GOD. There is a Promise of GOD, in which I Exhort you, to value an Interest, above all that was ever yet seen in the richest Inventory ; Heb. XIII 5. *He hath said, I will never Leave thee, nor Forsake thee.* Tho *Your Father and your Mother forsake you,* you are still Happy, if God will please to *Take you up.* Now that you may enjoy this Happiness, attend unto the *Nurture and Admonition of the Lord.*

I will *Premise* & *Presume* Two Things.

First, It is to be taken for granted, *Orphans,* we could not be so Abominable as to *Desire* the Death of our *Parents,* and we cannot now be so unnatural, as not to *Lament* it. We are *True Mourners,* Mourners in *Heart* as well as in *Habit.* God sees the Frame of *Heart,* with which the *Mourners walk about the Streets.* We walk after our *Dead Parents,* with the *Mourning of the Floor of Atad !*

Secondly, We Loath & Judge our selves before the Lord, for all that ever was *amiss* in our carriage towards our *Parents,* before their Death. Altho' we carried it never so *well* to them, we might have done *Better.* If we never heard them chide us, yet we

may

may fee caule to chide our felves for the
Defects in our Good Behaviour towards
them: we are always Defective in all we
do. If we have ever grieved them at all,
it fhould now be a grief to us, little fhort of
Inconfolable. *Petrarch* very properly
made this one of his beft *Remedies*, when
Dead Parents were Mourned for. *My Fa-
rent is dead*! Well, *Coluifti Parentem, et cum
licuit pia femper in illum officia congeffifti :*
You carried it well to them ; did you not ?
Yet there is enough to humble us.

But they are fome other Directions,
that are chiefly to be infifted on.

I Let *Orphans* firft of all fecure this,
That the Great **GOD** be their *Father*, fince
they are deprived of their *Parents*. You
have been more than a Thoufand times
minded of fuch a Priviledge as that of, An
Adoption by GOD. Children, There is
nothing, Oh! Nothing of fuch importance
for you, as this Priviledge. *To become the
Adopted Children of God.* Now, you are
well-apprifed of the way to obtain this
Priviledge ; An *Efpoufal* to the Eternal
SON of God, brings you into it. You

read ; Gal. III. 26. *Ye all are the Children of God by Faith in Christ Jesus.* You read ; Joh. I. 12. *As many as received Him, to them gave He Power to become the Sons of God, even to them that Believe on His Name.* Well then ; Orphans, O *Set your Hearts* unto this thing ; *It is your Life!* The Son of God makes unto you His aſtoniſhing overtures ; The aſtoniſhing Propoſals of your Great Saviour are ; *Child, Art thou willing to be Mine! Shall I take Poſſeſſion of thee: Wilt thou Live upon my Stores? And wilt thou by me bring forth Fruit unto God?* Oh! Don't Reject theſe Motions. With an aſtoniſhed Soul, Comply ; and Reply, *Lord, I am willing! Oh! Do thou make me willing! I am Thine; Save me!* From this Moment, thou art Eſpouſed unto thy Redeemer ; *His Father is thy Father, His God is thy God!* From this Moment, ſure of being well provided for ; ſure of a *Father* that will never *Forſake* thee: ſure of a *Father* that is *from Everlaſting to Everlaſting.* And, *from this time,* thou mayſt ſay unto God, *Lord, Thou art my Father, and the Guide of my Youth.*

But now, My Orphans, To keep up the
Aſſurance

Assurance of your *Adoption*, You must continually pay to the Blessed GOD, the Respects which are due to such a *Father*. You must render it unquestionable, That the Blessed GOD is your *Father*, by the Disposition of His *Children* operating in you. He sayes, Mal. I. 6. *A Son honoureth his Father; if I be a Father, where is my Honour?* If you would see the plain Evidences of it, That *God is your Father*, You must then *Honour* Him. You must be Afraid of *Sin*, which is a *Dishonour* to Him. You must be Troubled at the *Dishonour* which is done Him in the wickedness of other People. You must place your *Dependence* on Him for every Thing. You must Refer your selves to His *Disposal* in every Thing. You must yield a most entire *Obedience* unto Him, and *have Respect unto all His Commandments*. And you must be *Followers of God as dear Children*. *Orphans*, Do such Things, and you shall never want a *Father*. You shall also be before the Lord, as *One whom his Mother comforteth*.

I will conclude this, with an uncommon Hint upon it.

There

There is a very Surprising passage, which I find quoted, of the Ancient *Jewish Rabbi's*; That God in the Scripture, pleases to call Himself, *Our Brother*; and that hereby it was intimated, That the *Messiah*, who is God, should also take the Nature of *Man*, and be born of a *Woman*. To prove this, they bring that Scripture; Prov. XVII.17. *A Brother is born for Adversity.* Ah, My Poor Children; Make sure of an *Interest* in your Saviour, by putting your selves under His conduct. Your Saviour will condescend then to be as your *Elder-Brother*. His *Father* will be your *Father.* In your *Pupillage* you must look for *Adversity*. Behold, A Matchless *Brother born for your Adversity* !

II. Let *Orphans* go unto the Great GOD, as unto their *Father*, in all their *Wants*, as they did use to go unto their *Parents.* You are now Perhaps wishing, *O that it were with me, as in Months past, when I was in a Tabernacle, which had those Lights of God in it, that are now Extinguished! How would I go unto a Parent, that would have Enlightened me, and accommoda-*
ted

ted me, *in all my Difficulties!* Well, Children, Tho' you cannot go unto your *Parents*, you have a GOD still to go unto. And the more you go to Him, *In forma pauperis*, or as *Poor Orphans*, the more welcome to Him! If the *Spirit of Adoption* be in you, He will be a *Spirit of Supplication* in you. You will visit your *Heavenly Father* with your *Prayers* every day. You will make your *Prayerful Visits* unto Him, in every Thing. When any Thing ails you at any time, You will think; *I will go tell my Father of it.*

That I may the better describe the Deportment, which is to be Expected from you, I will make some observation of a *Star of the first Magnitude* in the Firmament of the Scripture; Gal. IV. 6. *Because you are Sons, God hath sent forth the Spirit of His Son into your Hearts, Crying, Abba, Father.* Our *Filial Familiarity* in Approaching unto God, is here expressed in the same Words, that our dear JESUS used unto Him. And the *Oxford Paraphrase* has a Guess, That the Expression might be taken up, in conformity to our Saviour. *Orphans,* You may with a *Filial Familiarity,* make

make your Approaches unto God ; your
dear JESUS has led you the way ; Go as
your Saviour did, and go in His Name.
There is a further Thought of *Luthers* upon it, which you will doubtless find Ex-
emplified.   Here is first used a foreign
Term, *Abba*; a Term in a Strange Language, the *Syriac* : Then comes on, a more
Familiar Term, a Vernacular one.   Thus,
*Initium tantæ erga Deum Fiduciæ, homini-
bus insolitum ac plane peregrinum.* At first
it will seem Strange unto you, to call the
Holy GOD, your *Father. What ? Such
a Wretched, forlorn, filthy Sinner as I am, go
to the Holy God as my Father, and expect
from the Holy God the Kindness of a Father !
O Strange Allowances, which the Grace of
God makes unto me !*   But go on ; Pray on ;
Hope on ; The Thing will grow more *Familiar.*   Anon you will plainly understand it ; plainly say, *Doubtless, Doubtless, O
Lord, Thou art my Father ; Tho' my Father
be now Ignorant of me, and my Mother acknowledge me not ; Thou O Lord, art my Father, thro my Redeemer.*   I will bestow
one Touch more upon it.   One of our
Great Literators, the Renowned *Selden*,
having

having searched into the ancient Laws of *Succession* and *Inheritance*, reports to us, That it was Lawful for a *Freeman* to accost another *Freeman*, with the Name, *Father*; and thus complementally Invite him to treat him with all the Favours of an *Adoption*. If the Gentleman thus complemented, would own the Title, and use the Name, *Son*, unto him who thus courted it; *This* being proved, a Right of *Succession* and *Inheritance* would be convey'd unto that Person. But Persons in a *Servile State*, might not presume to use this Compellation unto any one that could bequeathe any thing unto them; it affronted one of any Fashion, thus to offer the bringing a Mark of *Servility* upon his Family. Here may now be an Allusion to that Custom. They that were *Servants* under the *Law*, are brought into *Liberty* by our Lord JESUS CHRIST; Such *Liberty*, that they may bespeak a *Father*; yea, the most Glorious *Father* that ever was. The *Spirit* of God Himself, which also is the *Spirit* of the Lord JESUS CHRIST the *Son* of God, acknowledges them to be the *Children* of God, by enabling them to go

unto

unto Him as their *Father.* Orphans, make use of this your *Liberty*; prove your selves the *Children* of God, by repairing to Him, with *unceasing Supplication.*

III. Let *Orphans* take more *Satisfaction* in the Great GOD their *Father,* than ever they took in their *Parents.* It was the just Exclamation, 1 Joh. III. 1. *Behold, what manner of Love the Father has bestowed upon us, that we should be called, the Sons of God.* I will now say; Behold, *Orphans,* Behold, what a Satisfaction the *Love of God* has bestow'd upon you, That tho' your *Father* (and your *Mother*) do *Forsake* you, yet you have a transcendently Better *Father,* that never will *Forsake* you! *Nulli fit Injuria, cui Deus Praeponitur.* You have a *Father,* not only more *Able* to do you Good, than the *Parents* of which you are now bereaved; A *Father* that can *Supply all your Wants from His Glorious Riches*; A *Father,* to whom you may say, *O Lord, I know that thou canst do every thing*; A *Father,* that will One day bring you to *Inherit all things.* But you have also a *Father* that will be more *Tender* of you.

Shall

Shall I fay, your *Heavenly Father*, will be as *Tender* of you, as ever your *Parents* could be ? As Ready to hear you and help you, in all your *Uneafineffes* ? He has permitted me to fay fo. Plal. CIII. 13. *Like as a Father pitieth His Children, fo the Lord pities them that fear Him.* Yea, I have a Permiffion to fay more than this. Call to Mind, How gladly your *Parents* did ufe to do for you, while they were yet with you; and think, *It is much more Pleafing unto my God, that I fhould ask Him to do for me!* What Ravifhing words are thofe! Matth. VII. 11. *If ye that are Evil, know how to give good Gifts unto your Children, how much more fhall your Father which is in Heaven, give good Things to them that ask Him ?* And, Ifa. XLIX. 15. *Can a Woman forget her Sucking Child, that fhe fhould not have compaffion on the Son of her Womb? Yea, they may forget ; yet I will not forget thee.* If you had offended your *Parents*, yet upon a Penitent Confeffion, how readily did they *Pardon* your offences ? Child, Go to the Merciful God with a Penitent Confeffion of thy Mifcarriages, and with a contrite Heart fay, *Father, I have*

H　　　　　　　　　　*finned*

sinned against Heaven, and in thy sight !
Thou wilt much more find Him, *A God
Ready to Pardon*.   When you told your
Parents of any Need wherein you were to
be *Defended* from such as would have hurt
you ; with what a zeal did they appear to
Defend and *Shelter* you ?   Child, If any
ill People seek thy Ruine, go make a Re-
monstrance unto the Lord, and say, *O my
Father, Help me, or my Enemies will rejoyce
over me* !   Thou wilt find thy self Shelter-
ed under the *Shadow of His Wings* ; He
will say unto thee ; *Fear not, I am thy
Shield*.   Orphan, Thy *Heavenly Father* will
open the Rich Stores of His Goodness to
thee, with more *Alacrity*, and more *Liberality* than ever thy *Parents* did of Theirs.
And if thou canst but bring a *Prayer* unto
Him, Lo ! He has put into thy Hand, the
Golden Key of the Stores !   The God who
so often threatens to punish them, who do
not *Judge the cause of the Fatherless*, will
Himself, especially when Sought unto,
most certainly *Plead their Cause*.

My *Orphans*, There is One vast Kindness which your *Heavenly Father*, will upon your Asking, do for you, beyond what
would

would or could be done, by all the Parents
upon Earth. You Read; *Luk. XI. 13. If
ye being Evil, know how to give good Gifts to
your Children, how much more will your Heavenly Father give the Holy Spirit unto them
that ask Him?* I will show you now from
hence, how to *Order your cause before Him;*
how to *fill your Mouths with Arguments;*
how to Fetch down, what will bring all
Blessings with it, & what could not be had
from the Kindest *Parents* in the World.
Thus manage the suit. 'Lord, If I should
' have gone to my *Earthly Parents,* and
' say, *My Parent, There is one thing that
' would make me Perfectly and for ever Hap-
' py; and it is a thing that you can do for
' me, by Speaking one Word; will you please
' to Speak it?* I am sure, they would have
' done it; I am sure, they could not have
' deny'd me. Now the *Heart* of the
' Kindest Parents on Earth, is not to be
' compared unto the Lords. Wherefore
' I now come, and say unto thee, *O my Fa-
' ther, There is One thing that would make
' me wondrously Happy. One word of Thine
' can do this thing for me. Yea, and I am
' sure, tis infinitely pleasing unto thee, that I*
H 2 'shou'd

' *fhould ask for this thing.* Tis, That thou
' wouldeſt pleaſe to beſtow thy *Holy Spi-*
' *rit* upon me !

What, Oh ! What, will the *Heavenly
Father* do, for the *Orphans,* which thus
draw near unto Him !

I will add only This. He is, Iſai. IX 6.
The Everlaſting Father.   Once yours, and
you never *Loſe* Him.   You have *Loſt* the
Parents, whoſe *Breath was in their Noſtrils* !

IV. Let *Orphans* Religiouſly ſtand unto the *Covenant* of God, which thro' Religious *Parents,* they have convey'd unto
them.   If *Parents* that had a part in the
Covenant of God *forſake you,* they leave
that Warning with you, which One ſuch
once did unto a Son ; *If thou forſake Him,
He will caſt thee off for ever.*   Orphans of
Iſrael, You muſt Reſolve, That the God
of your *Father,* and of your *Mother,* ſhall
be *your God.*   With what an Awe of the
Holy Covenant, was it ſaid by *Jacob, The
Lord ſhall be my God,* when the Lord had
ſaid unto him, *I am the Lord God of thy Father* !   And by *David, O Lord, I am thy
Servant,* becauſe he could ſay, *I am the Son*
of

of thy Hand-maid! The Choice and the Voice of such *Orphans,* ought to be that ; *Exod.*XV 2. *The Lord is my God, and I will prepare Him an Habitation ; my Fathers God, and I will Exalt Him.*

There is a COVENANT of *Grace* : Tis thus to be conceived of. The Great GOD engaged unto our Saviour to *Assist* Him, and *Accept* Him in His Undertaking to bring His Chosen People unto Blessed-ness. Our Saviour Undertook, That He would make *Expiation* for the Sins of His People ; and then, that He would bring them Home unto God ; *Enlighten* them, *Sanctify* them, Write *His Laws* in their Hearts, Help them to walk in *His Wayes,* Embitter their *Sins* unto them, Incline them to the Things that *Please God,* Make them Victorious over the *Flesh,* and the *World,* and the *Devil*; and anon *Raise them from the Dead.* This *Covenant of Redemption,* being propounded unto *You,* with an Invitation unto you to receive the *Sure Mercies* of it, becomes the *Covenant of Grace.* You are now to come into the *Covenant of Grace,* by becoming Willing, to have the Blessed JESUS for your *Prince of Life,* and to

to be Saved and Ruled by Him, in the Methods Established, by the Eternal Agreement between God the Father and your Saviour. Declare, *O Great God, I am Willing, Thou hast made me Willing, to belong unto that Body whereof thy Blessed* JESUS *is the Head; I am Willing to be Thine according to the Covenant thou hast made with Him; & to be by His Lovely Hands brought home unto thee.* Make this Declaration, *O Children of the Covenant.* You should be moved unto this Transaction, by considering; Your *Parents* were in this *Covenant*; Yea, They *Laid hold* on it, not only for *Themselves*, but also for *You.* And they brought you unto the *Baptism* of the Lord, that so being under the *Seal* of the *Covenant*, you might never want a *Monitor* of your Duty. *Orphans,* If you prove *Apostates* from the *Religion,* and *Covenant* of your *Parents*, God will punish you as *Deserters.* Their *Covenant* shall be your *Condemnation.* The *Water* that *Baptised* you, shall Scald your Guilty Souls beyond a River of burning Sulphur. *If any Draw back, my Soul shall have no Pleasure in him, saith the Lord.* Oh! Let my *Orphans*
never

never forget that Word; Pfal.CIII.17,18. *The Mercy of the Lord is from Everlasting to Everlasting upon them that fear him, and His Righteousness unto Childrens Children.* But unto whom? *Unto such as keep His Covenant, and unto those that Remember His Commandments, to do them.*

V. Let *Orphans* not Forget the Holy In-structions, and those Truths and Wayes of God, in which their Pious *Parents* have Instructed them. There is One Word, which, Oh! That it were more frequent-ly fulfilled among us! Gen. XVIII. 19. *He will command his Children after him, & they shall keep the way of the Lord.* How accurately did the Wise Man keep in Re-membrance, what his *Father taught him, and said unto him;* and the *Prophecy which his Mother taught him!* It shew'd his Wis-dom to do so; it caus'd his Wisdom. It is thus Exprets'd; Prov. VI. 20. *My Son, keep thy Fathers Commandment, & forsake not the Law of thy Mother.* If we take it for the Precepts of God, then by, *The Fathers Commandment,* some will understand, the *Ten Commandments;* called also, *The Law of of the Mother,* because of the Exposition thereof made in the Church. But we may take it for the Precepts of *Pious Parents.* These, you see, the Great GOD makes them His Own ; Requires, that you hearken to them. *Phile* of old placed the *Fifth Commandment* in the *First Table* ; inasmuch as our Parents represent the Great GOD unto us ; and we Despise Him, if we dont Honour them and Hearken to them. *Orphans ;* Did not the *Parents* which have now *Forsaken* you, once Tell you, " That you are by Nature the "Children of Wrath, and that without a " work of Grace Changing your Nature, "you cannot escape the Wrath of Hea- " ven ? *Did not they tell you,* That with- " out an Interest in a Glorious CHRIST, " you are beyond all Imagination Mise- "rable ; and that you must Embrace Him " as your Priest, and Prophet and King, " if you would have an Interest in Him ? Did not they tell you, That you can't ex- pect the Favour of God, except you up- hold the *Religion of the Closet* ; and, ex- cept you Shun all *Wicked Company* ; and except you Watch against the *Snares* which

a

a *Worldly Mind* eafily runs into? Don't Forget fuch Things. *Tour Parents where are they?* You fee they don't *Live for ever.* But, Oh, Let the *Words* of God which you heard from them, *take hold* of you; and a Saving *Hold,* a Lafting *Hold.* Yea, Let the *Death* of your *Parents,* be the *Refurrection* of their *Inftructions*; & give a *New Life* unto thofe *Inftructions of Life,* which they formerly dropt upon you. Think, *What was it my Parents told me, they would have me to do!* *Receive* their *Inftructions, & not Silver; and their Knowledge rather than Gold.* There is a Sentence of the Son of *Sirach* in the *Apocrypha, Whofo honours his Father makes an Expiation for his Sins.* This don't Sound well. But *Grotius* has reliev'd it, with noting, That an *Expiation* of Sin, in the Style of Antiquity fometimes intended a *Prefervation* from Sin; He takes it in that Senfe, *Reverentia Parentum multos cuftodit a Peccato.* Children, If you pay a due Reverence and Deference to the Documents of your Parents, you will find it a *Prefervation* from Sin. And, God will *take you up!*

VI. Let *Orphans* make a Right Improvement,

I

ment, of the *Estates* which their *Parents*, if they were men of *Estates*, have left unto them. Sometimes it is so ; A Good Man dies, & then tis as we read, Psal. XXV. 13. *His Soul shall dwell in Goodness*, (in a *Good Place*, with the *Good One*, gone to *Paradise* :) and then, *His Seed shall Inherit the Earth* ; (His Children are *Heirs* of some Wealth left unto them.) Now let the *Children* reckon these *Estates* as *Talents* where-with God has Entrusted them ; *Talents* whereof they must give an Account unto God. *Orphans*, Beware of that *Venom*, which *Mammon* too often carries with it. Seriously set your selves to think, *What shall I now do, that I may best answer the Just Expectation of God ; & how shall I best apply my New Interest unto the Service of the Glorious Lord ?* It is Enjoyned, *Honour the Lord with thy Substance.* Our *Estates* are the most *Accidental* Things that can be ; They are *Things that are not.* Why would the Spirit of God call them, Our *Substance* ? Why, *Honour the Lord* with them, & that will make them so. They'l be *Substantial Things* ; They'l yield *Substantial Joyes* ; They will be turned into a *Lasting Substance in the Heavens.* O

Stewards of the manifold Grace of God, Be perswaded fo! There came fome of old, with Prefents unto the Houfe of God; and there-upon twas ordered; Zech. VI. 11. *Then take the Silver & the Gold, & make Crowns.* The *Crowns* to be Placed firft on the Head of the *High-Prieft*; and then to be laid up in the Temple, as *Monuments* of the Piety in the Offerers. Truly, your *Silver* & *Gold* will be turned into *Crowns,* and the *Crowns* will be fet on your own *Heads,* when you Serve the Houfe of God with it, and His Caufe in the World, & contribute unto the Glory of our *High-Prieft,* our JESUS. Mr. *Hutchefon* of *Edinburgh,* in his very Savoury *Expofition of this Prophecy,* more than threefcore years ago, has two very Pathetical obfervations upon this Paffage. One is, *Albeit any thing we can offer to God, be if no worth before Him, yet He gracioufly makes more of our Offerings, than we could well expect*; He makes *Crowns* of them. Another is: *They who in times of Great Difcouragement appear to ftrengthen the Hands of the Church, are fingularly taken notice of by God, and may Expect fingular favour from Him:* Their coming to *Jerufalem* with offerings,

I 2

when others are lingring in *Babylon*, must *be to them for a Memorial.*

When we read, Prov. X. 2. *Treasures of Wickedness profit nothing; but Righteousness delivereth from Death.* I remember the Jewish Rabbi s take it thus ; They are *Treasures of Wickedness*, which are hoarded up ; which do no Good ; which are not made *Profitable* : But then *Righteousness* display'd in works of *Charity* not only deliver the Needy for whom they are done, from *Death*, but also are follow d with Retaliations and Deliverances to the Doer of them. *Orphans* that have *Treasures* fallen to You ; *Do Good* with your *Treasures* ; use them for the *Profit* of others, & they will be for your own. And let one of your first Considerations be, *What shall I now do for Poor Orphans?* Are there no Poor *Orphans* of whom you should be able to say with the great Man of the East ; *I delivered the Fatherless, & him that had none to help him* ? And, *The Fatherless has eaten of my Morsel & was brought with me, as with a Father* !

VII. Let *Orphans* Imitate what was Imitable & Laudable, in the *Parents* that have now *Forsaken* them. It may be, You have

have had *Parents*, very Exemplary for the
Things that are *Holy & Just & Good.* Now,
*Remember them, & Follow their Examples,
Confidering the End of their Converfation.*
One of the *Parents* in the *Tears of Ancient
Times,* could fay ; Prov.IV 2. *I have taught
thee in the way of Wifdom ; I have led thee in
Right Pathes.* The words are thus placed
in the Original ; *In the way of Wifdom I have
taught thee.* Being firft *in the way of Wifdom*
himfelf, he *taught* his Children, how to come
into it, & walk in it. No fuch *Teachers* of
Wifdom, as thofe that are Themfelves in the
way of it. *Orphans,* It may be your *Parents*
were fuch *Teachers.* Oh! Learn from their
Way, how to be *Wife* ! To be the *Heirs* of
their *Vertues.* will be far better than to be
the *Heirs* of their *Eftates.* How deplora-
ble, the Degeneracy, when the Offspring of
a *Jofiah,* incur the Fulminations of fuch a
Rebuke as that ! Jer.XXII.15,17. *Did not
thy Father do Judgment & Juftice, & it was,*
(and is) *well with him? But thine Eyes &
thine Heart are not but for thy Covetoufnefs !*
But King *Theodoricus* beholding the Good
Children of One *Cyprianus,* he made him,
this agreeable Complement, *Quando talium*
                                    Filiorum

Filiorum Pater es, Natura ipsa videris esse Patritius. Truly, Sir, Such *Sons* as these were enough to render you a *Patrician.* Such Sons, put an Honourable, and even a *Patrician* Figure, on the Happy Parents, whose Quivers have them. Children, If your Parents were in themselves of an Honourable & *Patrician* Figure, Oh! do not procure your selves a *Degradation* by your *Degeneracy!*

Thro' the Grace of Christ, the Neighbours assure themselves of a Succession of nothing, but what is Hopeful, in the *Family,* with which we are now more directly concerned.

A *Family,* in which both the *Parents,* lately *Forsaking* us, had the *Fear of God,* shining in such Sensible Exercises & Expressions of it, that it Illuminated the Whole Neighbourhood: Both the *Parents* were *Conscientious* Christians, *Regular* Livers, Constant *Worshippers* of God: Both the *Parents* were Devout *Sabbatizers;* & it is easy to make an Excellent Inference, if it be considered, what Influence the *Religion of the Sabbath* will have, where tis Cultivated.

In One Word, A *Family of Good Orders,*
and

and where no Sin could hope to be harboured.

A *Family*, in which the FATHER was a Faithful *Magistrate*; A *Counsellor* continued by Annual Election with the esteem of the People at the *Board*, for the more than thrice Six [The brief Character of the Honourable JOHN FOSTER Esq]

years that have ran since his Name was inserted in the *Royal Charter* of the Province ; A *Judge* of Inviolate Integrity in the course of his proceedings on the *Bench* ; Mindful of His own Appearance before the just *Judge of all the Earth* ; In Both, by his withdraw making a *Vacancy*, not easily to be filled up. One *Just* in his Dealings ; & *Charitable* to the Poor. An Exact and a Wellbred *Merchant*; but as truly acquainted with the *Best Merchandise*. One Proudly Patient & Silent under the *Losses* in which these our Calamitous Times gave him now and then a Share ; but sometimes refreshed with Encouraging Rewards of a Submission to the Will of God in such Things. One who Loved both our *Liberties*, as an *English* man, and our *Principles* as a *New English-man* ; and often appeared for them

A

A *Family*, in which the MOTHER, was One to all the Indigent, as well as to her own Houſehold ; a *Matron*, adorned with the *Ornaments* of a Spi-rit, which is *in the Sight of God, of Great Price* ; and the true *Spirit of a Gentle-woman*.

[The brief Cha-racter of Mrs. ABIGAIL FOSTER]

One full of Humble *Conde-ſcenſions* ; Courteous, Affable, Obliging One of a *Peaceable* Temper ; an *Hater* of Diffe-rences, and an *Healer* of them. One who diſpenſed her *Alms*, with an uncommon *Generoſity*, an unfailing *Liberality* One who was mightily *Wean'd* from *this World*, Sick of its Vanities & Flatteries, while She was in the midſt of its Enjoyments. One who kept up an Intimate Communion with God, eſpecially in the *Prayer of the Cloſet*, where-to She not only Retir'd every Day, but ſome-times Devoted *whole Dayes* for Interviews with Heaven. One who Long'd for *Hea-ven*, long before She took her Flight from *Earth* ; and had her Mind no leſs affected with the *Glory* of her Saviour there, than aſſured of her *Portion* in Him.

The Beſt thing, that can be Spoke to the *Children* of Such *Parents*, or that can be wiſh'd for them, is ; *Let them go and as far as they may, do Likewiſe.*

F I N I S.

RULES

OF THE

SOCIETY

OF

ST. GEORGE:

ESTABLISHED AT NEW-YORK,
FOR THE PURPOSE OF RELIEVING
THEIR BRETHREN IN DISTRESS.

———————

NEW-YORK: PRINTED BY J. M'LEAN, & CO.
No. 41, HANOVER-SQUARE.
M,DCC,LXXXVII.

INTRODUCTION.

THE Author of our Being intended Man for Society, and has imprefled him with Principles of a focial Nature.—A Difpofition to Benevolence is implanted in his Heart; and, unlefs eradicated by the prejudices of Education, will extend itfelf in fuch a Manner as to comprehend the Human Race.

THE Effects of this amiable Difpofition cannot, however, be exerted in the fame Manner towards all mankind: our Family, our Friends

and

and our Countrymen have Claims upon our Affections, prior in Order and superior in Strength to those that result merely from our common Nature.

Even in particular Societies, besides the Ties of Friendship and Family, other Circumstances will exist by which Individuals find themselves more intimately connected with each other, than with the rest of their fellow Citizens.—Thus the Graduates of a particular University, or the Natives of a particular Province, consider themselves, in all Countries, as bound to each other by a more immediate Relation than that in which they stand to others of the Community.

In a country like North-America, the Inhabitants of which have derived their Origin from different Parts of Europe, it is not surprising that they should be attentive to that Circumstance.

Though now blended in one political Body, they are still distinguished by the Places from which they sprang, and look back to England, Scotland or Ireland as the Country of their Ancestors.

Hence have arisen Societies, distinguished by Names peculiarly adapted to each Country; and so far from prejudicing, they promote the general Interests

Interefts of Humanity, by directing and fixing the Attention to particular Objects.

MANY Acts of the moft beneficial Charity have owed their Exiftence to thefe Societies:— And Merit in Diftrefs might frequently have paffed unnoticed, if there had not been a Body, to whom it could make Application with Confidence of Succefs.

EVEN in a political View, confidering this Country as deriving infinite Benefit from the emigration of Foreigners, thefe Societies have their Ufe.—They may afford Counfel and Affiftance to Strangers upon their firft Arrival, and by leading them to Profperity encourage the Emigration of others.

SUCH being the Tendency and Nature of thefe Societies in general—the Subfcribers confider them as truly laudable, and being all either Natives of England or Defcendants of Englifhmen, have agreed to form themfelves into a SOCIETY, and be fubject to the following RULES for the good Government thereof.

RULES

OF THE

SOCIETY

OF

ST. GEORGE.

RULE I.

THAT this Society be called the *SOCIETY of ST. GEORGE*, eſtabliſhed at New-York for the Purpoſe of relieving their Brethren in Diſtreſs.

RULE II.

THAT no Perſon who is not an Engliſhman, or the Deſcendant of an Engliſhman, ſhall be admitted a Member of this Society.

RULE

RULE III.

THAT no Perſon ſhall be admitted a Member of this Society unleſs choſen by Ballot, and no one ſhall be balloted for unleſs he is nominated at a Meeting previous to a Ballot being held, (excepting honorary Members who may be propoſed and elected at the ſame Meeting). That no Election ſhall be held unleſs twenty-four Members be preſent, and no Perſon ſhall be admitted a Member unleſs he be choſen by three-fourths of the Members preſent.

RULE IV.

THAT the Society ſhall meet four Times every Year, to wit, on the 23d Day of January, on the 23d Day of April, on the 23d Day of July and on the 23d Day of October. That the Society ſhall Dine together on ST. GEORGE's DAY, and that the other Meetings ſhall be in the Evenings.

RULE V.

THAT a Preſident, Vice Preſident, Treaſurer, Secretary, four Stewards and a Charitable Committee, to conſiſt of ſeven, ſhall be appointed annually (the ſame Officers who ſerved the preceding Year may be re-choſen); and that the 23d Day of January ſhall be the Day of Election.

RULE

R U L E   VI.

THAT every Member ſhall pay an annual Subſcription of *Thirty Shillings* to the Treaſury, on or before the firſt Day of April. And every Member neglecting to pay his Subſcription, ſhall no longer be eſteemed a Member of the Society, unleſs he be re-elected by Ballot.

R U L E   VII.

THAT the Charitable Committee ſhall, with the conſent of the Preſident, Vice Preſident and Treaſurer, or any two of them, diſtribute any Sum or Sums in Charities between the Times of Quarterly or Special Meetings, provided ſuch Diſtribution does not in the whole exceed one Fourth of the annual Funds of the Society.

R U L E   VIII.

THAT every Member abſenting himſelf from the annual Dinner, ſhall pay to the Treaſurer *Ten Shillings* as a Fine for ſuch Abſence, and *Four Shillings* for abſenting himſelf from the Quarterly Meetings, unleſs prevented by Sickneſs.

R U L E   IX.

THAT no Reſident of this City who is eligible to be a Member of this Society ſhall be admitted as a Viſitor.

B   R U L E

RULE X.

THAT a majority of Votes shall decide every Question (the Chairman to have a casting Vote) except to annul or alter any former Rules ; in which case three-fourths shall be requisite. That no Number under twenty-four shall constitute a Meeting for the Purpose of making or altering Rules.

RULE XI.

THAT the President, Vice President and Officers shall have Power to call Special Meetings, on giving three Days Notice to every Member residing in this City of such Meeting and the Business. And as great Inconvenience may result from Members not attending pecial Meetings, any Member neglecting to attend any Special Meeting that may be called, shall pay a Fine of *Four Shillings* towards the Charitable Fund, unless prevented by Sickness.

RULE XII.

THAT any non Resident, being an Englishman or the Descendent of an Englishman, who may apply to become an Honorary Member of the Society, may be proposed and admitted, agreeable to the Rules of the Society, on paying *Forty Shillings* to be applied to the Charitable Fund.

LIST

LIST

OF THE

MEMBERS

OF THE

Society of St. George,

ESTABLISHED AT NEW-YORK.

A

Atkinfon, Francis
Appleby, George
Anderfon, Samuel
Allingham, Charles

Bache, Theophylact
Berry, John
Bayley, Richard
Barrow, Thomas

B

Banyar, Goldſborow

C

Corp, Samuel
Cafey, James

Cockle,

(12)

Cockie, Frederick
Chapman, Henry*

D

Dewhurft, John*
Dale, Robert
Dickinfon, Gilch-i?
Lilver, Thomas

E

Evers, John
Ellis, John
Evening, Abraham
Elmes, Thomas
Evans, Charles
Elam, Samuel*

F

G

H

Harifon, Richard
Hamerfley, Andrew

I

Johnfon, James

Ketland.

Kenyon K. William
Ketland, Thomas*
Kirkman, Samuel*
Kirkman, John

Maule, Thomas
M'Kinnon, Daniel

N

Nash, Henry

L

Laight, William
Ludlow, Gabriel William
Ludlow, Carey
Ludlow, Daniel
Ludlow, William
Ludlow, George
Lucas, David*

O

P

Philips, Henry*
Parsons, William

M

Moore, Rev. Mr.
Morewood, Gilbert

Q

R

Randall, *Thomas*
Randall, Paul Lobert
Rowlett, William
Rolton, Edward King
Rivington, James
Roberts, Michael
Roberts, Thomas

S.

Seton, William
Smith, Richard
Staples, Henry
Snaith, John
Startin, Charles
Shaw, John Charles
Sadler, John
Sherbrooke Miles
Smith, William x
Smith James x

T

Taylor, John
Thompson, John
Tucker, Daniel
Thurman, John
Thomas, William
Thomas, Francis
Taylor, William.

V

Venning, William

W

Waddington, Joshua
Waddington, Henry
Walton, William
Walton, Gerard
Walton, Abraham
Woodriffe, Robert
Wilkes

Wilkes, John
Wilkes, Charles
Williams, William
Wilson, Richard

Y

Young, William
Yates, Lawrance Reade
Yates, Adolphus.

⁂ Those whose Names are marked with a STAR, *are Honorary Members.*

SOME
ACCOUNT
OF THE
Charitable Corporation,

LATELY ERECTED

For the Relief of the WIDOWS and CHIL-
DREN of *Clergymen,* in the Communion of the
Church of *England* in *America*; with a Copy of
their CHARTERS, and FUNDAMENTAL RULES.

AND ALSO A
SERMON,

Preached in *Chriſt-Church,* PHILADELPHIA, *October* 10, 1769, before the ſaid CORPORATION,
on Occaſion of their FIRST MEETING.

By WILLIAM SMITH, D. D. *Provoſt of the
College and Academy of* Philadelphia.

Publiſhed, by Order, for the Benefit of the CHARITY.

PHILADELPHIA:
Printed by D. HALL, and W. SELLERS, oppoſite the *Jerſey* Market. MDCCLXIX.

TO

THE MOST REVEREND AND HONORABLE

FREDERICK, Lord Archbishop of *Canterbury*;

THE MOST REVEREND AND HONORABLE

ROBERT, Lord Archbishop of *York*;

AND THE RIGHT REVEREND

RICHARD, Lord Bishop of *London*.

Most worthy PRELATES!

THE CORPORATION lately erected " for the relief of the WIDOWS and CHILDREN of Clergymen, in the communion of the church of England in America," having honoured me with their commands to publish the following SERMON, together with some account of the rise and progress of the pious and charitable design which it recommends; permit me to offer Both to the world under your patronage----not only as, by Charter, the management of the Charity itself is committed to the inspection of the Archbishops of Canterbury and York, and the Bishop of London, for the time being; but likewise as an humble acknowledgment of the obligations which each of you, my Lords, who now adorn those Sees, have been pleased to confer on,

Your most dutiful, and

most obedient son and servant,

WILLIAM SMITH.

Philadelphia,
October 14, 1769.

Some Account of the Rise and Progress of the Charitable Corporation, " for the Relief of the Widows and Children of Clergymen, in Communion of the Church of ENGLAND in America."

THE diftreffed circumftances, in which the Epifcopal Clergy in the more northern provinces of America, and efpecially the Miffionaries in the fervice of the Society for the Propagation of the Gofpel, have too frequently been obliged to leave their families, had long been matter of difcouragement to many from entering into the miniftry of our Church, as well as of regret to pious and worthy members thereof.

AFTER fundry overtures, from time to time, it was at length refolved, at a meeting of the clergy at Elizabeth-Town, in New-Jerfey, October 1767, to appoint a committee to frame fome plan of provifion for the diftreffed widows and children of fuch of our clergy as fhould die in narrow or neceffitous circumftances. In purfuance of this appointment, the reverend Dr. Auchmuty, Rector of Trinity Church, the reverend Dr. Cooper, Prefident of King's College, both of New-York, the reverend Mr. Cooke, Miffionary in Monmouth county, New-Jerfey, and myfelf, met at Perth-Amboy, May 12, 1768; and drew up a fcheme for the approbation of our brethren; recommending it to them to follicit charters in each of the three provinces of New-York, New-Jerfey and Pennfylvania, that we might be a body corporate, in which ever of thefe provinces we might have occafion to meet.

THIS

THIS scheme having obtained the approbation of several succeeding meetings of the clergy, and a draft of a charter being settled, two persons were appointed in each province to sollicit the passing thereof; viz. the reverend Dr. Auchmuty, and Dr. Cooper, in New-York; the reverend Mr. Cooke, and Mr. Odell, in New-Jersey; and the reverend Mr. Peters *, and myself, in Pennsylvania. And justice requires, that the most public and grateful testimony should be given of that readiness and cheerfulness, with which the several Governors consented to the grant of the charters in their respective provinces.

THE charter for Pennsylvania was obtained the 7th of February last; the honorable JOHN PENN, Esq; the Governor, having ordered the seal to be put to it on the first application. And the worthy and honorable Proprietaries of the province, as soon as the design was made known to them in London, took the earliest opportunity to signify their hearty approbation of it, and wishes for its success. His Excellency, Governor FRANKLIN, shewed the same readiness, and the charter for New-Jersey was compleated in May. That for New-York, altho' cheerfully assented to by his Excellency Sir HENRY MOORE, Baronet, was delayed by his indisposition and death; but the passing it was one of the first acts of his successor, the honorable Lieutenant Governor COLDEN, who put the seal to it, the 29th of September last.

As it will be of use, to the members of the corporation especially, that each of them should have a copy of their charters to have recourse to, as occasion may require, I shall here insert that for New-York; not meaning thereby any other preference than what is usually claimed by that colony, in virtue of seniority, among her sister ones.

CHAR-

* Rector of Christ-Church and St. Peters, Philadelphia.

CHARTER

Of the CORPORATION, for the Relief of WIDOWS and CHILDREN of CLERGYMEN, in the Communion of the CHURCH of ENGLAND, in America.

GEORGE the Third, by the Grace of God, of Great-Britain, France and Ireland, King, Defender of the Faith, and so forth; TO all to whom these presents shall come, GREETING. WHEREAS our loving subjects, the clergy of our province of New-York, in North-America, in communion of the church of England, as by Law established, by their humble petition, presented to our trusty and well-beloved Sir Henry Moore, Baronet, our Captain General and Governor in Chief in and over our province of New-York, and the territories depending thereon in America, Chancellor and Vice-Admiral of the same, and read in our council for our said province, on the twenty-second day of March now last past, Have set forth, that the clergy of the church of England in the American colonies, and especially the missionaries in the service of the Society for the propagation of the gospel in foreign parts, are, with great difficulty, able to provide for their families, so that their widows and children are often left in great distress; that for remedy thereof corporations have, by charters, been erected in the provinces of Pennsylvania and New-Jersey, for receiving, managing and disposing of such sums of money, as may be contributed and given as a fund towards the support and re-

lief

lief of the widows and children of the said clergy; and for the further promotion of which laudable and charitable design, the petitioners humbly prayed our royal charter, under the seal of our said province of New-York, to create them, and such other persons as should be named therein, a body politic and corporate, with the like powers and immunities as are contained in the above mentioned charters, granted in the colonies of Pennsylvania and New-Jersey, or such other powers and privileges, as might be thought expedient by our said Captain General and Governor in Chief. WHEREFORE we, favouring the said useful and laudable design, and being fully convinced of the loyalty and affection of the clergy in America, in communion of the church of England, as by law established, to our royal person and government, are graciously pleased to grant to the Petitioners their reasonable request---KNOW YE, that of our especial grace, certain knowledge, and meer motion, We have given and granted, and by these presents, for us, our heirs and successors, Do give and grant, that our trusty and well-beloved Cadwalader Colden, Esq; our Lieutenant-Governor and Commander in Chief of our province of New-York, Sir William Johnson, Baronet, John Watts, Charles Ward Apthorpe, and Henry Cruger, Esquires, of the province of New-York; William Alexander, Esq; claiming to be Earl of Stirling, Peter Kemble, Charles Read, James Parker, Samuel Smith, and Frederick Smythe, Esquires, of the province of New-Jersey; James Hamilton, Lyn-Ford Lardner, Benjamin Chew, and James Tilghman, Esquires, of the city of Philadelphia, in the province of * Pennsylvania; the Reverend William Smith, Samuel Auchmuty, and Thomas Bradbury Chandler, Doctors in Divinity; Myles Cooper, Doctor of Laws; Richard Peters, William Currie, Richard Charlton, Philip Reading,

* The gentlemen named before the clergy, are of the councils of the different provinces.

ing, George Craig, John Ogilvie, Samuel Cooke, Samuel Seabury, Thomas Barton. Charles Inglis, William Thompson, Jacob Duché, Leonard Cutting, Alexander Murray, Ephraim Avery, John Beardsley, Jonathan Odell, Samuel Magaw, John Andrews, Abraham Beach, William Ayres, and William Frazer, clerks; Joseph Galloway, Alexander Stedman, John Ross, Richard Hockley, Samuel Johnson, Thomas Willing, John Swift, Samuel Powel, Francis Hopkinson, and William Atley, Esquires, and Doctor John Kearsley, of the province of Pennsylvania; John Tabor Kempe, John Livingston, Elias Debrosses, James De Lancey, James Cortland, Isaac Willet, Nicholas Stuyvesant, James Duane, Jacob Le Roy, Benjamin Kissam, Jacob Walton, and William Axtell, of the Province of New-York, Esquires; Cortlandt Skinner, Daniel Coxe, and John Lawrence, Esquires, of the province of New-Jersey; and such other persons as shall be hereafter elected and admitted members of the corporation erected, and to be erected, by these presents, according to the tenor hereof, and of such bye-laws and constitutions, as shall hereafter be made by the said corporation, be, and for ever hereafter shall be, by virtue of these presents, ONE BODY CORPORATE AND POLITIC in deed, fact and name, by the name of, THE CORPORATION FOR THE RELIEF OF THE WIDOWS AND CHILDREN OF CLERGYMEN IN THE COMMUNION OF THE CHURCH OF ENGLAND IN AMERICA, and them by the same name, ONE BODY CORPORATE AND POLITIC in deed, fact and name, we do for us, our heirs and successors, fully create, constitute and confirm, by these presents; and Do grant that by the same name they, and their successors, shall and may have perpetual succession, and shall and may, at all times hereafter, be persons able and capable in the law to purchase, take, have, hold, receive, enjoy and transmit to their successors lands, tenements, rents and hereditaments, within our said province of New-York,

York, to the value of One Thousand Pounds Sterling by the year in the clear, above all out-goings and reprizes, in fee simple, or for any other estate, term or interest, whatsoever; and to take, have, hold, receive, enjoy and transmit to their successors, goods, chattels, monies, and effects, but at no one time to exceed the sum of Twenty Thousand Pounds Sterling in the gross, within our said province of New-York, And may and shall, by the name aforesaid, do and execute all things touching and concerning the same, for the benefit, succour and relief of the WIDOWS and CHILDREN of such deceased clergymen, who have been in communion of the church of England, as shall or may be contributors to the funds of the said corporation, and in such manner, rates, proportions and annuities, as shall be reasonably settled, adjusted, agreed to, and expressed in the bye-laws and regulations, which shall be made, from time to time, by our said corporation, and their successors. And also, that they, and their successors, by the name aforesaid, be, and shall be for ever hereafter, persons able and capable in the law to sue and be sued, plead and be impleaded, answer and be answered unto, defend and be defended, in all or any courts of justice, and before all or any judges, officers or other persons whatsoever, in all and singular actions, plaints, pleas, suits, causes, matters and demands, of what nature, kind or sort soever. And that it shall and may be lawful to and for them our said corporation, and their successors, for ever hereafter, to have a Common Seal for their use, and in their affairs and business, and the same, at the will and pleasure of them, and their successors, to change, alter, break and make new, from time to time, as they shall think best: And for the well governing and ordering the affairs of our said corporation, we do, for us, our heirs and successors, further grant, that it shall and may be lawful for them, and their successors, to meet together on the First Tuesday after the feast of Saint Michael, in every year, and at such

B   other

other time and times, and in such places, upon such public notice given, as may be fixed and agreed upon by certain fundamental regulations, to be first duly made and enacted, by a majority of our said corporation, and never afterwards to be altered, but by a like majority of the members for the time being: And they our said corporation, being so met, in such number, and agreeable to such notice, as shall be fixed by the said fundamental regulations, shall have full power and authority, from time to time, to make other necessary laws and regulations, and to transact, manage and settle, all such matters and things, touching and concerning the affairs of our said corporation, as they shall be impowered and authorized to transact, settle and manage, by virtue of the fundamental laws and regulations of our said corporation, once duly made and enacted by a majority of the contributors and members as aforesaid. And all the bye-laws and regulations so made, whether concerning the election of officers and servants, or concerning the Government, and management of the estate, goods, chattels, revenue, business and affairs, of our said corporation, shall have full effect and force, and be binding upon, and inviolably observed by, all the members of the said corporation, from time to time, according to the tenor and effect of the same; PROVIDED that the same be reasonable in their own nature, and not contrary to the laws of that part of Great-Britain, called England, or of our said province of New-York. AND FURTHER, we do hereby constitute and appoint Richard Peters, of the city of Philadelphia aforesaid, clerk, to be the First President of this our corporation; and Thomas Bradbury Chandler, doctor in divinity, to be the First Treasurer; and Jonathan Odell, clerk, to be the First Secretary; who shall continue in their respective offices until the first Tuesday after the feast of Saint Michael, now next ensuing, and from thenceforwards until one president, one or more treasurer or treasurers, and one secretary be

chosen

chosen in their rooms, in such manner, and for such term and period, as shall be settled by the fundamental regulations, to be made for that purpose by a majority of the said corporation, duly met and convened. AND LASTLY, we do hereby, for us, our heirs and successors, ordain, order, and appoint, that the accounts and transactions of the said corporation, legally and properly vouched and authenticated, shall, from time to time, and as often as demanded, be laid before the Lords Archbishops of Canterbury and York, and the Bishop of London, for the time being, or such person and persons as they may from time to time appoint for that purpose, in America, in order that the said Archbishops of Canterbury and York, and the Bishop of London, for the time being; or such person and persons, appointed by them as aforesaid, may ratify and confirm the said accounts, or subject them to such revisal, check and confirmation, as may be thought just and reasonable. IN TESTIMONY whereof, we have caused these our letters to be made patent, and the great seal of our said province of New-York to be hereunto affixed, and the same to be entered on record in our Secretary's office, in our city of New-York, in one of the books of patents there remaining. WITNESS our said trusty and well-beloved Cadwalader Colden, Esquire, our Lieutenant Governor and Commander in Chief of our said province of New-York, and the territories depending thereon in America, at our Fort, in our city of New-York, by and with the advice and consent of our council for our said province of New-York, the twenty-ninth day of September, in the year of our Lord one thousand seven hundred and sixty-nine, and of our reign the ninth.

CLARKE.

THE Charters granted in Pennfylvania and New-Jerfey being, in every article, the fame as the above, it would be needlefs to infert copies of them here. The names of the perfons incorporated are the fame in all of them, and ftand in the fame order; excepting only, that the names of thofe who are of the Council for each province, ftand firft in the charter granted in that particular province.

As the firft meeting appointed by each charter, was to be on the Tuefday and Wednefday next following the Feaft of St. Michael, 1769, which were the 3d and 4th of this prefent October; moft of the Clerical, and fundry of the Lay Members, met accordingly at Burlington, in New-Jerfey, on Tuefday October 3d; and the Prefident having taken the chair, the different Charters were read, and compared with each other.

ON the day following, the members who were met, being 19 in Number prefented an Addrefs of Thanks to his Excellency Governor FRANKLIN, which he anfwered with the warmeft wifhes for the fuccefs of the pious defign for which the corporation had been erected; and added, that it would always give him pleafure to render any acceptable fervice to the members of the Church of England.

As humble Application had been made fome time before to the venerable Society for the Propagation of the Gofpel, praying their countenance and affiftance in carrying the defign into execution; their Anfwer, figned by their worthy Secretary, the reverend Dr. Burton, was produced and read as follows, viz. " That as a mark of their earneft de-
" fire to forward fo benevolent an undertaking, they wil-
" lingly charge themfelves with an annual contribution of
" Twenty Pounds Sterling to the Scheme for each of the
" provinces of New-York, New-Jerfey and Pennfylvania;
" that is, SIXTY POUNDS STERLING per annum in the
" whole; for which the treafurer of the Corporation for
" the relief of the WIDOWS, &c. may draw on the trea-
" furer

" furer to the Society, for propagating the gofpel, com-
" mencing from the time that the Charters fhould be ob-
" tained, and the Subfcriptions of the Clergy themfelves
" take place here."---The Thanks due to the venerable Society for fuch a frefh mark of their goodnefs and kindnefs
to the Epifcopal Clergy in thefe parts, are ordered to be
properly tranfmitted to them.

FINDING that a majority of the members of the Corporation could not be conveniently convened at Burlington,
to enact Fundamental Rules, agreeable to the tenor of the
Charters, it was found necefſary to proceed to Philadelphia,
without breaking up; and a committee was appointed to
have all the necefſary papers in readinefs. It was alfo a-
greed, that there fhould be an Anniverfary Sermon before
the Corporation; and that each of the Clerical members
fhould preach in turn, agreeable to the Order in which
their names ‖ ſtand in the charters. By this regulation it
fell to my fhare to be prepared to preach the following
SERMON at Philadelphia, as foon as the requifite majority
fhould be convened; and I fincerely wifh it may be found
an introduction in any degree worthy of a Charity fo truly
founded in the beft principles of Religion, as well as Humanity!

THE remainder of the bufinefs being tranfacted after the
fermon, will be taken notice of in its place.

‖ The names were placed in the charters according to feniority of degree among
thofe having a Doctor's degree, and after them according to feniority of Prieſt's
Orders.

A SER-

A SERMON,

Preached in Christ-Church, Philadelphia, October 10, 1769, before the Corporation for the Relief of the Widows and Children of Clergymen, in Communion of the Church of ENGLAND, in America.

JOB xxix. 11----13.

When the ear heard me, then it blessed me; and when the eye saw me, it gave witness to me; BECAUSE I delivered the POOR that cried, and the FATHERLESS, and him that had none to help him. The blessing of him that was ready to perish came upon me, and I caused the WIDOW's heart to sing for joy.

JEREMIAH xlix. 11.

Leave thy FATHERLESS CHILDREN, I will preserve them alive; and let thy WIDOWS trust in me.

JAMES i. 27.

PURE RELIGION and undefiled, before God and the Father, is this-----To visit the FATHERLESS and WIDOWS in their affliction; and to keep ourselves unspotted from the world.

MY RESPECTED HEARERS!

IT is from no affectation of singularity, that I have introduced this discourse to you, with Sundry texts of scripture, instead of One; but to shew how rich are the sacred oracles of God, as in exalted lessons of BENEVOLENCE in general, so particularly that amiable branch
thereof

thereof which I am to recommend to your present regard. Thro' the whole inspired books of the Old Testament, as well as the New, we shall scarce find a writer that hath not made the cause of the FATHERLESS and WIDOWS peculiarly his own.

AMIDST a very imperfect system of Morality, even in the Heathen-world, the voice of God, speaking in the hearts of men, had carried their Lessons of Benevolence to a more exalted pitch, than most other branches of their Doctrine; in so much, that some of their Sages could embrace, in the calm Wish of PHILANTHROPY, the whole * human species.

BUT it was from the Scriptures of GOD, and particularly from the divine Documents of our SAVIOUR and his Apostles, that the doctrine of UNIVERSAL LOVE AND CHARITY, received its finishing lustre, and was placed on its true foundation. Altho' the motives to this heavenly virtue be strong, both in the Old and New-Testament, yet are they carried infinitely farther in the Latter, and pressed home upon nobler and more animating principles.

TRUE it is, that no writer can express a more amiable Spirit of Benevolence, nor recount his acts of Mercy and Kindness, with more conscious delight and complacency, than the author of the book of Job; as well in the passage before us, as elsewhere----

" WHEN the ear heard me, then it blessed me; when
" the eye saw me, then it gave witness to me"---and why?
" BECAUSE I delivered the Poor that cried, and the FA-
" THERLESS, and him that had none to help him. The
" blessing of him that was ready to perish came upon me,
" and I caused the WIDOW's heart to sing for joy."

THE principles upon which he acted in all this, may perhaps be understood from what he says afterwards----

FOR---" If I have withheld the Poor from their desire,
" or caused the eyes of the WIDOW to fail; if I have eaten
" my

* Homo sum ; humani nihil a me alienum puto.

" my morsel myself alone, and the FATHERLESS hath not
" eaten thereof; if I have seen any perish for want of
" cloathing, or any Poor without covering, and his loins
" have not blessed me---and he were not warmed with the
" fleece of my sheep---If I have made Gold my hope, or
" have said to the fine Gold, thou art my confidence---this
" were an Iniquity to be punished by the Judge; for I should
" have denied that God is above *."---

So that the sum of his argument seems to amount just to
this---That if out of the Good Things wherewith my Almighty Creator hath abundantly blessed me, I should refuse to communicate and provide for the Destitute, I should
be worthy of the highest punishment. For this would be,
in effect, to claim all those things as my own absolute and
perfect property, which are only given me in trust by my
benevolent Maker. It would be denying that the Almighty
reigns in heaven Above, the sole and absolute source of every thing we enjoy here Below. In such case, justly might
He re-claim his own, strip me of all his bounty hath given
me, turn me naked into the world, leave the wife of my bosom destitute, and my children, in their turn, to beg in vain
for that bread which my unfeeling heart refused to others.

SCARCE any higher than this will the Old Testament documents of Love and Beneficence be found to run; and no
small height it is---but founded, however, on arguments of
Almighty justice and judgment, seemingly reaching no farther than to secure the divine favour in this world. Wholly in this strain is the language of the old law itself---

" YE shall not afflict any WIDOW or FATHERLESS
" CHILD; for if ye afflict them in any wise, and they cry
" unto me, I will hear their cry, and my Wrath shall wax
" hot, and I will kill you with the Sword; and YOUR
" WIVES shall be WIDOWS, and Your Children FATHER-
" LESS †."----

SUCH

---

* Job xxxi. 16-----28.   † Exod. xxii. 22.

SUCH denounciations of Wrath and Punishment, like the Thunderings and Burnings of the Mount, were suited to bend and awe the hearts of a people, whose Genius was too gross and servile, or too stubborn, to be woo'd and won by the soft breathings of Everlasting LOVE. And here the danger was, that attentive only to the Letter of the Law, and its awful Sanctions, but not discerning its divine Spirit, the outward offices of LOVE and BENEFICENCE, might be fulfilled from Carnal motives---to secure the Divine favour in this world---as considering that the more liberally they might give, the more liberally they would be supplied, of God's infinite bounty. Or the fond Praise of Men might be no small motive----that " the ear which heard them " might bless them, and the eye which saw them, bear " witness to their good deeds."----

OF this Spirit were those who affected " to bestow their " Alms before men." But when JESUS CHRIST came to give a more noble foundation to the Law of LOVE and CHARITY, this Ostentatious Spirit met with his early reprehension. Altho' he did not annul the Old Testament motives to Love and Alms-giving, he added new ones, infinitely more powerful and animating. He placed Life and Immortality before us. He taught us that we were Candidates for an Eternity of Glory, which none could be fit to inherit, but they who, having the LOVE OF GOD shed abroad in their Hearts, did, for his sake, Love all his CREATURES, and prepare their Souls for the final enjoyment of Him, thro' the constant exercise of every act of Kindness and Mercy here below. And in the rapturous glimpses he gives us of this future and eternal bliss, and of that awful process and sentence which is to fix the doom of mankind---- CHARITY to the Poor, the Sick, and the Needy, is made the grand Preparation of the Heart, for all that we can hope to enjoy from him.

C

Nor was it by Doctrines alone, but by conſtant and living Example, that this heavenly Temper was inculcated by Him.   As his Errand into the world was at firſt proclaimed by choirs of Angels to be " Glory to God on high, " with Peace and GOOD-WILL to Men on earth"----ſo GOOD-WILL to Men was the leading principle of his whole life ; which was at laſt cloſed with an act of GOOD-WILL ſo ſtupenduouſly great, that both Men and Angels were left aſtoniſhed at the Benevolence thereof---For *be died to ſave ſinners*----He breathed cut his laſt in " LOVE which paſ- " ſeth knowledge ‡,"---- conſtituting LOVE as the grand criterion, whereby all who ſhould afterwards profeſs his name, might be truly known § as his.

In this evangelic view, well might LOVE be ſtiled a New Law ; as founded not in a mere Regard to almighty Juſtice, or Fear of almighty Judgment ; but in a Heart that is caſt into the very Mold of LOVE itſelf----in a Temper that is Angelic, nay, even Seraphic, Godlike, Divine, and already ſo raiſed above this world, as to be daily ripening for the world to come !

Following this Doctrine of LOVE, given by our bleſſed SAVIOUR, nay, Living in it, and Feeling it in all its divine efficacy, his faithful Apoſtles conſtantly preſſed it home to men, upon his own heavenly principles.   Thus we find St. James, in the Text read to you, placing all Religion in a Heart thus ſet looſe to the world---thus breathing the dictates of Humanity and Love.

" PURE Religion, and undefiled before God (our Savi- " our) and the Father, is This----To viſit the FATHER- " LESS and WIDOWS in their affliction, and to keep our- " ſelves unſpotted from the world."

But the fervent Apoſtle St. Paul, of all others, with his uſual zeal, enters the fulleſt into this ſubject.   His 12th and 13th chapters to the Corinthians, are one continued

lecture

‡ Epheſ. iii. 19.   § John xiii. 35.

lecture on our SAVIOUR's heavenly Doctrine of CHARITY; which, by a sublime train of argument, he exalts above all other Virtues and Graces---even above those truly Evangelic Ones---FAITH and HOPE.

IF therefore, we would wish to understand this essential Doctrine aright, and to be truly actuated by the Life and Spirit of Heavenly Love, a short analysis of our Apostle's arguments, will be of the utmost use; and also be the best introduction I can give to the recommendation of that particular Branch of Charity; for which I have the honor to be appointed an humble advocate before you.

THERE had started up, in the Church of Corinth (as there hath, alas! in many churches since) a sett of men, who being elated with an over-weening conceit of their own Spiritual Gifts---the strength of their FAITH, and the ardor of their HOPE, in Christ Jesus---made that a plea for lording it over their brethren; and for Spiritual Pride, rash Condemnation, and censorious contempt of others; contending that those endowed with superior Gifts and Acquisitions, were as the Head, Heart, and Vital parts of the Body, while others were as the meaner Members.

SAINT Paul attacks them on their own Principles; and, by a beautiful Allusion to the Body Natural, proves that Christians of lower attainments, were as much members of Christ's Mystical body, as those of the highest; and that to condemn or judge uncharitably of them, was as much a Schism in the Body Mystical, as if in the Body Natural, " the Foot should say, because I am not the Hand; and " the Ear, because I am not the Eye---that therefore, they " are not of the Body. For if the whole were an Eye, " where were the Hearing? If the whole were Hearing, " where were the Smelling?"

JUST so in the Body Mystical. " Are all Apostles? are " all Prophets? are all Teachers? are all Workers of Mi- " racles? Have all the Gifts of Healing? Do all speak with " Tongues? Do all Interpret?"

You

You do well, fays he, to covet earneftly thefe "beft of Gifts." But, would you have the true Spirit of your Mafter Christ, and be his Followers indeed?---Behold, I will fhew you " A MORE EXCELLENT WAY," than that of ftriving to make yourfelves great by Boafting of any your own Acquifitions, however eminent.

He then begins his divine Sermon on CHARITY; and furely, my Brethren, he could not have delivered himfelf with a more glorious and fervent Zeal, had he lived to fee thofe fiercer Contentions, that Havock and Deftruction, which the want of this Gofpel-virtue of CHARITY hath introduced into modern times---that Spirit of Bitternefs and Violence; that Thirft of Imperioufnefs and Dominion; that prefumptuous Cenfure and religious Railing; that Strife for modes and opinions, uneffential to Chriftianity; that Defire of obtruding our own diftinguifhing Tenets on thofe around us, rather than the common Commandments of Christ; that Earneftnefs of Compelling their FAITH, ra- ther than provoking their LOVE and OBEDIENCE by our good example---all which unchriftian Temper hath been, like the worm at the root of Jonah's Gourd, eating out the very Vitals of Religion; and hath often made this world more like an Aceldama, or field of Blood, than the peace- ful Heritage of the meek and lowly Jefus. For moft cer- tain it is, from fad experience, that when once this Temper begins to prevail, not only the LOVE OF GOD is forgotten, but along with it the LOVE OF OUR NEIGHBOURS alfo; and the Heart, by Habits of Bitternefs, Cenforioufnefs, Con- tention, Violence and Revenge, becomes gradually callous, and dead to all the fofter impreffions of Humanity, Mercy and Good-will.

Saint Paul, determined to give an early check to this growing evil in the Churches, attacks it with an undaunted firmnefs, and truly Apoftolic ardor.

SUPPOSE,

SUPPOSE, fays he, that you had all thofe Gifts and Acquifitions, whereof you fo fondly glory---fuppofe your Eloquence fo great, that you could fpeak with the tongues of Men
and Angels; your Knowledge fo enlarged, that you could
underftand all Myfteries, and interpret all Difficulties; your
defire of Alms-giving fuch, that you could beftow all your
Goods to feed the Poor; your Mortification to the world
fo ftrong, that you had fubdued all carnal appetites; your
FAITH fufficient even to remove mountains; your HOPE
in CHRIST fo fervent, that you could give your Bodies to be
burnt for the Truth of his Doctrines---Yet, for all this, I
tell you, that " if you have not CHARITY, you are NO-
THING!" All thefe Gifts and Acquifitions---all thefe good
Deeds---are of no eftimation in the fight of GOD, if they
are not minifterial to that LOVE which is the fulfilling of
the whole Law; and are not performed in " that more ex-
" cellent Way of CHARITY," which is the Spirit of the
Gofpel, and the very badge of Chriftian Perfection!

FOR Eloquence, employed to puff up the vanity of the
poffeffor, and not exerted, in the fpirit of Love and Truth,
to propagate Univerfal Holinefs, " is but as the founding
Brafs, and tinkling Cymbal."

ALMS-GIVINGS, Mortifications, Zeal for Doctrines, or
Zeal againft them, fanctimonious Appearances, the moft
confummate Knowledge---all of them are dead and unpro-
fitable, if not accompanied with the unfeigned LOVE of
God and our Neighbour. Nay, even the divine virtues of
FAITH and HOPE are fruitlefs, unlefs productive of CHA-
RITY, which is Greater than They!

BUT altho' this vaft preheminence is given to CHARITY
over FAITH and HOPE, let us not think that St. Paul meant
to derogate from the latter. On the contrary, he every where
magnifies Them, that CHARITY, on the Comparifon, may
appear the more illuftrious. And in this very place, he
paints before us, in the ftrongeft colours, the FAITH and
HO!

HOPE of Abraham, of Mofes, the Patriarchs, and firſt Martyrs; ſhewing that, by theſe divine Graces, they were led to perſevere in Love and Obedience thro' all the trials of life.---

WOULD we truly know the Apoſtle's diſtinction on this head, methinks it may be rendered obvious in a few words, however needleſly perplexed it hath been.

FAITH and HOPE with him are indeed ever made the foundations of true RELIGION. But LOVE is the fuperſtructure; or it is Religion itſelf, in all its perfection and glory. FAITH, in his comprehenſive language, is the " Subſtance of Things Hoped for, the Evidence of Things " not ſeen"---That is to ſay---a ſtrong Belief in the adorable Perfections of God, and in the worth and reality of Inviſible things---a Belief that as his Veracity hath never failed us in the Paſt, fo neither will it fail in the Accompliſhment of thoſe glorious Future Things which he hath promiſed, altho' they may be too high and mighty for our preſent Comprehenſion. And thus thoſe future Inviſible things become Evidenced to us, and preſented before us, as if already enjoyed in Subſtance and Reality; leading us to lay hold of Chriſt as offered to us in the goſpel; all which is connected with, or neceſſarily productive of, the next divine grace and virtue, ſtiled by our Apoſtle HOPE, or " the HOPE of Righteouſneſs by FAITH"---a firm and joyous Confidence, that our ſincere, tho' imperfect, Services will be accepted thro' Him, inſtead of that unſinning Obedience required by the ſtrict tenor of the Law; and that we ſhall be Juſtified, Sanctified, and finally Saved by coming to God, in this " *new and living way.*"

Now, can ſuch Views of God's Goodneſs as theſe, be without LOVE? Or would theſe views be of any uſe at all, but for leading us to that LOVE, which begets Obedience and Conformity to what is ſo Lovely and Venerable?

JUSTLY

JUSTLY therefore is this living FAITH ftiled the foundation of that EVANGELIC Religion, whofe effence is LOVE. For furely we cannot have LOVE to Him in whom we have not HOPE; nor have HOPE in Him in whom we have not BELIEVED. But ftill, if our FAITH and HOPE were to ftop fhort of LOVE and OBEDIENCE, they would be of no value; for Love and Obedience are their end; and are the only perfections that can affimilate us to Angels, or in any wife make us fit for that heavenly Communion, where LOVE is to conftitute our eternal Felicity.

THUS, my brethren, I have endeavoured, as briefly as I could, to ftate St. Paul's great argument for the Preheminence given to CHARITY. And, I truft, what hath been faid, will not be deemed a deviation from my fubject. For it was my exprefs purpofe, by taking a Text from both Teftaments, to fhew how infinitely more powerful are the Motives to LOVE and Beneficence, under the New than the Old covenant; and that, therefore, if we do not fhine fuperior in all acts of Love and Mercy, under fo Loving and Merciful a Difpenfation; even the men of Nineveh, and the Queen of the South, fhall rife in judgment againft us---feeing neither Jew nor Gentile, before the coming of CHRIST, had thofe gracious and tender Calls to LOVE, which the Gofpel is now conftantly founding in our ear!

YE Sages! ye Rabbi's! ye venerable names of antiquity! we honor you for your Leffons of Benevolence; and rather blufh for ourfelves that you proceeded fo far, than wonder that your progrefs was no greater.

YET fay, O thou JEW, whoever thou wert, in antient times, whofe heart was made to glow for thy fpecies, on the principles of thine own Law---fay, what would have been thy raptures of Benevolence, hadft thou known the true Meffiah, and been tutored in his mild and evangelic doctrines of Love?

SAY

SAY alſo, thou GENTILE-SAGE! whoever thou wert, that by conſidering God only as the common Creator, and all Men as the work of his hands, couldſt from thence infer the duties of Mutual Love among the whole ſpecies---ſay further, whoever thou wert, that, by beholding His ſtars in the firmament mix their friendly rays in aid of each other, couldſt from thence conclude, that all his creatures here below ought to mingle in like friendly offices---ſay, how would thy ſoul have been enflamed towards God, and towards Man, had any Star or Conſtellation, in all thy Catalogue, pointed § to Chriſt the Power of God, dying in an Act of LOVE to thee---nay, ſetting LOVE before thee, as his laſt great Command, and the ſum total of everlaſting bliſs?

BUT here thy perſpective was limited---where (bleſſed be God) ours is infinitely extended; for CHARITY (to crown our Apoſtle's eulogium on it) never Faileth, but endureth for ever: It hath a place among the perfections of God, which neither FAITH nor HOPE can have; ſince, where all is pure VISION, there can be no exerciſe for FAITH; nor, where all is perfect FRUITION, can there be room for HOPE. Our FAITH and HOPE can give us no reſemblance of God; but our CHRITY makes us, in ſome ſort, what He himſelf is in a Superlative manner---the Helpers of the Helpleſs, and partakers of his own joy in beholding a happy world! Our FAITH and HOPE may ſerve us as the Handmaids of LOVE here below; but leaving them behind us, as of no further uſe, our LOVE is all that we ſhall carry hence with us, as our Dowery from Earth to Heaven!

As yonder majeſtic * Delaware is fed and ſupported in its courſe, by tributary rills and ſprings flowing from each mountain's ſide, till at length it comes to mix its waters with

§ See a thought ſomewhat to this purpoſe in Hartley, Serm. 7th.
* One of the largeſt rivers in North-America, on which the city of Philadelphia ſtands.

with its Parent Ocean, where it no longer ſtands in need of their ſcanty ſupplies; ſo FAITH and HOPE are the nouriſhing Springs of our LOVE in our journey Heaven-wards; but when once arrived there, we ſhall no longer ſtand in need of their Aid. " When that which is Perfect is come, that " which is in Part ſhall be done away." Our FAITH ſhall be ſwallowed up in VISION, and our HOPE in FRUITION; but our CHARITY and LOVE ſhall remain for ever, mixing and blending in the unbounded ocean of PARENTAL and ETERNAL LOVE!

O CHARITY, thou heaven-born Virtue! Can the tongues of Men, or even of Angels, ſpeak more excellent things of thee? Or can a more tranſcendent rank be now aſſigned thee---than, that the Saviour of the world hath thus made thee the badge of Chriſtian perfection; and his inſpired followers have enthroned thee as the Queen of all Evangelic Graces and Virtues; declaring, that neither the Martyr's zeal, nor the ſelf-denial of the Saint, nor all Languages, nor all Knowledge, nor any Virtue beſides, can profit or adorn the man any thing, who is unadorned with thy ſweet celeſtial garb! But he who is thus adorned, is the moſt auguſt ſpectacle upon earth---whom even Angels ſurvey with delight, as cloathed in that peculiar garb, which Chriſt himſelf vouchſafed to wear here below, and which ſhall not need to be put off in Heaven above.

WE ſee, then, my brethren, that Goſpel-Charity, thus explained, includes in it almoſt unſpeakable things; its ſhorteſt character, to ſum up all in a few words, being no leſs than this---

" An ardent and ſeraphic LOVE OF GOD, grafted in a ſtedfaſt Belief of his adorable Attributes, a firm Reliance on the goodneſs and juſtice of his Moral Government, a rapturous and comprehenſive view of his ſcheme of Providence, a Heart thoroughly touched and melted with that aſtoniſhing Plan of Love manifeſted in Chriſt, and a Mind

D

darting

darting forward to thofe everlafting fcenes of blifs promifed thro' him, in a well grounded and triumphant Expectation of their fure accomplifhment. Now the true LOVE OF
GOD, founded on fuch exalted principles as thefe, cannot
but be accompanied with the fecond branch of Gofpel-
Charity, the LOVE OF OUR NEIGHBOUR alfo---engaging us
in an affectionate Concern for the welfare of our Whole Species, with a quick and pervading Senfe of all the Good or
Evil that can befal them in this world ; confidering them
as Brethren---made by the fame PARENT-GOD; Redeem-
ed by the fame SAVIOUR-JESUS; travelling together to the
fame heavenly Country, and commanded to alleviate each
others burdens, " and not to fall out by the way."

To you then, who have this juft conception of the nature of Gofpel-Charity, and have the true Love of God, and
of Mankind, reigning in your hearts, my intended Application will be eafy. For if all acts of Love and Beneficence,
fo far as our abilities and opportunities reach, be branches of
this heavenly virtue, I have the authority of Scripture to
fay, that the Caufe of the FATHERLESS and WIDOWS,
claims a primary and moft fpecial regard.

IN the Text, taken from Jeremiah, the Almighty
himfelf, in the midft of the fevereft denounciations againft
a rebellious people, yet feems to relent in mercy towards
the FATHERLESS and WIDOWS---" Leave thy FATHER-
" LESS CHILDREN, I will preferve them alive; and let
" thy WIDOWS truft in me."

UNDER the Law, remarkable was the attention paid to
the STRANGER, the FATHERLESS, and the WIDOW.
" When thou cutteft down thine Harveft, and haft forgot-
" ten a Sheaf in the field, thou fhalt not go to fetch it---
" it fhall be for the STRANGER, the FATHERLESS, and
" the WIDOW---when thou beateft thine Olive-tree, thou
" fhalt not go over the boughs again---when thou gather-
" eft the Grapes of thy Vineyard, thou fhalt not glean it
after-

" afterwards---it fhall be for the STRANGER, the FA-
" THERLESS, and the WIDOW *."

EVEN David, altho' he refifted his own natural affections, and continued inexorable to the recal of a favourite
Son, who had offended him, yet could not withftand thofe
mournful accents of the WIDOW of Tekoah---" Help,
" O King---I am indeed a WIDOW-WOMAN, and my Huf-
" band is Dead"---

THE ftory is truly tender, tho' feigned. And if this
WIDOW's Apparent Diftrefs could procure an oath of David, that a hair of her fon (whofe life was forfeited to the
public) fhould not fall to the ground, only by pleading,
that if this fon was loft, " her coal, which was alive,
" would be quenched, and neither name nor remainder be
" left to her hufband on earth"---I fay, if this ftory of
Feigned Diftrefs could fo far prevail, furely the voice of
Real Diftrefs will have a ftill greater influence---the voice
of WIDOWS indeed! not pleading for lives forfeited to the
law, but for Themfelves, and their Children---for the
Names and Remainders of your own Clergy, that they may
not be wholly loft upon earth---the Names and Remainders of men, who have once been your dear Friends
in CHRIST-JESUS; men who, in their life-time, have
adminiftered to you heavenly Counfel, and fweet Comfort,
in his precious Word and Covenant; and men who may
have often opened your Souls to flow in thofe godlike
ftreams of Benevolence and Charity to others, wherewith
thofe Helplefs Remainders of themfelves now ftand in need
to be relieved and refrefhed at your hands.

MANY words are not needful to explain the nature and
propriety of fuch a Charity as this, nor need I mention the
long Call there hath been for its eftablifhment.

You well know the fituation and circumftances of the
Clergy of the Church of England, in thefe Northern Co-

D 2   lonies;

Deut. xxiv, 19---21.

lonies; for the Relief of whose families, when left in diftrefs, this defign is more particularly fet on foot. Except
in a few places, their chief fupport depends on the Bounty
of our fellow-members of the Church in Great-Britain;
and that venerable Society, who have the Diftribution of
this bounty, have of late been obliged, and will be ftill
more obliged, to retrench their allowance; that, like faithful Stewards, they may be likewife able to reach out their
helping hand to thofe numerous Petitioners for New Mif-
fions, which arife from the conftant encreafe of People in
thefe Colonies.

The additional Support which our Clergy receive from
their Congregations, is generally fmall, and exceedingly
precarious; decreafing fometimes in Nominal, often in
Real value; while the expence of every Neceffary in life
is proportionably encreafing.

Decency, a regard to Character, to their own Ufefulnefs, to the credit of Religion, and even your Credit,
among whom they minifter, require them to maintain fome
fort of Figure in their families, above thofe in common
profeffions and bufinefs; while, certain it is, on the other
hand, that any fober reputable Tradefman, can turn his Induftry to more account than They.

The like regard to Decency and character alfo forbids
our Clergy to follow any Secular employ, in aid of their
circumftances; unlefs, perhaps, here and there one, by
Education, fhould have been qualified for fome Practice in
the Healing Art of Medicine, which is not deemed incom-
patible with the Paftoral duty, where it is not too large.

On the whole, this I will venture to affert, that were the
generality of our Clergy to make their calculation according
to the way of the world, the money * expended in their
education at Schools and Colleges, a Voyage for Holy Orders,

* The money expended this way can fcarce be eftimated at much lefs than £ 500
fterling, and many of our miffionary clergy do not receive £ 30 fterling per annum
from their congregations, fome not more than half that fum, and not a great
number much above it.

ders, and the purchafe of neceffary books (if it had been laid out at firft as a common Capital at Intereft) would bring them a greater annual return, without any trouble or fatigue, either of Body or Mind, than they can procure by the labour of their whole lives, in difcharge of their paftoral duty, exclufive of the Bounty of benevolent perfons in the mother country.

I am far from mentioning thefe things as Complaints ; I know they are of Neceffity in many places; and I truft none of my brethren among the Clergy will ever make their Calculation in this way ; but keep their Eye on their Master's Service, looking forward to the " Recompence of Reward." Yet what I mention is fo far neceffary, as it fhews inconteftibly the great propriety of the defign before us.

It certainly requires little attention to what paffes around us, to fee that the families of our deceafed Clergy are often left among the moft diftreffed in their vicinity. The Father, by ftrict œconomy, and good Example, may be able to fupport them in fome degree of Reputation, during his own Life, altho' not to flatter them with the hopes of any Patrimony at his death. By his own Care, and fome conveniency of Schools, he may give the Sons the rudiments of an Education for his own profeffion, or fome other ufeful one in the world. The Mother, with the like anxious Care, and fond Hopes of rendering the Daughters refpectable among their Sex, may employ her late and early toil to train their Minds to thofe virtues, and their Hands to that Diligence and Induftry, which might one day make them the fweet accomplifhed companions of worthy men in domeftic life.----

But alas! amidft all thefe flattering dreams and fond prefages of the heart, the Father, perhaps in his prime of years and ufefulnefs, is called from this world. The Prop and Stay of all this promifing Family is now no more! His Life was their whole dependence, under God, even for daily
Bread !

Bread! His Death leaves them almoft deftitute----deftitute, alas! not of Bread only, but even of Council and Protection upon earth!

FATAL reverfe---Ah! little do the world in general, and efpecially they who bafk in the eafy funfhine of affluence and prosperity---little do they know the various complicated fcenes of private anguifh and diftrefs---Here they are various and complicated indeed!

THE Bereaved and Difconfolate MOTHER, as foon as Chriftian Reflection begins to dry up her tears a little, finds them wrung from her afrefh by the melancholy Tafk that remains to her. She is now, alas! to reduce the once flattering hopes of her tender Family, to the ftandard of their prefent fad and humbled condition! Hard Tafk indeed! The Son is to be told that he muft no more afpire to reach the ftation which his Father filled; and the Daughter is to learn that, in this hard and felfifh world, fhe muft no longer expect to become the Wife of him, to whom fhe once might have looked on terms of equality---The Son, perhaps, muft defcend to fome Manual employ, while even the poor pittance neceffary to fettle him in That, is not to be found; and the Daughter muft ferve ftrangers, or be yoked perhaps in Marriage for Mere Bread; while the mournful mother (without the flow-procured help of Friends) can fcarce furnifh out the decent Wedding-garment!

WHAT did I fay? the decent Wedding-garment, and a Marriage for Mere Bread? This were an Iffue of troubles devoutly to be wifhed for!---But, ah me! The Snares of POVERTY in a Mind once bred up above it---fhall every unguarded unprotected Female be able to efcape them? Alas! no----Some VILLAIN-DECEIVER, with Vows and broken Oaths, with LOVE in his Mouth, and HELL in his Heart, taking advantage of Innocence in Diftrefs, lays his fcheme of deftruction fure; and with the ruin of the Daughter,

ter, brings the Mother's grey hairs down to the grave with accumulated sorrow!

JUST, but indignant, Heaven! Is there no chosen Vengeance in this World, to heap on the heads of such perfidious monsters, to SAVE them from that Vengeance, which they have merited, tho' yet we dare not with them, in the World to come!

THIS sad part of the Catastrophe of many Females, descended from fathers, once venerable and pious in their day, we would willingly have passed over in silence; were not the experience of what has happened in other countries, more than sufficient to awaken our apprehensions in this.

THE picture here drawn, is no exaggerated one; and when the Children of Clergy, in low circumstances, are in an early age deprived of both Parents---then are they ORPHANS indeed! and every distress, every temptation, falls upon them, with aggravated weight!

To be FATHERS, then, to such FATHERLESS CHILDREN; to take them by the hand, and lead them out, thro' the snares of the world, into some public Usefulness in life, that the Name and Memorial of our dear Brethren and faithful Pastors deceased, may not be wholly lost upon earth--- I say, to Do THIS, and give some Gleams of comfort to the afflicted WIDOWS and MOTHERS that survive---must surely be one of the most delightful Actions of a BENEVOLENT Mind; and THIS, my brethren, is the glorious object of the CHARITY for which we are Incorporated, and which we have undertaken to sollicit and conduct.

BLESSED, therefore, be all they in this world and the next (Laity and Clergy) into whose Hearts God hath put it, to associate for so noble and pious a purpose. In like manner, may that venerable Society in England be blessed, whose annual Subscription hath laid so liberal a Foundation for the work; and blessed also be those Governors of Provinces,

who

who have fo cheerfully and readily given us their Charters for carrying it into execution!

HAPPY in fuch Beginnings and fuch Countenance, let us fet ourfelves earneftly to the difcharge of our Part; leaving the Iffue to GOD, and the Benevolence of good Men.

SOME *, perhaps, there may be, long accuftomed to view every Tranfaction of our Church on this Continent with a jealous eye, and who being loudly tenacious of every privilege of their own, tho' fparing in their allowance to others---may therefore conceive more to be Intended by this undertaking than is Expreffed.

To fuch, however, if it may have any weight with them, I will declare, that altho' every thing relative to this defign from the beginning has paffed thro' my own hands, affifted by a few others, appointed for that purpofe, I have never known the leaft hint or thought of any thing further expected from the execution of it, than what our charters exprefs.

BUT fhould it have all that happy Effect to us which fome may apprehend from it, namely---that of producing a more intimate Connexion and UNION among our Clergy and Church-members; furely it is what we ought moft ardently to defire and purfue, at this time efpecially.

WHEN we fee our Church and Miniftry unreafonably oppofed, and borne down in their common and effential rights; when we behold men feemingly Leaguing together to perpetuate this oppofition from Father to Son; it can certainly be no Harm in us, but our bounden Duty, to look to our own Concerns alfo; and particularly to take fome
Thought

* I have reafon to think that fuch perfons are far from a majority of any denomination. Many of all perfuafions have expreffed their hearty wifhes for the fuccefs of the defign; and I am particularly bound to acknowledge the ready affiftance received from a worthy friend of mine, who had a principal fhare in framing the plan for the relief of the widows and children of Prefbyterian minifters; and who communicated to me not only feveral ufeful papers, but likewife whatever remarks he thought might enable us to improve our Plan, on the experience of any difficulties or deficiencies that had occurred in the execution of theirs.

Thought, that our Children be not left wholly Deftitute in a world where We, and They on our account, are likely to meet with fo little favour from many----

But my fubject is CHARITY---I would not violate that fubject; and I blefs God that it hath not been violated, on our part, on this trying occafion; and that our general conduct hath been fuch, as not to difcredit the long-approved Moderation of that Church to which we belong.

In the fpirit of meeknefs and fober argument, firm, but (we hope) decent, our endeavour hath been to fhew---That the Fears and Jealoufies muftered up concerning us, could have no poffible Foundation, without a total Abolition of the whole fyftem of Law and Policy in thefe Colonies; that the Contingency which could render fuch an Abolition poffible, is as unlikely to happen as any thing that can well be imagined in this world; and that therefore, on the whole, it refts with the Confciences of our opponents themfelves, to reconcile their own conduct to any principles of BROTHERLY LOVE and CHARITY, or to any other principles whatever, not bordering on Intolerancy of Spirit, and an undue luft of Dominion on their own part.

So far, we may felicitate ourfelves. And if to have acted thus can be thought a breach of CHARITY, we muft reply, that there is a CHARITY to Truth and Right, fuperior to all others. We have now but one ftep further, my brethren, to fecure a Conqueft, equally compleat and glorious---Let us, in the continuance of every act of Moderation, Love and Well-doing, be a LIVING ANSWER to Gainfayers; and the time may yet come, when, every other Strife being fufpended, we fhall all be fo mollified one to another, fo poffeffed of the Spirit of Gofpel-Love, that we fhall think it our mutual Honor, as it is our mutual Duty, to mix our whole endeavours in the Propagation of our Common Chriftianity, only ftriving whofe Zeal fhall be foremoft---nay, and even to mix our Deeds of Charity to

E   the

the diftreffed, they with us, and we with them, as God
fhall give us abilities, without regard to Sect or Party.

Happy time, fhould it ever-take place! For then would
Men indeed feel a Truth, now little attended to; and
which I wifh I could write in letters legible to the whole
Univerfe——" That there is a greater Weight and Moment
of christianity, in one Deed of Benevolence, where
we have the Power to do Good, or in one Sigh for Diftrefs,
where we have not the power (proceeding from a heart that
is right towards God, and towards man) than in all the
doubtful Points of Controverfy, all the Oppofition to Modes
and Forms, that have bufied and enflamed the world ever
fince the reformation——and which will never deferve
the true name of a reformation, till this foul Reproach
is wiped away from it alfo!"

But till that happy time arrives, it is to thofe of our
own Communion we muft chiefly look, for the fuccefs of
the pious Charity before us. Humane and benevolent as
they are known to be in all cafes of Diftrefs, the fatherless and widows of their own Clergy will never be without Advocates and Benefactors among them.

The particular Rules by which this Charity is to be con-
ducted are open to all; and the main fupport of the Fund
is to be the annual Subfcriptions of the Clergy themfelves,
with fuch cafual Benefactions as, by the Providence of God,
may be added to it.

If Succefs fhould, in any Degree, be anfwerable to our
hopes and wifhes, it will furely be a high Satisfaction to
the members of our Churches, to behold their Minifterr fo
relieved from thofe anxious cares, which every man muft
have on the profpect of leaving a diftreffed Family behind
him, as to proceed cheerfully in all Duty; knowing, that
altho' they can acquire little, and leave lefs of their own in
this world, there is fome fmall provifion to place their
children

children above total want, and some Protectors and Friends to guard their Infant-years.

But a still higher Satisfaction will arise at the last Day, to all who have participated in such LABOURS OF LOVE—to hear those whom their Benevolence hath relieved, testifying for them before their ALMIGHTY JUDGE—or rather to hear their ALMIGHTY JUDGE himself testifying in the name of those relieved Destitutes, and embracing them with the following glorious sentence—

" COME, ye blessed of my Father! inherit the Kingdom
" prepared for you from the foundation of the world—

" FOR I was an hungred, and ye gave me meat; thirsty,
" and ye gave me drink; a stranger, and ye took me in;
" naked, and ye clothed me; sick, and ye visited me; in
" prison, and ye came unto me."—

THAT all of us may be so Habituated to acts of Mercy and Love in the present world, as to be found fit for this happy sentence in the next, may GOD, of his infinite Mercy, grant thro' JESUS CHRIST! Amen.

———————————————————

AFTER the conclusion of the foregoing SERMON, a very generous collection was made at the Church-doors for the benefit of the Charity, as will appear by the annexed list of donations. And the members of the corporation, having continued in church till the congregation was dismissed, proceeded from thence to present an address of thanks to the honourable Governor PENN, for his Grant of a Charter; requesting that their thanks might, in like manner, be transmitted, thro' him, to the honourable Proprietaries of the province, THOMAS PENN, and RICHARD PENN, Esquires, for the hearty approbation they had given of the design; to all which his Honour was pleased to return a very affectionate answer, expressive of his readiness, at all times, to serve the interest of the Church of England in general, and this Charity in particular.

AFTER dining together, the corporation applied themselves to the business for which they were met; and the great attention paid to it by the lay members---the accuracy and care with which all the proposed articles and fundamental rules were examined, digested and corrected, especially by the gentlemen of the law, deserve to be held continually in grateful remembrance by the Clergy. Some of the gentlemen who were present, had been kind enough to come from 30 to 60 miles distance, to make up the requisite majority. The same zeal would have been manifested by the respectable Lay-members residing at New-York, notwithstanding their great distance, if their presence had been absolutely necessary. But it was resolved to spare them as much as possible till the next year's meeting. The members present at this meeting of October 10th, 1769, were as follow.

Reverend

Reverend Richard Peters, Prefident.

Hon. * John Penn, Efq; Lieutenant-Governor of Pennſylvania,

Hon. † James Hamilton, Eſq;

† Benjamin Chew, Efq; Attorney-General of Pennſylvania,

† James Tilghman, Eſq;

‡ Charles Read, F.ſq;

‡ Frederick Smythe, Efq; Chief Juſtice of New Jerſey,

Joſeph Galloway, Eſq; Speaker of the Aſſembly of Pennſylvania,

Alexander Stedman, ⎫
John Roſs, ⎬ Eſquires.
Richard Hockley, ⎪
Samuel Johnſon, ⎭

Thomas Willing, Efq; one of the Judges of the Supreme Court, Pennſylvania,

John Swift, ⎫
Samuel Powel, ⎬ Eſquires.
Francis Hopkinſon., ⎭

Dr. John Kearſley,

Daniel Coxe, Efq; of Trenton, New-Jerſey,

John Lawrence, Efq; Mayor of Burlington, New-Jerſey.

Rev. William Smith, ⎫
Samuel Auchmuty, ⎬ D.D.
Thomas Bradbury Chandler, ⎭

Myles Cooper, L. L. D.

William Currie, ⎫
Richard Charlton, ⎪
George Craig, ⎪
Samuel Cooke, ⎪
Thomas Barton, ⎪
William Thompſon, ⎪
Jacob Duché ⎪
Leonard Cutting, ⎬ Clerks
Alexander Murray, ⎪
Jonathan Odell, ⎪
Samuel Magaw, ⎪
John Andrews, ⎪
Abraham Beach, ⎪
William Ayres, ⎪
William Frazer, ⎪
Henry Muhlenberg, ⎭

The above Members being a full majority, agreeable to the tenor of the Charters, the following FUNDAMENTAL LAWS and REGULATIONS were unanimouſly agreed to and enacted.

N. B. SAMUEL ATLEE, Efq; did not arrive time enough for this meeting, but was preſent the day following.

FUN-

* To the 67 charter names are to be added the four following, elected at this meeting, viz.

Hon. John Penn, Efq; Lieutenant-Governor of Pennſylvania.

His Excellency William Franklin, Efq; Governor of New-Jerſey.

Rev. Mr. Muhlenberg, firſt Miniſter of the Lutheran churches, Philadelphia.

Rev. Mr. Preſton, Miſſionary at Amboy, New-Jerſe,.

The names of the Governors were not inſerted in the charters, as members ex officio, it being thought more reſpectable to obtain their own leave to elect them, from time to time. The Hon. Cadwalader Colden's name was inſerted, during Sir Henry Moore's government.

Thoſe marked thus † are of the Council for Pennſylvania, and thoſe marked thus ‡ are of the Council for New-Jerſey. The Council of the provinces are ſtiled — honourable."---The names ſtand above, in the order in which they were taken into the Minutes, from the Pennſylvania charter, under which the meeting was held.

FUNDAMENTAL LAWS *and* RE-GULATIONS, *of the Corporation for the Relief of the Widows and Children of Clergymen in the Communion of the Church of* ENGLAND *in America, duly made and enacted at Philadelphia, on the 10th Day of October, 1769, by a Majority of the Members of the Corporation met for that Purpose, according to the Tenor of their Charters.*

LAWS relative to ANNUITIES, &c.

I. THE yearly contributions of the clergy, whofe widows and children fhall be hereby intitled to annuities, fhall not be lefs than eight Spanifh milled dollars, of the prefent current weight, namely, feventeen penny-weight and fix grains, nor more than twenty-four fuch dollars, or the value thereof, in current money of the province, where each contributor lives.

II. No annuities fhall be paid but to the widows and children of fuch clergymen as fhall have been contributors to the fund; and the refpective annuities to be paid to the widows and children of fuch clergymen, fhall be five times the fum of their annual contributions.

III. In order to have a certainty, both as to the quantum, as well as the payment of the annual rates, each contributor fhall abide by that rate or clafs which he firft choofes; unlefs he fhall change into another clafs, on fuch terms as to the corporation fhall appear to be reafonable: And each

contri-

contributor shall pay his annual contribution to the corporation, on or before the first Wednesday after the feast of St. Michael in every year, under the penalty of one penny in the pound for every day's default : And if the said penalty of one penny in the pound, together with the whole contributions due, shall not have been paid up during the life of the contributor, then his widow and children shall receive only an annuity proportionable to the payments made by the husband or father.

IV. Every yearly contributor, who shall marry oftner than once, shall pay one year's contribution extraordinary on every such marriage, as he makes the chance in general worse against the fund.

V. If the husband or father of any person or persons, intitled to an annuity on this plan, shall not have paid five annual contributions into the fund; then the widow and children shall only be intitled to ten per cent. per annum for thirteen years, on the amount of the contributions paid by the deceased.

VI. If any contributor shall have paid for five years, or any number of years under fifteen, and exceeding five, the annuitants shall receive only half the annuity which belongs to the rate or class subscribed to by the deceased, until such time as the yearly deduction of half the annuity, added to five or more payments, made by the deceased (without computing interest) shall together make a sum in the fund, equal to the sum of fifteen annual payments in the rate or class to which such deceased contributor belonged; which partial annuities, payable agreeable to this article, shall be proportioned between the widow and children as hereafter fixed, in respect to full annuities, viz.

VII. If there be no children, the widow of every contributor, if fewer than fifteen payments shall have been made by the deceased, shall receive the whole annual sum due by the last preceding article; and if fifteen such pay-

ments

ments shall have been made complete by the deceased, then the widow shall receive the whole annuity due on the husband's contribution during her widowhood; and if she marry again, she shall, from the time of such second marriage, receive only half such annuity during her natural life.

VIII. If there be a child, and no widow, such child shall be intitled to the whole or partial annuity for thirteen years, agreeable to the foregoing articles; but if there be more than one child, and no widow, the annuity, whether whole or partial, shall be equally divided among them, to be laid out, in case they are minors, in their education or apprenticeship, with the advice and approbation of such executors or guardians as the father may have nominated; and if none such shall have been nominated by the father, then in such manner for the benefit of the child or children, as the corporation shall direct.

IX. If there be a widow, and one child, the annuity, whether whole or partial, shall be equally divided between them, under the limitations aforesaid: And if there be a widow, and two or more children, she shall have one third during her widowhood, or one sixth during her natural life, if she should marry a second time; and the remainder for thirteen years, shall be laid out for the use of the children as aforesaid.

X. The corporation may, if they think proper, with the consent of the annuitants, or of their guardians, if they be minors, pay the child or children of contributors such a sum in hand, as shall be equal to the annuity of such child or children, according to the number of years for which such annuity should be paid, deducting legal interest, and taking into the account the chances against the life of such child or children, for the term such annuity is to be paid.

XI. The corporation shall have power to increase the rates of annuities, as the state of the fund shall admit; and for that end, all benefactions that shall be made to this fund shall,

ſhall, for the term of ten years to come from this day, be put out to intereſt, on good land ſecurity, and the ſaid intereſt, annually collected, and again put out to intereſt, ſhall be appropriated as an augmentation of the capital ſtock, for the ſaid term of ten years; and, after the expiration of the ſaid term, the intereſt of all benefactions ſhall be equally divided among all the children of contributors for the term that their annuities reſpectively ſhall continue payable, according to the foregoing articles.

LAWS relative to MEETINGS and BUSINESS.

I. AT every annual meeting, agreeable to the charter, there ſhall be one preſident, one or more treaſurers, and one ſecretary choſen for the enſuing year; and if any of the ſaid officers ſhould be abſent from any meeting, the members met ſhall chooſe another to officiate in his ſtead, during that meeting. At any annual meeting, the members met as aforeſaid, ſhall have power to elect ſuch new members as they ſhall think fit, and likely to promote the good purpoſes of the charity; and all elections whatſoever, ſhall be by ballot; and the majority of votes ſhall be ſufficient for the election of the preſident, treaſurer or treaſurers, and ſecretary; but no new member ſhall be admitted, unleſs four fifths of the whole votes be in his favor.

II. There ſhall at each annual meeting be choſen a ſtanding committee of ſix members, conſiſting of two out of each of the three provinces, who, together with the preſident, treaſurer or treaſurers, and ſecretary, ſhall direct and carry on the neceſſary correſpondence of the corporation, and from time to time aſſiſt the treaſurer or treaſurers, in managing the rents and eſtate of the corporation, and in putting out at intereſt the monies coming into the ſtock, either by the annual contributions of the clergy, or the occaſional donations of benevolent perſons, for which good land ſecurity ſhall be taken, at leaſt to double the value of

F　　　　　　　　the

the monies lent, payable in Spanish milled dollars of the
present current weight, namely, seventeen penny-weight
and six grains each, or the value thereof in current money
of the province where the loan is made.

III. The annual meetings of the corporation, appointed
by the charter, shall be alternately held in the provinces of
New-York, New-Jersey and Pennsylvania; and six weeks
previous notice of the time and places of all annual meetings,
shall be given by the secretary, in one or more of the public
News-papers, published in New-York, and in Philadelphia.
And if an occasional meeting of the corporation should be
found at any time necessary, and the standing committee of
business, to be appointed agreeable to the rules of the society, should apply in writing to the president of the corporation, to call such meeting at any particular place within
the said three provinces, the president shall call such occasional meeting at the place requested by the committee,
giving such public notice thereof, by the secretary, as is directed above. And at all such meetings, whether occasional or stated, any number of members met, not being less
than fifteen, shall have power to make bye-laws, and in general, have all the powers granted by charter to this corporation, other than the making, altering or repealing fundamental laws and regulations; provided always, that when
any part of the stock of the corporation is to be disposed of,
or any augmentation of annuities to be made, the same shall
be expressed in the previous public notices hereby directed
to be given of such meetings.

IV. The treasurer or treasurers, shall give such security to
the corporation every year, or as often as thereto required, in
such sum or sums as the corporation at any annual meeting
may judge sufficient, for the faithful discharge of the trust
reposed, and to be reposed, in him or them; and farther,
he or they shall, at each annual meeting, exhibit his or
their accounts to the corporation, for their inspection and
approbation.   AFTER

AFTER paſſing the Laws, the following Officers were elected for the enſuing year.

PRESIDENT.

Reverend Mr. Richard Peters.

TREASURERS.

For New-York.	For New-Jerſey.	For Pennſylvania.
Rev. Dr. Auchmuty.	Rev. Dr. Chandler.	Francis Hopkinſon, Eſq;

STANDING COMMITTEE of CORRESPONDENCE, &c.

Rev. Dr. Cooper,	Daniel Coxe, Eſq;	Rev. Dr. Smith,
John Tabor Kempe, Eſq;	John Lawrence, Eſq;	Samuel Powel, Eſq;

SECRETARY.

Reverend Mr. Jonathan Odell.

THEN adjourned, to meet to-morrow at 10 o'clock.

At a Meeting of the Corporation, October 11, 1769.

Twenty-two Members preſent.

The following EXPLANATORY RULE was made and agreed to.

WHEREAS in the foregoing Fundamental Rules, &c. of this Corporation, which were paſſed yeſterday, upon as full and mature conſideration, as the time would admit, there ſtill appear ſome things, relative to the payments to be made by the Clergy, whoſe widows and children are to be entitled to annuities, which ſeem to have been tacitly IMPLIED, and which it might nevertheleſs be better to EX-PRESS fully, that there may be no miſapprehenſion of the

F 2

ſenſe

sense of the articles afterwards; WHEREFORE, we the Sub-scribers, being all the Clergy, who were present at the settlement of the said Fundamental Articles, and who are the Parties to be bound by them in the matters to be now mentioned, DO hereby declare, That we apprehend the sense of the Articles to be, that every Clergyman, who shall become a Contributor, in order that his WIDOW and CHILDREN may be entitled to an Annuity at his Decease, is to continue the payment of his yearly Contribution during his life, and not to stop at the end of fifteen years; the whole calculations being on the principle of payments for life. And if any Clergyman should die in Arrears of his annual Payments, our sense of the Articles is further---that all his Arrears, with the Penalty of one Penny in the Pound per day, is to be deducted out of the Annuities payable by the foregoing articles to the WIDOWS and CHILDREN: And, as we declare ourselves to be as much bound by this explanatory Article, as if it had been included in the Fundamental ones, so every other Clergyman, who shall become a contributor, in order that his WIDOW and CHILDREN may be entitled to an Annuity, shall make and subscribe this Declaration. And we recommend it to the next Annual Meeting, where a Majority of the whole Corporation shall be met, to give this Declaration such further Sanction as may be thought necessary.

Signed by the twenty Clergymen who were present.

An address of thanks to the Honourable Cadwalader Colden, Esq; Lieutenant Governor of New-York, for his grant of a charter, was drawn up, and ordered to be presented to him, in the most respectable manner, by the members of the Corporation residing in that province.

THEN adjourned, to meet at New-York, the first Tuesday after the feast of St. Michael, 1770, unless sooner called by the President, agreeable to the Law made to that effect.
LIST

LIST of BENEFACTIONS to this CORPORATION.

AS but one week hath intervened since the opening of this Charitable Scheme, it cannot be expected that the List of Benfactions should yet be large, or extend beyond a few individuals in the city of Philadelphia. The foregoing Sermon was the first public notification of the design; and, excepting the collection at the Church-door, no application hath yet been made to benevolent persons, it being judged best to delay every thing of this nature till the Plan should be first laid before the world. The thanks of the Corporation are, however, to be sincerely offered, for the following Benefactions already come in, viz.

Pennsylvania Money.

	£	s	d
To the Congregation of Christ-Church, Philadelphia, for their generous contributions at the church-doors, amounting to	40	10	0
To a Gentleman, for 6 l. sent by Dr. Smith,	6	0	0
To a Gentleman, for 3 l. by Dr. Chandler,	3	0	0
To a Gentleman, for 6 l. by Ditto,	6	0	0
To a Gentleman, for 10 l. by Mr. Cooke,	10	0	0
To a Lady, for 1 l. by Dr. Smith,	1	0	0
To a worthy and benevolent Clergyman, a member of the Corporation, for his generous benefaction paid into the hands of Mr. Treasurer Hopkinson,	200	0	0
The Subscriptions of the Clergy already entered for the present year, are	141	0	0
	£ 407	10	0

THE names of the different benefactors, where they are known, are inserted in the treasurer's books; but are not at present published, as their leave has not been yet requested for that purpose.

The

Three Pounds, Pennsylvania Money, make eight Dollars.

The FORM of a LEGACY

To the Corporation for the Relief of the WIDOWS and CHILDREN of Clergymen in the Communion of the Church of ENGLAND in America.

ITEM. I GIVE to the "Corporation for the Relief of the Widows and Children of Clegymen in the Communion of the Church of England in America," the sum of   to be raised and paid, by and out of all my ready money, plate, goods, and personal effects, which by law I can or may charge with the payment of the same (and not out of any part of my lands, tenements and hereditaments) and to be applied towards carrying on the charitable purposes, expressed in the charters granted to the said Corporation, in the provinces of New-York, New-Jersey, and Pennsylvania, in America.

N. B. IT will be necessary to observe the above Form in any legacy in Great-Britain and Ireland; but in the Colonies, where Charters are granted to the Corporation, a legacy in lands, or in money, payable out of the sale or rent of lands, will be valid; and then the form may be thus-----

ITEM. I give to the "Corporation for the Relief of the Widows and Children of Clergymen in the Communion of the Church of England in America," and to their successors for ever,   acres of land, situated, lying and being in [here describe the lands] or, if it is money payable out of lands-----

ITEM. I give to the Corporation [using the charter stile as before] the sum of   to be paid, within   after my decease, out of all my effects, goods and estate what-

whatfoever, whether real or perfonal, and to be applied towards carrying on the charitable purpofes, expreffed in the
charters granted to the faid Corporation, in the provinces of
New-York, New-Jerfey, and Pennfylvania.

A BENEFACTION to the Corporation may be fent to either of the Treafurers, or other Officers, mentioned in the
lift of officers for the prefent year.

E   N   D.

POVERTY, U. S. A.

THE HISTORICAL RECORD

An Arno Press/New York Times Collection

Adams, Grace. **Workers on Relief.** 1939.

The Almshouse Experience: Collected Reports. 1821-1827.

Armstrong, Louise V. **We Too Are The People.** 1938.

Bloodworth, Jessie A. and Elizabeth J. Greenwood.
The Personal Side. 1939.

Brunner, Edmund de S. and Irving Lorge.
**Rural Trends in Depression Years: A Survey of
Village-Centered Agricultural Communities, 1930-1936.**
1937.

Calkins, Raymond.
**Substitutes for the Saloon: An Investigation Originally
made for The Committee of Fifty.** 1919.

Cavan, Ruth Shonle and Katherine Howland Ranck.
**The Family and the Depression: A Study of
One Hundred Chicago Families.** 1938.

Chapin, Robert Coit.
**The Standard of Living Among Workingmen's Families
in New York City.** 1909.

**The Charitable Impulse in Eighteenth Century America:
Collected Papers.** 1711-1797.

Children's Aid Society.
Children's Aid Society Annual Reports, 1-10.
February 1854-February 1863.

Conference on the Care of Dependent Children.
**Proceedings of the Conference on the Care
of Dependent Children.** 1909.

Conyngton, Mary.
How to Help: A Manual of Practical Charity. 1909.

Devine, Edward T. **Misery and its Causes.** 1909.

Devine, Edward T. **Principles of Relief.** 1904.

Dix, Dorothea L.
On Behalf of the Insane Poor: Selected Reports. 1843-1852.

Douglas, Paul H.
**Social Security in the United States: An Analysis and
Appraisal of the Federal Social Security Act.** 1936.

Farm Tenancy: Black and White. Two Reports. 1935, 1937.

Feder, Leah Hannah.
**Unemployment Relief in Periods of Depression:
A Study of Measures Adopted in Certain American
Cities, 1857 through 1922.** 1936.

Folks, Homer.
**The Care of Destitute, Neglected, and
Delinquent Children.** 1900.

Guardians of the Poor.
**A Compilation of the Poor Laws of the State of
Pennsylvania from the Year 1700 to 1788, Inclusive.** 1788.

Hart, Hastings, H.
Preventive Treatment of Neglected Children.
(Correction and Prevention, Vol. 4) 1910.

Herring, Harriet L.
**Welfare Work in Mill Villages: The Story of Extra-Mill
Activities in North Carolina.** 1929.

The Jacksonians on the Poor: Collected Pamphlets.
1822-1844.

Karpf, Maurice J.
Jewish Community Organization in the United States.
1938.

Kellor, Frances A.
Out of Work: A Study of Unemployment. 1915.

Kirkpatrick, Ellis Lore.
The Farmer's Standard of Living. 1929.

Komarovsky, Mirra.
The Unemployed Man and His Family: The Effect of Unemployment Upon the Status of the Man in Fifty-Nine Families. 1940.

Leupp, Francis E. **The Indian and His Problem.** 1910.

Lowell, Josephine Shaw.
Public Relief and Private Charity. 1884.

More, Louise Bolard.
Wage Earners' Budgets: A Study of Standards and Cost of Living in New York City. 1907.

New York Association for Improving the Condition of the Poor.
AICP First Annual Reports Investigating Poverty. 1845-1853.

O'Grady, John.
Catholic Charities in the United States: History and Problems. 1930.

Raper, Arthur F.
Preface to Peasantry: A Tale of Two Black Belt Counties. 1936.

Raper, Arthur F. **Tenants of The Almighty.** 1943.

Richmond, Mary E.
What is Social Case Work? An Introductory Description. 1922.

Riis, Jacob A. **The Children of the Poor.** 1892.

Rural Poor in the Great Depression: Three Studies. 1938.

Sedgwick, Theodore.
Public and Private Economy: Part I. 1836.

Smith, Reginald Heber. **Justice and the Poor.** 1919.

Sutherland, Edwin H. and Harvey J. Locke.
Twenty Thousand Homeless Men: A Study of Unemployed Men in the Chicago Shelters. 1936.

Tuckerman, Joseph.
**On the Elevation of the Poor: A Selection From His
Reports as Minister at Large in Boston.** 1874.

Warner, Amos G. **American Charities.** 1894.

Watson, Frank Dekker.
**The Charity Organization Movement in the United States:
A Study in American Philanthropy.** 1922.

Woods, Robert A., et al. **The Poor in Great Cities.** 1895.